# 1 MONT

# FREE
## READING

at

# www.ForgottenBooks.com

By purchasing this book you are eligible for one month membership to ForgottenBooks.com, giving you unlimited access to our entire collection of over 700,000 titles via our web site and mobile apps.

To claim your free month visit:

www.forgottenbooks.com/free67937

# UP THE
# AMAZON AND MADEIRA RIVERS,

## THROUGH

## BOLIVIA AND PERU.

BY

## EDWARD D. MATHEWS,

ASSOC. MEM. INST. C.E.

LONDON:

SAMPSON LOW, MARSTON, SEARLE & RIVINGTON,

CROWN BUILDINGS, 188, FLEET STREET.

1879.

LONDON:
PRINTED BY WILLIAM CLOWES AND SONS,

# PREFACE.

A FEW years ago I was Resident Engineer of the
projected Madeira and Mamoré Railway, to be constructed in the Province of Matto Grosso, in the
Empire of Brazil, and as nearly as possible in the
centre of the Continent of South America. From
various causes the prosecution of the enterprise fell
into abeyance for some considerable time. When
the works were temporarily stopped, several reasons
combined to induce me to return home by way of
Bolivia and Peru. During that journey I kept up my
ordinary custom of keeping a rough diary, and I have
since dressed up my notes into something of a con-
secutive form. The resumption of the railway works
has led me to think that some interest would attach
to a description of a route across South America that
has yet been but little travelled over. It has also
occurred to me, that nowadays, when the Eastern
trip to India, China, Japan, and home *viâ* San
Francisco and New York, has been done by so many

there may be adventurous spirits in search of new worlds to conquer, who would be pleased to know of a journey offering the combined attractions of canoeing on the magnificent affluents of the Amazon and a journey in the saddle across the Andes. My endeavour therefore has been to give all the information in my possession regarding the method and expense of travelling over the route indicated.

In grateful remembrance of many kindnesses received, I have dedicated my labours to the indefatigable worker who, for many years past, has devoted his life to the noble enterprise of opening a way to the markets of Europe for the many and varied products of the Republic of Bolivia and the Province of Matto Grosso in the Empire of Brazil.

# CONTENTS.

——◆——

## CHAPTER I.

## CHAPTER II.

## CHAPTER III.

## CHAPTER IV.

## CHAPTER V.

## CHAPTER XII.

The rapid of Araras—Farinha and sardines for supper—Difficulty of
treating the Indians successfully when they are sick — The
current of Periquitos—Arrival at the Rabo do Ribeirão—The
Bolivian Indian's chaunt at night—Passage of the Rabo do
Ribeirão—Quantity of farinha consumed by boatmen, in the
form of "shebee"—Canoe aground in the bay below the main
fall of Ribeirão—The river Ribeirão—The portage of Ribeirão—
Curious marks on rocks ... ... ... ... ... ...

## CHAPTER XIII.

Bad arrangements of the Bolivian patrons for rationing their men—
The rapid of Misericordia—Tradition attached thereto—Meeting
with canoes from Bolivia—The Madeira rapids and the junction
of the river Beni—Nomenclature of the river Madeira in its
different sections—The rapids of Layes—Wild cocoa trees—The
Falls of Pao Grande ... ... ... ... ... ...

## CHAPTER XIV.

The river Yata — Meeting with another party descending from
Bolivia—The rapids of Bananeiras—Abandoned settlement—
Variability of the Bolivian character—The cabeçeras of Bananeiras
—The Sierra da Paca Nova—The rapids of Guajará Guasu and
Merim—A few hints on leaving the last of the rapids ... ...

## CHAPTER XV.

Start made up river above rapids with drums beating—The islands of
Cavalho Marinho—A party of Baure Indians met with—Rate of
progress calculated at two miles per hour—Otters, alligators, and
monkeys shot—Steam navigation practicable on the river above
the rapids—Stock taken of food-supplies left—Long hours worked

## CHAPTER XVI.

Junction of the river Itenez—Short description of the Itenez or
Guaporé and its affluents—Fires at night prohibited on account
of savages—A capybara shot—Abundance of game above the
rapids—False alarms of attack by savages—Cooking-stove rigged
up in the canoe—The river Matocari—Hard work towing canoe
—Open pampas—Strong gale from the south hinders progress—
Chocolotales of Exaltacion—Falling banks—Estancia de Santiago
—Value of oxen in the Estancias of Mojos ... ... ...

## CHAPTER XVII.

## CHAPTER XVIII.

## CHAPTER XIX.

## CHAPTER XX.

## CHAPTER XXI.

## CHAPTER XXVIII.

## CHAPTER XXIX.

# LIST OF ENGRAVINGS.

\* From a sketch by the Author.

# UP THE
# AMAZON AND MADEIRA RIVERS.

## CHAPTER I.

Brazilian coast—True and false Salinas—Dangers of the mouth of the
Amazon—Pará—Steamers on the Amazon—Amazon Steam Shipping
Company, Limited—Vicinity of Pará—European residents—Climate.

AFTER about twenty days' steaming from Liverpool
with southerly and westerly courses, the low-lying
coast of the north of Brazil appears, and navigators
who are not acquainted with the locality have
considerable trouble in making out the pilot station
of the Salinas.

The false Salinas are about half a day's steam to
the east of the true, which, again, are a few hours'
steam from the mouth of the Amazon River. At the
true Salinas there is a lighthouse and a small
village, a large red house, visible from the deck of
the steamer, being the barrack in which the pilots
for Pará live.

The steamer in which I had a passage had been
chartered specially for the conveyance of the railway staff to which I belonged. The captain knew
nothing at all of the spot to which he had under-

taken to navigate his ship, and took the vessel considerably to the east of the Salinas; we were therefore a night and a day coasting about in soundings. At dark, a slight gale gave the sea the most phosphorescent appearance that, in the course of a good many voyages, I have yet seen. Every wave, as it curled over, broke in vivid phosphorescent fire, and it appeared as though we were steaming through a sea of flaming spirits.

The mouth of the river Amazon has many shifting banks and reefs of which no accurate information exists, and vessels are frequently lost in attempting to get up to Pará without a pilot. In 1873, three vessels, laden with iron for the Madeira and Mamoré railway, were lost, one after another, on the reefs near the Braganza lightship, which had shifted from her moorings and remained away from her station for many months. More pilots are required at the station of Salinas, for it has often happened that captains of vessels have got tired of beating about, waiting for a pilot to come off, and have attempted to enter the river alone, only to lose their vessels and cargoes.

The river Pará may be termed an outlet or arm of the river Amazon, and on its right bank the city of Pará is situated. The land on the left bank of the river forms the island of Marajo, which appears to be subject to periodical inundations, but is valuable as a feeding-ground for cattle. The rise and fall of the river at Pará is about twenty feet at highest tides.

In front of the city the river affords splendid anchorage for almost any amount of shipping, but the wharfage is very badly arranged, as there is no pier or jetty at which vessels can unload, consequently much time is lost in transhipping cargoes from the vessels into launches, and from these to the wharves. The practice has been to build out these wharves into the river at low water; and as each successive wharf has been completed, the river has silted up its frontage, and so rendered necessary the building of a new one further out. The "Rua da Praia," which doubtless was the "Street of the Shore" some fifty years ago, is now the third line back from the river, and so the city is extending itself out into the water instead of backwards into the country. A wharf on screw piles, and a jetty with a cross-head wharf at its end, would probably not cause the silting, and would not cost more, while it would be more durable than the badly built stone walls that are now from time to time put up in front of each other.

The bay of Pará presents a cheerful aspect, from the number of vessels generally found there. The Red Cross line, owned and admirably maintained by Messrs. Singlehurst, Brocklehurst & Co., of Liverpool, Booth's line, Garrison's and another American line between Brazil and New York, all touch at Pará, and the Amazon Steam Shipping Company, Limited, always have some of their steamers lying in front of the wharves. The trade of the Amazon valley is already sufficient to maintain a considerable number of steamers in the river, the finest and largest of which, built by Messrs. Laird and Co. of Birkenhead, were formerly owned by the Baron Mauá. The Baron sold his steamers and workshops, with the

subventions from the Brazilian Government to the
Amazon Steam Shipping Company, Limited, formed
in London a few years ago.  This company, being
desirous of maintaining its purchased monopoly of the
trade of the Amazon, has bought up the two Brazilian
companies that also traded on the river.  One was
called the "Fluvial Paraense," and traded from Pará
to Manáos, and to several small towns on the islands
near Pará.  This company's boats were all built by
Messrs. Pusey, Jones & Co., of Delaware, on American
principles, with cabins on upper deck, and are very
suitable for river navigation.  The other company
was the "Alta Amazonas Company," owners of
three or four small steamers, built by Laird & Co.,
that traded on the upper waters of the Amazon, and
on its confluents—the Madeira, Purus, and Rio Negro.
There are also several other steamers on the river,
owned by private firms, which pick up all the
freights left by, and even give great opposition to,
the powerful English company.  A new enterprise
has lately been started in London, with the object of
placing tugs and barges on the Amazon, and the
Madeira and Mamoré Railway Company will doubtless run its own craft between Pará and San Antonio,
the terminus of its railway on the Madeira River.
The Amazon, therefore, is likely in future years to
bear a considerable increase of steam shipping on
its broad bosom, for attention seems to be almost
universally directed to the magnificent facilities that
it offers, for the ready export to the European
markets of the produce of Northern Brazil, Peru, and
Bolivia.

The city of Pará has not much to boast of in

architecture; nevertheless, from the river, it has an imposing appearance, from the number of its churches. The convent of San Merced and the president's palace, amongst old buildings, and the new theatre, a very elegant structure, are all worthy of notice. The streets are mostly broad and well paved, fairly lighted with gas by an English company, and kept decently clean. There is a very good market-place, and water is now being laid on to every house. Excellent hired carriages ply, at moderate prices, for the accommodation of the richer city merchants; while a tramway, worked by a locomotive and cars, takes the humbler individual out to join his family circle in the cooler districts of Nazareth, a very pretty suburb of Pará, where the principal merchants have built many elegant villa residences. As most of the roads run down avenues of very handsome palm trees, the effect of the whole is charming. There are also two public gardens, maintained with a good deal of taste.

The Europeans resident in Pará are extremely hospitable, and the staff of engineers and others to which I was attached, took away with them to the solitudes of the Madeira River most grateful recollections of the kindness, attention, and good wishes bestowed on them during their stay in Pará, more especially by the English and German consuls.

Pará does not enjoy a very good reputation for its climate, but I do not think it is so bad as is generally supposed. It has a fair alternation of wet and dry seasons, and the air is so pure that it is said that persons suffering from consumption rapidly recover after a short stay there. Yellow fever and small-pox sometimes linger a long time amongst the lower classes, being maintained a good deal, I believe, by the exhalations at low tides from the silted-up mud in front of the river wall. As I have said, it is probable that this silting up could in future be avoided by erecting a screw-piled pier instead of a wharf wall; and if the country behind the town were cleared further inland, the plague of mosquitoes might be materially decreased.

A trip up the Amazon is extremely pleasant, for the steamers of the Amazon company are commanded by very accomplished and amiable Brazilian captains. The table is very fairly found for one that can accustom himself to Brazilian cookery, and a liberal ration of Portugese "vino verde" is supplied to passengers. The upper deck, covered with a double-planked water-tight awning which protects one from the hot sun, affords an agreeable lounge during the day, whilst at night it forms the general dormitory where each passenger slings his hammock and mosquito net, if he has been thoughtful enough to provide himself with these indispensable articles of a travelling equipment for Brazil.

## CHAPTER II.

Bay of Marajo—Lighthouses—Rule of the road for steamers—Vegetation on the Amazon—Rubber trees—Boa Vista—Corralinha—Breves—Parainha—Gurupá—Mont Alegre—Cattle-feeding grounds —River Tapajoz—Santarem—American settlers—Obidos—Manufacture of charqui—Villa Bella—Serpa—Navigation of the Amazon.

THE start up river is generally made from Pará soon after midnight, in order that the wide estuary termed the Bay of Marajo may be passed before noon of the following day, as the trade wind that sets in towards the afternoon raises too high a sea for the steamers built with overhanging main decks.

In the immediate neighbourhood of Pará there are some sugar plantations and brick and tile factories, which have a pretty appearance on the river banks, but as soon as the steamer passes the bay and gets into the narrow channels which are at the junction of the river Pará and the main stream of the Amazon, the scenery becomes flat and monotonous. There are several well-kept lighthouses on the banks of the bay and on the islands therein, but more will be required as the navigation increases. Some of the channels through which the steamers work their way are so narrow, that there is hardly room for two steamers to pass each other in them ; some are therefore used for the ascending journey only, while others serve for the downward passage; and so well is this " rule of the road" kept by the Brazilian pilots and captains, that collisions are of very rare occurrence.  On the main river the rule is that ascending steamers should keep to either bank, by preference the right, whilst descending steamers have the centre of the river and the full force of the current let free for them.

The islands and the mainland in the lower part of the Amazon are covered with a dense vegetation, almost impassable by any living being but the tapir, or "anta" as it is there called, the lianas and water plants being closely intertwined and growing amongst the lofty trees of the forest.  In these low-lying lands a considerable population of Brazilian, Portuguese, negroes and half-castes live, their occupation being entirely confined to the collecting of the rubber for which the city of Pará is famous.  This tree (*Siphonia elastica*) grows in groups, small paths called "estradas" being cut through the localities where it most abounds.  The lands being mostly subject to flooding at high water, all the houses are built upon piles; and as no cultivation can be carried on, the dwellers therein are entirely dependent on the steamers for their supplies of provisions.  Nearly every house has a small wharf projecting out into the river, to which the steamers can haul up and receive the firewood prepared for them, or take in the rubber, on their return journeys to Pará.  In consequence of the daily flooding of these lands, it is not strange that the people have a washed-out and sallow look, and appear to suffer greatly from fever and ague.

Leaving Pará behind us, the first places passed

on the upward journey are Boa Vista and Corralinha, the latter a little town that, from the steamer, looks very pretty with its white church and houses. On the second day, Breves, a small town on a very narrow channel of the Amazon, is arrived at. It is a small, unimportant, and very unhealthy place, being built on land that cannot be a couple of feet above high water. Then Parainha and Gurupá, small villages, are passed, and Mont Alegré is reached on the third day. Here there are large pampas, on which cattle are reared in great numbers.

These " fazendas de ganado," or cattle-runs, are very valuable properties, especially those that have hilly lands on them, where the cattle can take refuge during the periodical inundations. The fourth day brings the steamer to Santarem, on the Tapajoz River, a short distance from its junction with the Amazon. The Tapajoz is a fine river of clear darkish-coloured water, very different in appearance to the whitish water of the great river, which always contains a certain amount of sediment.

Santarem is a very pretty town of about 3000 or 4000 inhabitants, and is built upon rising ground on the right bank, its fine church showing to great advantage. The climate of this place appears to be delightful and the lands of very good quality. On a range of hills a few leagues from the town, some American settlers have established themselves, and seem to be well satisfied with their location. They grow sugar-cane largely, selling their sugar and rum to great advantage in Santarem.

Obidos, about a day's steaming from Santarem, is the next town on the Amazon, and has more inhabit-

ants than any of the places yet passed. Here there
is a small fort, and a few artillerymen keep up a
show of barring the passage of the river to any
possibly hostile craft. Large stores of firewood are
kept on the river-side for the steamers, most of which
call here to embark bullocks or their necessary supply
of fuel. In Obidos a great trade in " charqui," or
jerked beef, is carried on, it being the emporium to
which the owners of the estancias send their stocks.
Obidos charqui appears to enjoy a special fame
throughout Brazil, and is preferred to that made in
the southern provinces of the empire. To acquire a
taste for it takes considerable time, although, " faute
de mieux," I have managed to make many a good
hearty meal from it. It is curious to note the clever
manner in which the fresh meat is cut out into great
sheets, called " mantas," or blankets. These sheets
of meat are rubbed with salt, and after being dried
in the sun and wind, are rolled up into bundles,
which are tied up with lianas and are then ready for
sale. The price of a Brazilian arroba of charqui,
weighing thirty-three pounds, varies from six to ten
milreis, say from fourpence to sevenpence per pound.
Obidos is about the highest place on the Amazon at
which the daily influence of the tides is felt, the river
rising and falling about two feet at this place,
against a tide of about twenty feet at Pará.

Above Obidos, high lands on the right bank of
the Amazon mark where the provinces of Pará and
Amazonas meet: these hills are known as the Serra
dos Parentins. The small town of Villa Bella on the
right or southern bank of the river being passed,
Serpa, opposite the river Madeira, is reached on

the sixth day's navigation from Pará.   Here, in view of the opening up of trade with Bolivia *viâ* the Madeira River and the Railway of the Rapids, the Brazilian Government has lately established a custom-house; and the town, though but small now, will doubtless become of importance in the course of a few years.   Unless the steamer in which one is voyaging is on a special trip up the Madeira, a visit will have to be paid to Manáos, the capital of the province of Amazonas, for it is there that the larger steamers remain, and passengers for the upper waters of the Amazon, the Purus, or the Madeira, have to take the smaller but still comfortable steamers that ascend these rivers.

The navigation of the river Amazon is free all the year round, between Pará and Manáos, for vessels of any tonnage or draught, if we except the alleged existence, in September or October of very dry years, of a sandbank near Villa Bella, on which it is said that vessels drawing more than eight feet have grounded; but if they have, it has, in my belief, been owing to faulty pilotage, for I think there must be good water always throughout the whole of the course.

# CHAPTER III.

MANÁOS, a small but well-built town of about 5000 inhabitants, is situated on the banks of the Rio Negro, whose black waters offer a great contrast to the white but muddy waters of the Amazon. The town is clean and fairly paved, and the stores, kept principally by Portuguese merchants, are extremely well filled with general articles. The authorities of the province, led by their intelligent and talented president, Doctor Domingos Monteiro Peixoto, are evidently desirous of improving the condition of the place by every possible means, and concessions and subventions are given to any scheme that promises to be of public utility. Premiums on cattle imported to Manáos are given ; a contract for lighting the town with gas, and a liberal subvention for a water supply are offered ; while the sum of £10,000 per annum was given to a *concessionnaire* for the organization of a company to run steamers direct from Manáos to Europe, six times during the twelve months. There is also a German house lately established, whose vessels are towed up the Amazon without having to unload at Pará, the house receiving a considerable drawback on the duties payable according to the general tariff. A good public school where boys are taught useful trades and handicrafts exists, and appears to be well managed. Some Germans were engaged in Hamburg, and brought to Manáos as teachers of carpentry, masonry, smith's-work, and other useful occupations, and were paid good salaries, but could not settle themselves down to steady work or to Brazilian fare; they were therefore sent back to Hamburg, at great loss and expense to the province.

There is at Manáos an obelisk erected to commemorate the opening of the river Amazon to free navigation by all flags. This took place in 1867, and was a politic act on the part of the Emperor of Brazil, which is much appreciated by all the dwellers on the river. For the present this privilege is only given as far as Manáos on the Amazon, and Borba on the Madeira, but there is no doubt but that it will be extended to all the navigable waters when commerce calls for further facilities.

As a field for emigration, Manáos offers many advantages; its climate is good, and there are no mosquitoes or other insect plague, for although these abound on the Amazon and other rivers, there are none on the lower part of the Rio Negro. The blackness of the water of this river is said to be caused by the tannin imparted to it by the trees on its banks, and the presence of this substance, though perfectly harmless to human beings, seems to be fatal to the production of insect life. After a stay in Manáos, one wishes that all the waters of South

America could be impregnated in like manner, so that the fearful plague of flies and mosquitoes might become unknown throughout the land. Grants of good agricultural land would doubtless be made by the provincial authorities, and as there is a well-established city, and constant communication by steamers with Europe at least once a week, emigrants would not feel so lonely as they do in districts less accessible.

The Madeira is much narrower than the Amazon, and may be said to have a general width of about half a mile to 1000 yards. The current is, however, much swifter than that of the Amazon, and runs, when the river is at half flood, at about four miles an hour. The banks are, as a rule, much higher and better defined than those of the Amazon, there being few, if any, lagoons on its course from Serpa to the rapids

The only trade of consequence at present on the river Madeira is the collection of rubber, the forests on either bank abounding in groves of the *Syphonia elastica*, the tree that yields this valuable product. The rubber trade, as at present carried on, on this river, is a most delusive one, and few, if any, of the speculators have gained fortunes from their labours. In consequence of the large profits that were made when the river was first opened up, the "seringueiros," as the collectors are called, devote all their time to working the trees already discovered, or to finding out new ones; therefore agriculture is entirely neglected, and all provisions have to be brought from Pará; for, in many cases, the seringueiros will not tell off an Indian to hunt or fish, labour being so scarce that, in order to send as much rubber as possible to their creditors in Pará, the seringueiros must get all the work they can out of their Indians in the season favourable for entering the forests. This season may be said to last from April to November. The "estradas," or roads of rubber trees, yield well on the Madeira, but some are much more prolific than others; trees on lands that are inundated at times only, yielding better than those on very low or on elevated grounds. The method of collection is, that small tin pots, possibly holding about a third of a pint, are hung on the tree closely under an incision made at an angle so that the sap of the tree may run into the pot. These are emptied daily into convenient vessels, which are carried to the peon's hut near by. Fires made from nuts of the motocu palm are then made, and the sap being emptied out into large vessels, the operator dips a kind of flat wooden shovel in it, and immediately holds the shovel over the smoke, which causes the sap to coagulate quickly. The smoke from these nuts is found to effect this much quicker than any other process; and from the large demand for them, these nuts are in some districts getting very scarce, the absurd practice of felling the tree for the sake of the nut having been much resorted to. The operation above described having been frequently repeated, the coagulated sap attains a thickness of about a couple of inches; it is then cut on one side, and the shovel is withdrawn, leaving the rubber in its marketable shape, its price being regulated according to its freedom from impurities. There is, however, very little difference in quality

of the " bolachas," or biscuits, as they are called, the
price generally being about 26 to 30 milreis, say
£2 12s. to £3 per Brazilian arroba of 33 lbs.,
according to the demand or the crop.    A low
quality, called " sernamby " in Pará and " negro-
head " on the London market, is a collection of all
the scrapings of, or droppings from, the vessels, and,
being full of impurities, fetches only about half the
price of the " bolachas."

The only other exports from the Madeira River
are Brazil nuts (*Bertholetis exelsa*) and Sapucaya
nuts (*Acythis ollaria*), which are collected and
shipped to Pará, principally for exportation to the
United States.

Guaraná, collected principally at the town of
Maués nearly opposite to Serpa, but situated
inland upon a small stream of the same name, forms
an item of considerable value in the trade with
Bolivia and the province of Matto Grosso, and is
a preparation of the fruit of the guaraná tree
(*Paullinia sorbilis*).

The beans are ground up, and pressed into
cylindrical masses of about eight or ten inches in
length by one and a half to two inches diameter.
The quality varies in accordance with the evenness
of the paste and its freedom from impurities.   The
taste is slightly acrid, and its property of astringency
renders it valuable in diarrhœa and other kindred
sicknesses ; but in the central parts of South America
it is freely taken as a beverage, and there are many
Bolivians who would fast all day, and even forswear
their beloved " chicha," rather than miss their glass
of guaraná and water, taken at daybreak, immediately

after rising. What the peculiar virtues of the guaraná may be, I cannot say; for, though I tried it many times, I discovered none at all. Some people consider it a specific for sick headache, but my experience does not allow me to recommend it as a perfect cure. Probably it sustains the body in a similar manner to the coca plant; for I have seen many Bolivians who positively could not begin their day's work without their glass of guaraná. In order to drink it, the mass is rasped down on the dried tongue of the **pirarucú** fish, until about a tea-spoonful of powder is obtained, and this is taken with half a pint of water sweetened to the palate. So great a sale exists for this article both in Bolivia and in Matto Grosso, that traders on the Madeira River never make the return journey without taking several hundredweights amongst their cargoes, and some are content to load up their canoes entirely with it.

## CHAPTER IV.

THE first village arrived at in the ascent of the
Madeira is Borba, an old Jesuit settlement about
twelve hours' steam from the junction of the Madeira
and Amazon.  Tobacco of excellent quality is grown
at Borba, and fetches about two milreis, or four
shillings, per pound.  The method of preparing the
tobacco is very simple, the picked leaves being
strung up in the roof of the hut until properly dried,
when they are, by hand, pressed into a stick-like
form of an inch and a half in diameter, and being
tied closely round with split cane, are sold in " masas "
of from four to six feet in length.

Ascending the river, Sapucaia-oroca and Arauna-
cuara, rubber gatherers' huts are passed, and the
Island of Araras is reached on the third day's
steaming in the river.  This island is of considerable
size, and is the property of the Amazon Steam
Shipping Company of Pará.  It is very rich in
rubber and nut trees, and sarsaparilla and other
drugs are found there, but no minerals.

About three hours' steam above this island, "Las Piedras de Uruás," or the Rocks of Uruás, are reached. These form the first danger to navigation, and, uncovered at low water, leave only a channel of about fifty yards wide, a rather tortuous passage for the steamer. A careful pilot can, however, always take a steamer drawing not more than eight feet through with perfect safety; while from high to half-flood water, the rocks offer no obstruction whatever.

Next in order, Cachoerina and Exaltacion are passed, the former a single house only, and the latter one of the largest rubber settlements on the river. On the fifth day the village of Manicoré is arrived at. It is a settlement of the Mundurucu Indians who have been brought into entire subjection, and who, though proverbially lazy, are quiet and well disposed. At this village are several storekeepers who trade with these Indians.

Marmélos, a collection of sandbanks requiring caution on the part of the pilot when the river is low, come next in order. Then **Bayetas** and **Juma**, both rubber stations, and San Pedro, a government mission under the care of Franciscan friars, are passed in succession. Crato, one of the best cleared spots on the river, is reached on the eighth day's journey : here there are good grazing grounds, and the place is now remarkable for its healthy climate, though strange to say, not many years ago, perhaps less than thirty, it was used by the Brazilian Government as a penal settlement where prisoners of very bad character were kept, the climate being then so bad that their term of imprisonment was soon cut short

by their death.   About three miles above Crato is
Umaitá, a thriving Portuguese settlement belonging
to Don Juan Montero, who is the wealthiest settler
on the Madeira River.   He has a small steamer of
his own that trades between Umaitá and Pará.   Das
Abeillas, a Brazilian rubber collector's head-quarters,
is the next station passed, and then an ascending
steamer enters on the reserve of the Parententin
Indians, and steams through some score or so of
leagues of lands where no settler has yet been able
to keep a footing.   It is supposed that, about two
centuries ago, these savages were Christianized by
the earlier Jesuit Fathers, and that, in consequence
of some bad treatment, they revolted, and are now
deadly enemies of any settlers, whether whites or
mestizoes.   The idea is strengthened by the fact
that a raid on one of their temporary settlements,
practised a few years ago by the Portuguese of
Umaitá, in retaliation for a murderous attack on a
rubber gatherer's hut set up near the territory
roamed over by these savages, found roughly carved
crosses and figures that might be supposed to represent
saints, in the huts of these Parententins.   However
this may be, they now have the reputation of being
cannibals, and no settler dares to set up a hut on
their territory, although it contains very rich growths
of rubber trees.

The Brazilian Government does not allow the
improvement of these savage races by the only
practical method, namely extermination, but trusts to
the efforts of the few missionary friars to whom is
entrusted the work of proselytizing the untamed
tribes of the interior of the empire.   These efforts

might doubtless be successful in partially civilizing milder tribes, such as the Mundurucus of the Amazon, the Pamas of the Purus, or the Caripunas of the Madeira, but they are perfectly unable to tame fierce tribes, such as the Parententins of the Madeira, the Ycanga Pirangas of the Jamary, or the Sirionos of the River Grande of Eastern Bolivia, tribes that refuse to hold any converse with the white faces, but attack suddenly with their arrows whenever they can come across an unprepared party. For these irreclaimable sons of the forest there is no taming method other than the rifle and bullet, and it is no use trying to shirk the fact that they must be removed out of the way of the opening up to commerce of the Amazon and its tributaries.

The termination of the Parententin territory is marked by the junction of the river Machado on the eastern or right bank of the Madeira. Above this point the huts of rubber gatherers are again met with, and on the ninth day's steaming on the Madeira, the "Praia," or sandbank of Tamandoa, which at low water forms a vast and barren deposit for many miles of the river's course, is reached. In the dry season, when the river is low, in the months of August and September, enormous numbers of turtles frequent these sandbanks for the purpose of depositing their eggs. On one occasion, passing this bank in a canoe at daybreak, I saw an extraordinary sight. For miles, as far as the eye could reach down the river, which hereabouts runs straight for some six or seven miles, were continuous rows of turtle at the water's edge; the rows being eight and ten deep, many thousands of turtle must have been collected together. The business of gathering the eggs of these turtles for making oil, and catching the turtles for food, is one of the regular occupations of the settlers on the river, who flock to these sand-banks in great number at the time of lowest water.

On the tenth day's journey on the Madeira, and about the sixteenth from Pará, the steamer should arrive at San Antonio, the first of the rapids of the Madeira River. The total distance from Parà to San Antonio is said to be about 1600 miles, the upward journey generally occupying fifteen to sixteen days, while the return has been made by a steamer belonging to the National Bolivian Navigation Company, in six days and seven hours.

# CHAPTER V.

Madeira and Mamoré Railway—Ocean steamers can ascend to the first
rapid—Brazilian outposts—Difference between high and low water
below the rapid—Rainfall—Temperature—Scenery—Marks on rocks
—Glossy black deposit on rocks—Trees of the forest—Brazil nuts—
Alligators—Peixebois, pirahybas, pirarucus, and other fish—Tapirs,
how shot—Onças, and other animals—Birds, wild turkeys, ducks,
etc.—Insects, mosquitoes, ants, etc.—Snakes, etc., etc.

FROM San Antonio the railway commences that is
in course of construction by the Madeira and Mamoré
Railway Company. This line, which is to run upon
the eastern side of the rapids, has for its object the
establishment of communication between the navigable waters of the Mamoré and Guaporé or Itenez
in Eastern Bolivia, and the Madeira and Amazon in
Northern Brazil. The length of the line will be
about 180 miles, and it is estimated to cost £6000
per mile, with a metre gauge. At foot of the rapid
of San Antonio the river forms a bay on the right
or eastern bank of the river, on which the wharf and
terminus of the railway will be built. For eight or
nine months of the year, ocean-going steamers could
ascend the Madeira and make fast alongside the
bank, but for three months of the dry season, August
to October, steamers that do not draw more than
three to four feet will have to ship the produce
brought down by the railway to San Antonio, and

tranship into the ocean steamers either at Manáos, Serpa, or Pará.

My object being to describe a route of travel, it would be out of place to remark at length upon the commercial importance of the enterprise of the Madeira and Mamoré Railway; I would therefore claim attention for it principally on the ground that it will afford means of rapidly passing the barrier placed by the falls of the Madeira River in the way of navigation from Bolivia and the province of Matto Grosso, in Brazil, to the Amazonian outlet to the Atlantic Ocean. No doubt exists in my mind that the railway will draw to itself a very considerable and important traffic, as it will open up provinces in Bolivia and Brazil that at present have no means whatever of exporting their valuable products of either mineral or agricultural industry.

San Antonio bears a bad reputation for ague and fever, but I lived there for nearly two years and did not suffer any serious attack, and the place is rapidly improving now that a somewhat extensive clearing has been made. A Brazilian outpost, or " destaca- mento," with about thirty soldiers under the charge of a captain-commandant, is maintained, the next destacamento being on the river Itenez, in the province of Matto Grosso. The Madeira River below the falls has a total difference of forty-eight feet and a half between the highest flood water in the rains, and its lowest water in the dry season. The highest water is generally reached in the month of March, while the lowest obtains in September. The rainfall at San Antonio, according to measurements taken by me in 1872 and 1873, may be said to be about ninety inches per annum. There are six months of dry season, from May to October inclusive, and from January to March seems to be the wettest quarter. The heat, at times, is great in the dry season, the thermometer sometimes rising to 95° Fahr. in the shade; but, speaking generally, the temperature is not nearly so high as might be expected

SAN ANTONIO—RIVER MADEIRA (LOOKING DOWN STREAM).

from the latitude of the place, the highest and lowest average temperatures for the year being 82° to 88° at day, and 69° to 75° at night.

At San Antonio on the railway side, or right bank, of the river, the land is hilly, and the islands forming the rapid have a pleasing look, as they are covered with foliage. Below the settlement is a spit of rock running out into mid river, and uncovered at

low water.   On these rocks are many peculiar
grooves or marks on the sloping surfaces ; they are
about a finger's depth, and cross each other at
different angles, while some are quite distinct and
separate from the others.   It has been suggested
that these marks are the work of some of the tribes
of the district, but my opinion would rather be, that
they have been caused by glacial action.   At the
rapid of Riberão there are some carvings on rocks
uncovered at lowest water only, that represent
animals, birds, and circles or squares, and these
of course are due to human agency ; but the
occurrence at all the rapids, and the great number of
the straight grooves, decidedly favours the view that
they are not the result of manual labour.   The rocks
at all the rapids are covered with a glossy black
substance, which seems to be a deposit left by the
waters during floods, and possibly enamelled by the
sun's heat during the dry season.   If I recollect
rightly, Humboldt noticed this deposit on the rocks
of the upper waters of the Orinoco, and defined it
to be a deposit left by the flood waters of the rainy
seasons, but as I have not his " Travels in South
America " at hand to refer to, I may be incorrect in
this reference.

The forests are of lofty trees, many being of very
valuable timber for house building and for railway
purposes.   Rubber trees are plentiful, also Brazil
nuts and cocoa trees, the latter in a wild state but
yielding very excellent fruits.   Sarsaparilla, vanilla,
copayba and annatto abound, also fustic and other
dyewoods, while many of the barks and bejucas or
sipoys might be utilized as fibres.   The Brazil nut

tree *Bertholetis excelsa* is perhaps the handsomest tree of the forest, its dark green foliage showing to great advantage over the top of its neighbours. The fruit when fresh is very agreeable and sweet, being very different to the nut as sold dry and tasteless in London.

Of fish and game, the forest and the river yield an abundant supply to the settler or traveller. Besides turtle in any quantity, alligators are in great numbers. The former is a favourite food of the Indian labourers of Brazil and Eastern Bolivia, who are also not at all averse to a dish of the latter; and I can vouch for the fact that the tail of a young alligator not more than three or four feet in length is a most excellent dish, being as nearly like filleted sole as can be imagined. When the reptiles grow to a larger size, the flesh has a very repugnant flavour and smell of musk. Amongst fishes may be mentioned—the boto, which has the shape of a large porpoise, but is white-coloured and has a snout or proboscis about a foot in length. The peixeboi and pirahyba are very large, many being seven and eight feet in length; they, as well as the botos, are only killed for the oil that can be extracted from their carcases by boiling. Pirarucus of very large size and weight are found principally in the back waters or lagoons bordering on the river, and are much sought after for salting down, in which state they form the staple food of the settlers on the Madeira. I have heard that a fair-sized pirarucu will give from five to six Brazilian arrobas (of 33 lbs. each) of salted fish, and as I have seen them over ten feet long and eighteen inches to two feet in diameter, I can give them credit for yielding such a large quantity of solid food. The pescado, a fish with scales, and to be caught from one to three feet in length, is the best eating fish in the river, and is equal in flavour to fresh cod or bream. This fish is curious from the fact of its having two stones situated in the broad bones at the top of the head, just above the eyes. The tambaqui, dorado, surubi, pintado, and the joão may also be named as good eating fish, while the fisherman will often wish heartily that the palometa fish could be exterminated at once and for ever. This fish is flat and small, seldom passing a foot in length, but has a very large mouth for its size, full of the sharpest possible teeth, with which it not only takes the bait from the hook without any danger to itself, but has also been known to take a good-sized piece out of a bather's leg.

The only large animal in the country is the tapir, sometimes called the " anta," and sometimes the " gran bestia." He is a very timorous and inoffensive animal, and must be shot at night-time, the practice being for the huntsman to set up what is called a " chapapa," or raised platform of poles, sometimes placed in the fork of a conveniently situated tree. This platform must command the pool of mud where the tapir comes for his nightly bath and supper of succulent roots ; and some hunters place a candle or small lamp near the pool, the light of which attracts the stupid beast. A moonlight night is, however, the best for the sport, if such it may be called, and as soon as the animal shows, the contents of one barrel are generally sufficient to bring down the game. The tapirs are as large as a fair-sized Brazilian bullock, and the flesh is much like beef in taste. There are also "onças," a species of small jaguar, and tiger-cats of small size; wild pigs, or peccaries, in great number; capybaras, or river hogs; squirrels and other small rodents, monkeys in great variety, small deer, sloths, ant-eaters, armadillos; "lapas," or "pacas," a rodent whose flesh is capital eating; and "lobos," or otters, of great size and fierceness.

Besides numerous small birds of great beauty in their plumage, such as toucans, humming-birds, "carpinteros," and "campaneros" or bell-ringers, there are hoopoes, or "ciganas," which are uniformly reckoned as unclean, and the ever-present forest scavenger, the vulture, or "souchu," called "urubu" in Brazil and "samura" in Central America. A more pleasant and useful list would comprise— "pavas" and "guachacas," species of wild pheasants; "mutuns," or wild turkeys; "perdrices," or wild partridges; "patos royales," or black ducks—the finest duck in the world; "marecas," or Orinoco geese—a brown duck equal, I should think, to a canvas-back; sheldrakes, snipes, widgeons, teal, herons, storks, and numerous other water fowl. From this list it may be seen that the locality offers plenty of occupation for the sportsman who is content with small game, and is not ambitious of leaving his name on the roll of the mighty hunters of "greater game."

The insect plagues of the district have still to be mentioned; and certainly, when one looks back upon the sufferings undergone from the attacks of these brutes, one is tempted to wonder greatly why such plagues exist. Many fine arguments have been brought forward by the advocates of the theory that everything in nature has its use, in order to prove that some good results from the existence of a mosquito, but I who have suffered for years from these pests have hitherto failed to discover any benefit in their attacks, and cannot see the excellence of the design that exposes a human body to be the breeding ground of a " gusanero," a beast of a fly that attacks you, you know not when, till after three or four months you know that he has done so, by the swelling up of the bitten part into a fair-sized boil, from which issues a maggot of perhaps an inch and a half in length. I have heard it said that the bite of a mosquito is beneficial, as it thins the blood of a dweller in swampy tropical regions ; but if this were so, they might be arranged to carry out this bene-ficial design without causing exquisite pain to the party operated upon ; but the theory is an incorrect one, for there are spots on the banks of the Ama-zonian rivers where there would be much less fever if the countless hosts of mosquitoes or " carapanas," " gusaneros," " marigueys " and " tavernas," could be exterminated. The ant tribes are also very numerous and objectionable, coming raiding at times in such numbers that there is nothing left to do, but, snatching up your clothes and bedding as quickly as you may, make tracks to a new location. The larger ants are very venomous, their bite causing intense pain, equal almost to that caused by scorpions or centipedes, which, also, are pretty numerous in the dead wood and rotting leaves of the forest. Snakes, also, are plentiful, the deadly coral snake, and a yellow and black fellow called the "tiger," being the species most frequently met with. The former is seldom seen more than about a foot in length, while the latter is frequently met with eight or ten feet long and four to six inches in diameter. A list of these insect and reptile plagues gives a rather horrible idea of the district, but the annoyances are lost sight of in the excitement and pleasure caused by travelling through new solitudes and territories so far removed from all civilization; and at nightfall, when on the march, one lays down perfectly at one's ease on an outstretched hide, without giving a thought to any of the venomous creatures that possibly pass over the sleeper just as they would over a log of wood intervening in their path. A good mosquito-net, or bar, as it is sometimes called, is a perfect safeguard to the intrusion of any of these creatures, provided that the falling sides and ends are well secured from being raised by wind during the night: but I would especially advise a traveller to avoid the ordinary net that outfitters and others always recommend so strongly. The mariguey of the Madeira is about the size of a midge, and will lodge on the net, and having walked inside will torment the inmate beyond belief. The only materials that circumvent him entirely, and yet allow for ventilation, are ordinary figured muslins, or a thin blue unglazed calico with a small check pattern, both of which can be had in Parà at moderate prices.

## CHAPTER VI.

Rapids of the Madeira River—Journey undertaken—Canoes, Indians, and
other requirements for the journey described—Articles good for
trading with savages—Provisions, etc.

THE journey onwards becomes rather laborious, as
canoes must now be the means employed for the
ascent of the rapids and the upper riverine systems
of Eastern Bolivia and Western Brazil.   I made this
journey in 1874, starting from San Antonio on the
24th of April, in company with some Bolivian
merchants who were returning to their country with
general stores purchased in Pará, for sale in the
department of the Beni in Eastern Bolivia.   When
prosecuting my journey, I endeavoured to note down
whatever might have called for notice during the
day's run, and although incurring, perhaps, the risk
of being rather tedious, I think it will now be the
best plan to copy the notes I then entered in my
diary, in order that the rapids and other portions of
the route travelled over may be described in proper
order.

   But, first, it is necessary to describe the arrangements requisite for the ascent of the rapids and the
Mamoré to the most eastern towns of Bolivia.   Large
canoes, called on the river " batelãos," or " igariteas,"
are the craft required, a good and useful one being

from eight to ten yards in length, by about four or five feet beam ; they draw from two to four feet of water, and will carry from three to six tons. A crew of not less than ten peons and a captain is required for a canoe laden with, say three tons, and the Bolivian Indians of the Beni are the best paddlers or " marineros," the Brazilian peons not being so expert in getting the canoes over the many miles of

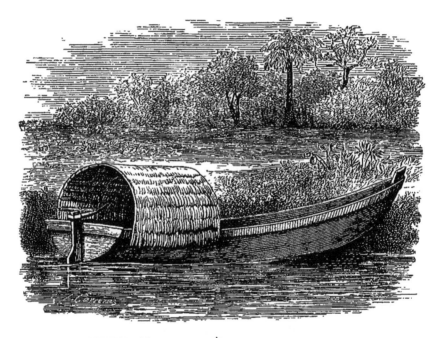

GARITEA, OR TRAVELLER'S CANOE, RIVER MADEIRA.

broken water that have to be encountered. It is unwise to attempt to make either the upward or downward journey with single embarkations, because at, at least three of the rapids, the canoes have to be totally unladen and dragged over the portages, which invariably have to cross a small but steep hill, and one crew is quite unable to haul the canoe over any one of these hills. It is best, therefore, always to

D

arrange a party of three or more canoes, before commencing the ascent or descent of the rapids.    Canoes
travelling singly are also much exposed to attacks
from the wandering families of savages on the river
banks, while parties of three or more canoes in
company have rarely if ever been molested.    A small
canoe, or "montaria," is extremely useful for the
purpose of sending the cable ahead of the large
canoe, when a strong current is met with that the
paddles are unable to overcome.    This cable should
be about fifty or sixty yards long, and may be of
good hemp or piassava; there should be one for each
canoe, and the test of the strain of at least thirty
men should be applied to each cable before the
journey is commenced, as breakages of bad cables
cause an immense amount of vexation, and a great
deal of danger.    The canoes have a cabin at the
stern end, made of palm leaves, covered with a
raw hide if possible.    In this cabin the "patron," or
owner, arranges his small stores, guns, books, etc.,
and, with the addition of a narrow hair mattress,
manages to make of it a very snug abode, which
serves for his parlour by day, and sleeping quarters
at night, except when amongst the rapids, when it is
always safer to sleep on shore, for fear of the canoe
breaking away during the night, and taking its
sleeping occupant over the nearest rapid below.
Besides, it is not advisable to trust one's self too
implicitly in the hands of the Indian marineros, for
cases are on record where an Indian, to be revenged
on his patron for some well-deserved punishment
perhaps, has cut the rope by which the canoe has
been made fast, and has sent his patron to his last

reckoning in a brutal and treacherous manner; and it must be borne in mind that, in a crew of Indians, there may easily be one black sheep, however tractable and good-natured the majority are. I have never had cause to complain of treachery or vindictiveness on the part of the Bolivian Indians, and believe that if they are kindly and honestly dealt with they are most trustworthy in every way; but discretion is the better part of valour, and it is well to be on the safe side, which is, amongst the rapids, the river bank, and not the cabin, or " camarota," of the canoe. It is also well to provide each canoe with a short length of chain and a good stout padlock, for securing it to a tree at nightfall.

The traveller will naturally furnish himself with firing-irons after his own heart, but I would recommend him to add to his own particular fancy, a Winchester sixteen-shot repeating rifle, for they make splendid shooting, are light, portable, and carry a good armament ready at hand in case of a brush with savages. A double-barrelled shot-gun; a pair of revolvers (not fitted with cartridge extractors, which invariably get rusted and clogged up unless they are taken to pieces and cleaned thoroughly every day—an almost impossible task), a good hunting knife, or " machete," for clearing one's path amongst the reeds on the river bank or through the forest, and a good assortment of fishhooks and lines, will about complete the inventory of " materiel de guerre " advisable. To preserve one's guns and knives from the rust which covers them completely in one night if they are left ungreased, I found that the best thing was " Andiroba oil," which can be obtained in any quantity in Pará or Manáos. This oil is expressed from the nuts of the Andiroba tree (*Xylocarpus caropa*), and is used in Brazil for lighting purposes principally. It makes, however, a first-rate lubricant for machinery, and the way it protects steel or iron from rust is simply marvellous. Guns and pistols should be rubbed clean about twice a week, and then, if the oil is laid on lightly with wool or tow, they will keep their polish and browning in the dampest spots. A stock of knives, axes, machetes, beads, fish-hooks, and ready-made canvas or common flannel shirts should also be taken, in readiness for the chance of an amicable " pow-wow " with the " barbaros," as the traveller will naturally be desirous of bringing away a record of his visit, in the shape of arrows, bows, necklets of seeds, feathers, teeth ornaments, etc., from these gentry. As for provisions, it is well not to despise the humble farinha, charqui, or bacalao, although most Europeans find it difficult to bring their palates to this plain diet ; but when the ducks have been wild, or the exigencies of the journey have hindered the traveller from procuring his supper from the fresh meats afforded by the forest or the river, he will find that the good appetite his day's work with the canoe has given him, proves a good sauce, even to a dish of charqui soup, rice, and farinha. I found that a spoon-ful of " Liebig's Extract," added to the " chupe," or thick soup, which is the only dish known to Bolivian peons, rendered it both palatable and nutritious. Some live fowls and a few tins of vegetables, salmon, herrings, or sardines would not be amiss, as one must prepare for a voyage of about seven weeks between San Antonio and Exaltacion, the first town arrived at in Bolivia. For liquors, the river affords good potable water for those that are tectotally inclined ; but temperance principles are good for those only that cannot keep their drinking propensities within bounds, and I do not think that a European can keep his health in any tropical climate without a small and regular supply of some stimulant. A bottle or two of brandy in case of illness, a box of claret, or a garrafão of "vino verde," will be as much as the traveller can find space in his canoe for, especially as it is vitally necessary to have a good supply of cachaça (ordinary white rum, made from sugar cane, and called aguadiente, caña, pisco, or cachaça, according to locality) for the Indian crew, who need a ration, about a wine-glassful, night and morning, and also whenever they have to work at hauling the canoes in the water for any length of time. The traveller also will not despise a nip of cachaça when the wind blows coldly, and at night a little in a bowl of tea is very agreeable. As a preservative against fever, I have found it a good plan to take, every morning at daybreak, before coffee or eating, a small quantity, say about two and a half or three grains, of quinine, in a small glass of any kind of spirit; and this plan, if carried out regularly, will, I believe, take a man safely through any of the most malarious districts of South America. A capital preparation which a traveller in the tropics should, in my opinion, always be provided with, is Angostura bitters, which are made at the city of Angostura, on the river Orinoco, in Venezuela. These bitters, besides having great preservative properties against fever, for cascarilla or quinine bark is doubtless their principal ingredient, are about the finest appetizers that I ever met with. A small cocktail made with Angostura will give any one an appetite for the roughest and plainest meal that can be imagined, and I am confident that the immunity that I have enjoyed from ague has been mainly owing to my use of these bitters, as I have thereby been enabled to keep up my appetite, and make a square meal where others have been quite unable to do more than look at, and perhaps turn away from, the dishes of charqui and farinha which are often the only fare to be met with in Brazil.

# CHAPTER VII.

A start made—Canoe heavily laden—San Antonio rapid passed—Slow
progress made—Method of passing over strong currents—The current
of Macacos—The Bay of Theotonio—Canoe nearly swamped in same—
The Falls of Theotonio—Fish at foot of falls—Franciscan mission to
the Pamas—The portage of Theotonio.

On the 24th of April, I woke up all hands at 3 a.m.,
and we had the last boxes packed, the fowls caught,
put in the coop, and all on board ready for a start
at seven o'clock. On calling over the roll of oars-
men, or " marineros," as they are called, we found
that a Bolivian boy was missing, having hid himself
in the forest, so as to be left behind; for there are
many of these Indians that are so lazy that they
would rather remain on the Madeira River than
undergo the hard work of the ascent of the rapids
on their way to their own country. The canoe was
very low down in the water, the top of the gunwale
not being more than three inches out, and she therefore leaked rather badly round the top seams; but as
the wood swelled from the immersion, the leakage
decreased. We took about an hour and a half to get
from the right or eastern bank of the river, below
the rapid of San Antonio, to the other side, where
the shortest land portage for the baggage is found.
On the passage across, the canoe hung several times

in the strong current, as the crew were not yet practised together, and I had a good deal of shouting and encouraging to do in order to avoid being carried some distance down stream. The Bolivian Indian's term for "putting on a spurt" is "churka," and a good crew of twelve or fourteen paddles will make even a heavily laden canoe almost leap in the water when the paddlers "churka" well together. A Bolivian paddle is oar-shaped, and about four or five feet in length, by six inches width at the blade ; but a Brazilian one is much shorter, has a crutch-shaped handle and a round blade fifteen or sixteen inches diameter : both paddles can do excellent work in strong hands. I had to send back to the other side for a few things that, of course, had been forgotten, including my two retriever dogs, " Jack " and " Burro," who got safely through the journey up the rapids with me, but had some narrow escapes from the alligators. By the time we got the baggage over the portage to the upper side of the fall, it commenced to rain heavily, so the tarpaulins were brought into service, and the night was passed above the fall, the empty canoes having been hauled up the rapid on the San Antonio side, and passed across the river above the fall. On the 25th, the cargo was all on board again by 7 a.m., and the ascent of the river recommenced, much hard work being met with in the frequent strong currents, or "correntezas." We stayed for breakfast in an igarapé, or small stream, opposite the Macacos hut, and in the afternoon passed the first current of the same name by roping, stopping at dark between the currents.

Any one who has not travelled in a canoe up

stream on a broad and rapid river like the Madeira, is almost unable to imagine the delays and vexations caused by the slow progress that is all that can be made. The canoes must always be kept as close as possible to the bank, for out in mid-stream the paddles would be quite unable to keep way on the boat, while near the banks there is generally a little quiet water. When currents are arrived at that cannot be surmounted without the use of the cable, roping must be resorted to, and then one can't do more than perhaps twenty yards in as many minutes, for the overhanging bushes give great trouble to keep clear of, while at the same time they are very serviceable to haul by.

The 26th, Sunday—but not a day of rest, for the men prefer continuing the journey, and one cannot carry provisions sufficient to allow for one idle day in seven—we started at 5.30 a.m., after a cup of tea, and soon came to some very hard work, roping over the second current of Macacos, which we passed quite through by about 10 a.m. The land hereabouts is rather hilly on the eastern or left side, the rocks in some places rising twenty or thirty feet above the water even when the river is full. We arrived at the cataract of Theotonio about mid-day, after being very nearly swamped in the rough water below the fall. The river widens out at the foot of each one of the principal rapids, and in the case of the Theotonio, the greatest fall on the river, the bay is of very considerable size. The water here is always in a more or less agitated state, from the effect of the principal fall, which is about twenty-six feet in height, and when the wind blows up stream, the waves rise so much that canoes run great danger of being swamped. The captain of my crew took us out too far in the centre of the river, as he was anxious to avoid being thrown into the surf on the bank; but the canoe was so heavily laden that the waves dashed over the sides, and we ran great danger of swamping. Some of the crew took fright, and by rising up and ceasing to paddle, endangered greatly the safety of the canoe, its occupants, and cargo. However, by encouraging them by words and prompt action in baling out the water that had entered the canoe, we happily got to the foot of the fall, and hauled up the canoe on the flat rocks.

The fall of Theotonio is at all times a most majestic one, but is more espcially so at low water, when the full effect of the cataract can be seen. The river here is probably more than a mile in width, the fall being divided into three parts by rocky islands. I had previously visited this fall at a time when the river was almost at its lowest, and was then able to walk on the uncovered rocks almost to its centre. One could then stand right in front of the horseshoe fall and thoroughly enjoy the grand sight of the foaming and splashing waters. Any amount of fish may be caught in the pools below the fall during the months of low water, and wandering bands of the savages are then frequently met with at this rapid. At my first visit the pools were so full of fish, that some Brazilian soldiers who accompanied me were able to spear, with the greatest ease, some very large tambaquis. The fish appear to attempt to ascend the river and get stunned at the foot of the rapid, for they can be seen in the pools, rolling about rather than swimming in a natural manner. On the right or western bank of the river, at this fall, there was, during my time, a mission established by a Franciscan friar, " Frai Luis Zarraga," an Italian of good education and most pleasing and courteous maners. He had at one time as many as 200 savages of the Pama tribe, that appears to have its hunting grounds between the Madeira and the Purus Rivers, which, near the Theotonio Fall, are probably not more than fifty or sixty miles apart. These savages appear to be very mild and tractable, but the Fraile found it impossible to keep them at the mission for more than about two to three months at a time; they would then leave him, promising to return in a certain number of moons. This wandering custom appears to be a characteristic of all the savage tribes of the interior of South America, and is doubtless governed or suggested by the exigencies of hunting. When the river is full, the ravines also have plenty of water, and the fish and game go up to the sources of the waters, following the water in its downward retreat during the dry season; and the savages, who have only their hunting and fishing to depend upon for food supplies, are thus forced to be almost continually on the move.

The afternoon of the 26th was occupied in transferring my garitea and baggage to the upper side of the fall. The portage is about 600 yards in length, and passes over a rocky hill about fifty feet in height, the canoe being passed over it on rough rollers made from boughs cut from the forest near by. The Bolivian merchants, in whose company I had arranged to make the journey, were waiting at

Theotonio for me, and I very soon saw how useless it would have been to have attempted to have made the journey alone. These other patrons sent about five and twenty men to assist my crew in passing the canoe over the hill, which was done in about an hour, safely and without much trouble. We also carried over about half the cargo before nightfall; and, my tent being set up, I passed a good night, the morning part being delightfully cool.

# CHAPTER VIII.

Currents above Theotonio—Loss of a small canoe—Theft of rum at night by one of the Bolivian boatmen—The rapid of Morinhos—Crew turn out to be very weak and slow—Plan for securing a good crew—The river Yaci-Paraná—Morning fogs—Igarapé of the Caripuna savages—Capitan Cinco's Island—Buena Esperanza—Rations given to the boatmen.

ON the 27th, the rest of the cargo was on board, and breakfast over by about mid-day, when we started in line, I being last of the total file of seven canoes. About a couple of miles above Theotonio, we came to a very strong current, and had to pass over a very dangerous point of rock, getting over safely with hard work and much shouting. About 5 p.m. we came to a current by an island, the current being very strong, and the worst we had yet passed. Señor Morales sent his montaria to assist me in getting to a point of safety for the night; but the montaria was badly managed in passing the prow of my garitea, which was tied in mid-current to a tree, and, owing to this mismanagement, she struck a rock, filled, and was sucked under my canoe, and away in a moment. The four men in her fortunately escaped, by jumping on the rock and clinging to the branches of the tree, from whence they passed into my canoe. We had a dreadfully hard time for about a couple of hours, and had my rope broken we should

have gone down stream at a rapid rate ; but, fortunately, all went well, and we got to where the other
canoes were made fast for the night, about 100 yards
ahead, by 8 p.m., and had a bad night, as, in consequence of arriving so late, we were unable to cook
a supper or set up the tent.

The next day, the 28th, we started at daybreak, about half-past five o'clock, and stopping
for a short time only, about ten, for breakfast, concluded a good day's work by half-past-five at night,
when we arrived at some small shanties of palm-
leaves, that had been set up by the engineers of the
railway when cutting a road through the forest for
the entire length of the river amongst the rapids.
Here we should have passed a tolerable night, had
it not been that one of my men got to my stores,
and stole sufficient cachaça (white rum) to make
him not only very drunk, but also so offensively
noisy, that I had to get up several times during the
night and quiet him, not only by threats, but also
by a mild application of corporal punishment.   It is
a very bad plan to be continually beating one's peons,
or Indian servants, for every fault they commit.
A patron who always has a blow or a bad word for
his men cannot expect even Indians to esteem him
or work willingly for him ; but it must be borne
in mind that there is no law or authority to appeal
to in the solitudes that have to be travelled through
in the centre of South America : in fact, the patron
must be the judge, and frequently the executioner
as well, of the law ; and for serious offences, such as
gross insubordination, theft, or continued drunkenness, there is no other remedy than a judiciously

applied whipping. The best plan will be found, when the necessity arises, to form a court of which perforce you must constitute yourself both judge and witness, condemn the criminal to a punishment proportionate to the offence, and have the sentence duly administered by the captain of the crew. Thus the men will see that they are not arbitrarily punished, and a proper amount of discipline will be maintained; but I am bound to say that the Bolivian Indians can be perfectly well managed with a very slight show of authority.

The next morning I had a good deal of trouble to get my drunken reveller on board, and very soon after starting he dropped his paddle in the river, probably doing so on purpose, in order that he should not be made to work. This was very annoying, but it was of little use punishing a man in his condition, so we had to make the best way we could with one paddle short. About half-past eight in the morning we got to the next rapid, called " Morinhos," during a heavy fall of rain, and made preparations for ascending by a channel on the right or eastern bank. The upper part only of the cargoes of the canoes was unloaded at this rapid, and the crews assisting each other, all the craft were passed through the broken waters in about four hours. Some 200 yards above the fall we had some heavy roping work, and my canoe again struck on a rock in a full current, giving us altogether five or six hours' hard work to get free; but at length we got off again, and roped ahead to where the other patrons had awaited us. Arriving by night at the resting-place, or " pascana," as it is

called, is very unpleasant, as the boys have not time
to put up my small tent or screen of waterproofs,
and paddling after dark is very dangerous. Hereabouts it became clear that my crew could not keep
up with the other canoes, so I asked the Bolivian
patrons to go ahead and leave me to my snail's pace ;
this, however, they refused to do. The reason for
my delay was clearly that I had a most wretched
crew in my canoe, great in number—being sixteen
in all—but worthless in quality ; and also they were
men of different villages, and therefore did not work
well together. To travel amongst the rapids with
any degree of pleasure, one must be able to do as
did one of the Bolivian patrons, Don Miguel Cuellas,
who owned three of the largest canoes ; two of the
others belonging to one Señor Juan de Dios Molina,
and the remaining one, besides my own, to Don
Ruperto Morales. Each of Señor Cuellas' canoes
was manned with men from one village, two
having none but Baures, while the other had
Itonamas only ; thus the men understand their
captains, and work with will like a machine. Where
practicable, the plan is to find a good captain and
let him select his men from amongst his own
" parientes " or relations.

On the 30th we did a good day's work, my crew
improving a little, and at night we stopped on the
left bank, opposite the mouth of the river Yaci
Paraná, that enters the Madeira on the eastern or
Brazilian side. The night was passed in a wild
cane brake, a kind of reed called in the district
" chuchia," and from the straight tops of which the
savages make their arrows. The morning of the

1st of May broke with a very heavy fog, which, hanging over the river, did not lift until the sun attained full power by about eight o'clock. We made our start, however, at 4.15 a.m., and during the whole day paddled straight forward, the only troubles being in places where the fallen trees stretching out from the banks forced us to go out into the river where the current is always very powerful. These awkward spots being of frequent occurrence, my poor fellows could not keep up with the other crews, but after a very hard day's work we got, at 6.30 p.m., to an " igarapé," or ravine, on the left bank, where one of the Bolivian patrons had waited for me. This igarapé is known as the " igarapé de los Caripunas," as these savages have a " malocal," or clearing, in the forest about eight miles from the river. They are often to be met with hereabouts, but I was not fortunate enough to come across them. The fogs were on again the following morning, but, nevertheless, we started at 4.30 a.m., and crossed over to an island known as Capitan Cinco's, this being the name of the head man of the savages of the Caripuna tribe. We coasted round this island until about 10 a.m., when we crossed over to the mainland on the railway side of the river, namely the eastern or Brazilian side. From 11.30 a.m. to 1.30 p.m. we stopped for breakfast about half a mile below where the other canoes had pulled up. In the afternoon we paddled on till half-past six at night, when we got to some huts left by the railway engineers, and known by the name of " Buena Esperanza ; " the Bolivian patrons having arrived there as early as three o'clock in

E

the afternoon.   Here I had a conversation with the
Bolivian patrons, and sought their advice as to the
slow rate at which my men managed to paddle
the canoe, and heard, to my disgust, that there was
a report going about that my rations to the crew
were insufficient, and that some of my men had said
so.   The rations I had been giving my men were
daily ¾lb. of charqui (jerked beef), 1½lb. of farinha
(yuca flour), some rice, flour, sugar, coffee, and a
liberal serving of cachaça (white rum) night and
morning.   The meat, rice, and farinha were, in my
case, larger rations than those given by the Bolivian
patrons to their men, while the sugar and coffee
were extras altogether ; and the other men only got
tots of cachaça after working in the water, or any
other specially trying work.   I was very much
annoyed at this wretched lie, the fact being that
my crew was composed of a thoroughly worthless set
of fellows, too lazy even to make themselves a cup
of coffee before starting in the early morning.

# CHAPTER IX.

The rapid of Calderão do Inferno—Attacks of fever and vomiting—
Caripuna savages—Death of a Bolivian boy—Earth-eating practised
by the Indians—Death of Mariano, a Bolivian boatman—Peculiar
custom prevailing amongst the Indians—The Falls of Girão—
Miseries of a wet night.

THE following day we arrived at the foot of the
rapid bearing the suggestive name of " Calderão do
Inferno," or " Cauldron of Hell." This name is given
to a succession of six rapids extending over about
a mile and a half of the river, the upper one being
the principal, with a fall of about eight feet; the
lower five are called the " Rabo," or tail, of the
" Calderão." These were all passed on the left or
Bolivian side of the river, the whole of the 4th and
part of the 5th being occupied in passing the
cargoes over the land portage used for overcoming
the upper rapid. This portage is very little short
of a mile in length, and the road being very rough
and rocky, the men had very hard work. The
canoes were hauled up empty through a creek or
channel between the islands and the mainland.
The mornings now were always foggy, and the sun
during the day seemed to be exceptionally powerful,
and several of my crew were sickening with fever.
I myself had rather a bad attack of vomiting, and
had to take as much rest as possible while the

cargoes were being carried round the fall. A cup of tea made from some sort of balsam, and given to me by one of the Bolivian patrons, had good effect in allaying the sickness, but I found the most relief from two or three draughts of Lamplough's "Pyretic Saline," a medicine that every traveller in South American forests should carry. At the upper portage of this fall we found two of the bark canoes, belonging to the Caripuna savages, who have a "malocal," or clearing inland, near this rapid. The canoes appeared to have been abandoned for some time, as they were full of mud, having probably been sunk on the bank, according to the custom of these savages, when the river was at its flood height. The savages did not show, and we had no time to spare to search for them in the interior. Travellers must be on their guard in the neighbourhood of this rapid, for the tribe bears a very bad and treacherous character; and although they have been friendly to many passers-by, and were so to the engineers who cut the track for the railway, they have attacked small parties with great ferocity.

On the 6th it was nine o'clock before the last of my packages was carried over, and all the canoes started, the Bolivian patrons having again kindly waited for me. Above the fall we had much roping and pulling up stream by the bushes, although some of the other canoes that had good strong crews were able to get on with paddles only. The sun was terribly hot and overpowering, so at mid-day I ordered my men to stop and finish their breakfasts, which they had had to take very hurriedly before starting in the morning. One of my Bolivian boys,

a lad about fourteen or fifteen years old, had been
complaining yesterday and to-day of fever, so I had
allowed him to leave his paddle and lie down on
the top of the cargo, the only available space for
idle hands.   Just as the canoe touched the bank I
saw him fall back from a sitting posture, and to my
horror, when I got from my cabin to him, I found
he was evidently dying.   I applied smelling-salts
to his nose, and bathed his forehead with cachaça,
the liquor nearest to hand, giving him also a
spoonful to drink; but he died quickly, and apparently without pain.   This was another blow to
add to our misfortunes, especially as we had a man
very ill at the time, and with too good reason feared
that the shock of poor Bruno's death would prove
too great for him.   The boy Bruno had been in my
service for nearly eighteen months before leaving
San Antonio, and was always a weak and sickly
boy, besides being afflicted with the disgusting vice
of " earth-eating," so common to many of the Indian
tribes of South America.   I had succeeded in
keeping him from this practice whilst I had him in
regular service at San Antonio, but it appeared that
at the rapid of **Morinhos** he had seen some particular
kind of earth that aroused the dormant habit, and,
indulging himself too largely, his stomach must have
got into a thoroughly disorganized state, so that he
was unable to resist the intense heat of the sun.

It was melancholy work, paddling up stream all
day with the dead body of the boy on board, and
another of the Indians in a dangerous state; but the
longest day comes to an end, and at 3.30 p.m. we
crossed over to the Brazilian side of the river, just

below the last rock of the Girão Falls. The hills near this fall show bold and high as one ascends the river, and we arrived at the port, a small bay at the foot of the fall, about seven o'clock. During the night my forebodings as to losing the other sick man, Mariano, were verified, as he died about daybreak. This was the man who at Morinhos stole liquor, and fell into the river during the night; he then caught cold, and had been ailing ever since. I gave him the best remedies that I had at hand, also wine, arrowroot, and beef-tea, made from Liebig's "Extract," and I could not see that there was any sickness that should cause his death; but, about a couple of days ago, his squaw and other relations evidently made up their minds that he ought not to recover, and in accordance with a custom that exists with many of the Indian tribes, they gave him numerous commissions to those members of his family and other friends that had preceded him in their last journey. I have frequently observed the existence of this custom amongst Bolivian Indians of the Beni: when one of them falls sick, his immediate friends and companions seem to settle amongst themselves whether the sick man shall recover or not; and if their verdict is unfavourable, the poor man gets no remedies and very little, if any, food or care. The prediction is therefore brought to realization, and as the fatal moment is seen to draw near, the friends deliver to the moribund messages to their relatives or acquaintances that have before-hand joined the majority.* It is quite useless to leave

* This custom of the Indians, seems by the following extract from Josephus to have had its prototype in eastern lands in times of very ancient date.

Josephus, " Wars of the Jews," book 7, chap. 8, s. 7. In Eleazar's speech a sick Indian to the care of his fellows only, and in all cases where these Indians are brought together in numbers, attendants and nurses of other races must be provided for the care of the sick. I myself was very unwell about this time, and was quite unable to do more for my sick than give out medicines and wine, or arrowroot, etc., for them. I could not sit up with them at nights, and, unfortunately, I had no companion or head man that could be depended upon.

The next day, the 7th of May, we buried poor Bruno and Mariano at about mid-day, side by side, at the foot of the fall, and setting up a rough wooden cross over the graves, left them to the solitudes of the forest. The crew in consequence of these deaths were very downhearted, and not much work could be got out of them this day; the canoes were, how-

to the Sicaril, when advising his followers to put themselves to death rather than fall alive into the hands of the Romans, occur these words:—
" We, therefore, who have been brought up in a discipline of our own, ought to become an example to others of our readiness to die; yet if we do not stand in need of foreigners to support us in this matter, let us regard those Indians who profess the exercise of philosophy; for these good men do but unwillingly undergo the time of life, and look upon it as a necessary servitude, and make haste to let their souls loose from their bodies; nay, when no misfortune presses them to it, nor drives them upon it, these have such a desire of a life of immortality, that they tell other men beforehand that they are about to depart; and nobody hinders them, but every one thinks them happy men, and gives them letters to be carried to their familiar friends that are dead; so firmly and certainly do they believe that souls converse with one another in the other world. So when these men have heard all such commands that were to be given them, they deliver their body to the fire; and, in order to their getting their soul a separation from the body in the greatest purity, they die in the midst of hymns of commendations made to them; for their dearest friends conduct them to their death more readily than do any of the rest of mankind conduct their fellow-citizens when they are going on a very long journey, who, at the same time, weep on their own account, but look upon the others as happy persons, as so soon to be made partakers of the immortal order of beings. Are not we, therefore, ashamed to have lower notions than the Indians ? "

ever, emptied of their cargoes, and hauled over the land portage, to the upper side of the fall. This portage is nearly half a mile in length, and is over very rocky ground; the canoes are therefore exposed to suffer damage if the men are not careful to keep them on the rollers. The whole of the 8th of May was taken up in repairing the canoes, and in getting the cargoes transported over the portage, and put on board again above the fall, ready for a start on the following day. The night of the 8th was very wet and miserable, the rain coming down in torrents nearly the whole night long. It was very late in the evening before we got all our baggage re-embarked in the canoes, and as we should have lost some time in the morning if I had ordered my tent and camp bedstead to be set up for the night, I had decided to pass the night on a hide with a water-proof sheet stretched on sticks and strings overhead, little guessing that we were to have such a wet night. I shall not easily forget the wretched night I passed. To have any light was impossible, and so I had to keep my blankets tucked in under the water-proof awning as well as I could in the dark. With all my efforts I could not keep the drippings of the sheet overhead clear of the outstretched hide, so after a very little time I found myself laying in a hide full of water, my gun and revolvers alongside of me also coming in for a good wetting. The men must have suffered far more than I did, for they had not put up any shelters at all, and were simply laying on the bank of the river, exposed to the full fury of the storm. I therefore looked forward to a fresh succession of fevers and other illnesses amongst them.

# CHAPTER X.

The rapid of Trés Irmãos—Meeting with the Pacaguara savages—The river Trés Irmãos—Wild turkeys.

ON the morning of the 9th, we left Girão at six o'clock, with all our blankets and clothes thoroughly wet, and with no chance of drying them. No coffee, either, could be had, as no dry sticks could be found; so we had to be content with a nip at the flask, and a tot of cachaça served all round to the crew. We had more rain during the day, everything in consequence being dull and dispiriting. I had a smart attack of shakes and fever at night, probably from the severe wetting endured the previous night. I stopped work at about four in the afternoon, so as to give time to get some kind of shelter ready and some supper cooked, passing the night in the camarote or cabin of the canoe, as I was afraid of the damp on shore after the heavy rain of the previous night.

For the 10th there was nothing special to note; the weather improved, and we made pretty fair progress. On the 11th we came, about 8 a.m., in sight of the hills of Trés Irmãos, or the "Three Brothers," the highest hills I had yet seen in the district. We passed the rapid of the same name

towards nightfall without any difficulty, and very
little towing work.   This rapid is only troublesome to
travellers when the river is low; when there is plenty
of water it becomes merely a corriente.   As we were
making our canoes fast for the night a short distance
above the rapid, we heard voices below us, and,
stealing up out of the deepening shadows, saw a bark
canoe approach, with three men and a child seated in
it.   They were the first " Barbaros," or savages, that
I had seen, and were objects of great interest to me.
They were of the tribe called " Pacaguaras," and
have their " malocal," or clearing, on the river Trés
Irmãos, which runs into the Madeira on the Brazilian
side.   They are not to be confounded with the
Caripunas that are generally met with at the rapid
of Calderão do Inferno, and were very careful to let
us know that they were Pacaguaras, and not Caripunas.   The three men were of very fair features,
two of them rather good-looking, and, except in their
adornments of feathers, very similar to the Bolivian
Indians of the Beni, although, perhaps, a shade
lighter in colour.  Their hair is jet black, cut
squarely above their eyebrows, and hanging down
behind almost to their shoulders; they have no
whiskers or beard.   The absence of these facial
appendages seems to be a characteristic of the savage
tribes of the interior of South America, and I
observed that these Pacaguaras seemed to be much
surprised at the length of these adornments of some
of the travellers, and would take hold of one's
whiskers, giving them a good pull, possibly with a
view to see if they were false; when, finding that
they adhered firmly to the faces, they would burst

out into a hearty laugh.  They were dressed in
shirts and trousers that they had received from the
engineering parties that had lately been up the river,
but in their natural state a few feathers and a little
string form the whole of their wardrobe.  It is said
that when once they put on an article of clothing
that is given to them, they never remove it until it
drops to pieces, and certainly the state of the shirts
I saw them in warranted the report.  Their language
appears to be a succession of semi-articulated sounds,
shrugs, signs, and much laughter, and the word
"shuma," which is said to mean "good," stands
them in great stead in their conversation with
passers-by.  Some of them have picked up a few
Spanish and Portuguese words, and the first question
they address to one is to ask one's name; and if they
hear a new one, they give it to the next child that is
born in their malocal.  The three men that paid us
a visit were named Patricio, Isiriaco, and Gregorio,
while the head man, or "Capitan," of the tribe is one
Mariano, who, however, is not a true Pacaguara,
but a runaway Cayubaba, from the town of Exaltacion
in the Beni.  They were very friendly to us, and
seemed to be very pleased to see my mayordomo
again, as they had known him some months before,
when he was up the river with the railway engineers.
We gave them some cachaça and some biscuits, and
they promised to bring us some yucas and maize in
the morning, and, bidding us good-night, they paddled
away in the dark at a rapid rate.  Their bark canoes
are wonderful structures, being about fifteen or sixteen feet long, and made out of one single piece of
bark, about half or three quarters of an inch in

thickness, tied up at either end, and stretched out in the middle, the stretchers forming the seats. These canoes are rather heavy to carry on land, but, sitting very lightly on the water, are driven along rapidly, with very little exertion on the part of the paddlers. They also appear to be very safe, and will go up or down all the smaller rapids. There is generally a small fire carried at one end, where a sufficient

CASCARA, OR BARK CANOE OF THE CARIPUNAS AND OTHER TRIBES OF THE RIVER MADEIRA.

quantity of earth is placed to prevent the canoe being burnt. If all the " Barbaros " were like these Pacaguaras, they would give but little trouble to travellers or settlers, a little stealing being probably the only annoyance to be anticipated from them.

The next morning, the 12th, we started early, and tried to go up the river Trés Irmãos to the malocal of the Pacaguaras, but were unable to go so far for fear of being separated from the other canoes. The river near its junction with the Madeira is about 200 yards in width, is very deep, and is very abundantly stocked with fish; indeed, all the rivers and ravines that debouch into the big river amongst the rapids are full of fish at the junction, as it would seem that the fish like to frequent the quieter waters there met with. While we were breakfasting at a small clearing about a mile or so above the rapid, three of the Pacaguaras came up with a quantity of fine fresh maize, but no yucas or plantains; and they made us understand by signs, and pointing to the sun, that they had not had time to go to their clearing, where the plaintains and yucas were growing. We bought the maize from them by barter, giving them an axe, a machete, or cutlass, and some fish-hooks in exchange; and I also obtained a couple of sets of the capybara teeth that they use as ear ornaments, for they can hardly be called ear-rings, as they are stuck behind the ear by a small piece of wax. I presented the Capitan Mariano with an accordion, with which he seemed highly pleased, and they parted from us evidently very contented with our treatment of them.

Up to the present time I had but little chance of shooting, but nevertheless generally managed to get a shot at a pava or a mareca while the canoe was *en route*, although, as I was always behind the other canoes, I only got other people's leavings, in stray birds that had escaped discovery, or that had returned to the river bank, possibly thinking that all the canoes had passed. To-day, however, I was fortunate enough to bag a "mutun," or wild turkey, a very handsome black bird, with a bright yellow horn-shaped wattle over his beak. He had a fine fleshy breast, and made us a capital supper. One of my best men, a Canichana Indian, was down to-day with a very bad attack of ague fever.

# CHAPTER XI.

San Louise—Track across the big bend of the river—Corrientes and Remansos—The rapid of Paredão—Violence of one of the Indian boatmen during a fit—The rapids of Pederneira—La Cruz—Probability that the country is level in the interior on the right bank of the river—As Penhas Coloradas.

ON the 13th, we started at daybreak, and passed the hut called " San Louise " about 8 a.m. From this hut the track cut by the railway engineers turns inland, and crosses the big bend of the river, coming out again at the hut called " La Cruz," near the rapid of Araras. From 8.30 to 9.30 a.m. we were roping through currents below the rapid of Paredão, so called from the wall-like appearance of the rocks, that break up the fall into several channels of broken water that one sees glistening about half a league before getting up to them. The approach to Paredão for the whole of this half-league is about the worst we have yet encountered. We came up on the right bank, and had to encounter a constant succession of " corrientes " and " remansos;" this latter being a return current that in many places, especially bays, runs up stream inshore with great force, until, meeting the down current at some projecting point, it again takes the downward course. The remansos hereabouts are particularly dangerous, for the river

bank is sheer rock, and the current drives the canoe
with such force towards the rocks, that it would
certainly break in pieces with the shock if it were
allowed to strike.  More by good luck than by good
judgment, we escaped the danger, although once or
twice we were running great risk; once in the
remanso, and once in a great "rebujo," or boiling
up of the water, which probably takes place over a
sunken rock.  Arriving at the foot of the fall, we
made fast for the night.  There was a slight wave
on from the cachuela; but, as we were moored
against a mudbank, it did not do us any damage.
We had to put off the unloading till next day, as
the creek up which the canoes have to be pulled for
this purpose is so narrow that only one boat at a
time can be got up it.  The cachuela is one of the
prettiest yet passed, being broken up with large
islands and rocks into three channels, up the eastern
one of which we are to pass.

The next morning, the 14th, we were occupied
till about eleven o'clock in getting our canoes over
the fall, and reloaded again at the upper side.  From
the top of a rock I superintended the hauling up of
my canoe over the projecting corner of a miniature
promontory, and was surprised to see the immense
amount of strain on the rope, although the canoe
was being pulled through water; and I looked on
with some fear and trembling, not only on this
occasion, but always when I saw my only means of
locomotion dependent entirely upon the holding
together of a few strands of hemp, and my ropes
were unfortunately of very inferior quality, and far
from new.  To-day, two of my men were ill, the one

with fever and the other with an epileptic fit. So violent was this poor young fellow in his throes, that we had to tie him tightly with cords, or he would not only have done himself some injury, but would probably have ill-treated some of the other men. I never before saw such a curious case; for the sufferer, a young man of about eighteen or twenty, did not seem to lose consciousness, although he refused to answer, or even to speak, but ground his teeth, and, foaming at the mouth, would seize a stick or paddle, and, rushing at those nearest to him, would scatter them far and wide. He put me very much in mind of what I had often heard of in India, but fortunately had never seen—a mad Mussulman running amuck in a Hindoo bazaar. We managed, with difficulty, to get a lasso over our madman, and then to tie him securely, and in about a couple of hours he came to his senses, but was not thoroughly well for at least a week after the attack. We paddled on through quiet water all the afternoon until, about 5 p.m., we made fast about a league below the next cachuela, called Pederneira.

On the 15th we started in good time, and by 7.15 a.m. were at the Pederneira Falls, which we passed in three ropes' lengths. The river was much broken in centre, and the waves were rather high; but on the right side there was no other difficulty than that caused by a strong current. It is said that, at low water, this rapid is a bad one, and I could see that there are many rocks below the level of water to-day. The country hereabouts appears to be level on both sides of the river, and is consequently uninteresting. At 2 p.m. we came to some

islands, and a rapid that has not had a name given
to it.   At low water it is said to disappear altogether;
but to-day it looks quite as formidable as Trés Irmãos
or Pederneira.   We crossed the river below the
islands, and had some tough pulling to avoid being
drawn into a current and on to rocks near the left
bank, getting successfully across about 100 yards
above the dreaded dangers, and, keeping on up the
river-side, came shortly to some rocky points and
strong currents.   Here one of the Bolivian patrons
sent the small canoe and four men to give me
some help, which was very acceptable, as my men
were almost knocked up after a hard and long day's
work; and we got to the sleeping-place by about
seven o'clock.

Next morning, the 16th, we started very early,
probably before 3 a.m., and at daybreak crossed over
to the right bank.   The mornings have generally
been foggy and cloudy for the last few days, and
this, together with the slight attacks of fever that
I suffered from at Calderão and Girão, entirely
prevented my endeavouring to fix positions by
observations; and, besides, I dare not stay behind
the other canoes, or I should be left to get over the
upper rapids with my weak crew, and probably break
down at Riberão, where the land portage is very
steep.   This morning, the pavas were very abundant.   I got a couple before breakfast; several others
that were wounded got away into the bush, and
there was no time to look for them.   At 3 p.m. we
passed by some high banks of rock and red earth on
the right bank, cut down straight by the river.   One
big lump from them has fallen down into the river,

and forms a conspicuous landmark, in the distance looking like a large canoe. In the evening I got three more pavas, and one of my men got a very fine " perdrix," as they call it, although to me it appeared more like a jungle fowl. It had a most wonderfully fleshy breast, and was as tender as a young chicken; so we were excellently well off for fresh meat to-day.

The 17th we made another early start, and passed the hut called " La Cruz " about 7 a.m. At this spot the track cut by the engineers of the rail- way across the big bend of the river comes out again, the distance between the two huts of San Louise and La Cruz being about eighteen miles. The whole of this distance was described to me as perfectly level and dry, by several of the Indians who had accompanied the engineers and Señor Ignacio Arauz, the Bolivian patron who furnished the peons for the work, and to whose energy and perseverance the successful cutting of the track alongside the rapids was mainly due. I had in my canoe a very intelligent Bolivian, of rather a superior class, who had been one of the " mayordomos," or foremen, under Señor Arauz, and this man assured me that from the track over the big bend, looking east- wards, no sign of hills could be seen, but only a vast undulating plain covered with low scrub or brush- wood. Señor Arauz has also assured me that there are no hills to be seen; and a short walk inland, together with all the evidence that I could collect leads me to the belief that a cut across the interior, entirely avoiding the greater bends of the River, say from the Trés Irmãos River to the Riberão Falls, would not only shorten the length of the line of railway, but would locate it where the smallest amount of earthwork and bridging would be met with.

After breakfasting about mid-day, we tried to pass under the high red cliffs called " As Penhas Coloradas," which rise straight up from the water a height of perhaps 100 feet. The current runs very strongly under these cliffs, and we found it impossible to pass underneath them, there being no foothold for the men to pass with ropes ; and there are no bushes available for the " ganchos," or long hook-ended poles, which are of great service all through the journey. We had, therefore, to cross over to the left or Brazilian shore, and thereby lost all the ground we had gained since breakfast; and we got across at 3 p.m., just in front of where we had started from after breakfast. We had some good sport with the pavas before nightfall, four of them falling to my gun; and about 5 p.m. we arrived at a very strong corriente, where, to my great joy, one of my Bolivian friends had left three men to assist me. With this extra help, we were able to overcome the current by paddles only, and arrived at the sleeping-place before dark.

## CHAPTER XII.

The rapid of Araras—Farinha and sardines for supper—Difficulty of treating the Indians successfully when they are sick—The current of Periquitos—Arrival at the Rabo do Ribeirão—The Bolivian Indian's chaunt at night—Passage of the Rabo do Ribeirão—Quantity of farinha consumed by boatmen, in the form of "shehee"—Canoe aground in the bay below the main fall of Ribeirão—The river Ribeirão—The portage of Ribeirão—Curious marks on rocks.

THE following morning, the 18th, another very early start was made, and at daybreak we heard a gunshot from the other side, and knew thereby that the Bolivian patrons had crossed over to the other side, to which I accordingly made haste to follow; but we soon had to recross, on account of strong currents amongst the islands that are below the rapid of Araras. These constant crossings of the river cause one to lose much ground, as in mid-stream the current always takes one a considerable distance down stream, and it requires very strong pulling even in a small canoe to cross from bank to bank in a straight line. After coasting round the islands we finally went over to the right bank again, and ascended the rapid by one rope's length of hauling for about eighty feet, so that this cachuela was, in the then state of the river, passed very easily. It is said that when the river is dry it should be ascended on the left bank at this rapid, but at full river there

is a very heavy "olada," or wave, on that bank.
We got to another of the engineering stations, called
" Barracão das Araras," about half-past eleven, and
called a halt for breakfast; but before we could get
our meal cooked, a heavy storm of rain fell and put
out all the fires, so that we had to eat our food in
a half-cooked state. A soup with farinha, rice, and
onions, in a semi-raw condition, is not the most
palatable of dishes, but a good appetite never fails
one up the rapids; so we make the best of circumstances, and thinking ourselves lucky even to get a
half-cooked breakfast, paddle on till 5 p.m., when
the rain again bothers us, and we pull up for the
night, and content ourselves with a dish of wetted
farinha and sardines for supper. Many people
would fancy this but a poor repast, but I found on
many occasions, when perhaps time or circumstances
did not allow any cooking to be done, that I could
satisfy my hunger very well indeed with these
homely articles. The mode of preparation is very
simple indeed : take a bowl full of farinha, and pick
out the small sticks and lumps that are always
found in Brazilian farinha, and then moisten with
sufficient water to make the grains soft but not
pappy, break up three or four sardines and mix
them with the farinha, pouring a little of the oil
over it as well. The dish is then ready, and wants
nothing but good appetite for sauce.

The next morning, the 19th, was damp and dull,
and we started somewhat later than usual, the men
being tired and downhearted with the rain. My
Canichana, Candido Cayuva, passed a very bad
night with the ague—and I do not wonder at it, for

he must have got thoroughly wet through during the day—and, indeed, it was a miracle that he did not die during the night. He complained last night of pains in his chest, and I gave him twenty-five drops of chlorodine, and some arnica to rub where the pain was most violent. He felt much better after this, and I found out this morning that, feeling so, he had, like a madman, bathed at night-fall in the river; consequently he had a strong return of fever during the night, and it was indeed wonderful that he survived. So difficult is it to treat these Indians with any chance of success, for at any moment they will commit some foolish act that may carry them off at a moment's notice.

We arrived at the corriente of "Periquitos" about half-past ten, and although the cachuela was rather fierce, and the wave somewhat high, we passed the canoe safely up the right bank without any very great deal of trouble or danger. We kept on at work till seven in the evening, when we got up to the last corriente of the "Rabo do Ribeirão," and, arriving after dark, had to make the canoes fast in a most awkward place, where they bumped on the rocks all night in a wretched manner, so that one got very little, if any, sleep.

Besides being kept from sleep by the constant bumping on the rocks, we were treated by our men to more than the usual nightly allowance of chanting. The Bolivian Indians of the Beni, having been civilized by the Jesuit missionaries, are exceedingly superstitious, and when on a dangerous journey are very regular with their nightly orisons, the refrain of which forms a prayer to the Virgin ("a livrar nos siempre de todo mal") to "deliver us always from every ill." These words are sung to a rather solemn chant, and as many of the men have very fair voices, and not at all a bad idea of harmony, the singing at night, if one be not too near to it, has a very soothing and pleasant effect. The passage of the rapids of Ribeirão, being considered both difficult and dangerous, accounts for an extra allowance of the chanting the night before the first corrientes were ascended.

The passage of the " Rabo," or tail, and the main fall of Ribeirão occupied us three whole days and part of the fourth. The Rabo extends for about five miles below the real fall, and is a succession of whirlpools and currents, extremely dangerous to canoes either on the upward or downward journey. The downward journey is by far the most dangerous, as the canoes have to be steered in full course through the boulders and rocks scattered over this length of the river, which here has an average fall of about four and a half feet per mile.

At daybreak on the 20th we commenced the arduous ascent, and by breakfast-time had overcome eight severe corrientes. The next one was about three quarters of a mile in length, being one continued current, running possibly about eight miles an hour for the whole distance. We failed to get to the top of this corriente before dark, and had to dodge inside a sandbank, which fortunately afforded a resting-place for the night.

On the 21st we started as soon as we could see— for amongst these strong currents it is impossible to move in the dark—and proceeded up the creek formed between an island and the right bank of the mainland. Here also the current is very strong, and forms, one may say, a continuous cachuela, up which we have to pass in ropes' lengths. The progress made was consequently slow, and as the greater part of my men were sick, I was greatly dependent on my Bolivian friends for assistance. Fortunately I had good stocks of cachaça (white rum) and farinha (yuca flour), and at each stoppage I plied the men of the other canoes with a tot of rum and a handful of farinha; so they helped me along willingly. This farinha they eat constantly during the journey, putting about a handful into a gourd or calabash ("tortuma"), filling up with water, and they seem to find much refreshment from this preparation, which they call "shehee." So fond are they of it, that frequent halts for "shebee"-taking have to be allowed, the mayordomos and others of a higher grade adding a little sugar to the mess when they can obtain it; but this latter luxurious addition the poor peons seldom get, although mine had it throughout the voyage, for I had taken a large stock of coarse sugar with me. In the afternoon we had to partially unload the canoes in order to ascend the current known as the " Cuerpo del Rabo," or the " body of the tail," and at dusk made fast at the top, and set to work carrying overland the cargo taken out of the canoes, so that we might be ready again for an early start next day.

Next morning, the 22nd, we started at 6 a.m., after having had to catch the fowls, of which I still had ten left, and which the boys had allowed to escape from the coop, that had got much broken in the work of carrying it over the land portages. I feared they would all be lost in the forest, but when free they appeared to be quite dazed, and were caught without very much trouble, a couple of wildish ones being shot as the quickest means of stopping them. Roping and hauling by the bushes, we proceeded but slowly, but soon got a sight of the "salto" itself. This is the main body of the fall, with a drop of about fourteen feet; and imposing enough it looked, being much broken up into islands, with huge waves breaking heavily over the numerous rocks. The river at the Rabo and at the fall is very broad, and this probably accounts for the name of Ribeirão, or "great river," being given to this part of it. Two corrientes were ascended by roping, and then a short stretch at the paddles brought us to another, the thirteenth of the series forming the "rabo," and which we ascended between the land and a large tree that forms a point. This is at times the last current before entering the remanso that takes the canoes up to the foot of the main fall. There proved, however, to be two more before we got into the bay with its "remanso" and "olada," that form the chief and most dangerous features of the passage of this salto. One of my Bolivian friends lent me a second captain, and I took the men out of the small canoe, or "montaria," so that I passed these dangers with fourteen paddles going and two captains aft, each using his big paddle for steering, one on either side of the "popa," or stern. It is a great help throughout the journey to have two good captains behind, for when strong currents or dangerous bits of river have to be encountered, one of them can keep the boat in its proper course ; while the other encourages the paddlers forward, keeping them together in their strokes by shouts and good sounding thumps of his heel on the projecting boards on which the captains have to stand behind the " camarota," or cabin.

The wave, or " olada," was not nearly so bad as that met with at Theotonio, and as the canoe was much lighter we passed very well, the only approach to a casualty being that we grounded on a sandbank in the bay, on which a canoe preceding us had struck also, but which it was impossible to avoid from the set of the current right on to it. However, the peons jumped into the water with great alacrity, and pushed us afloat again before the waves had time to swamp us. I had heard a good deal of the danger of this " remanso " and " olada," but with a good crew and captains, and a garitea well up at the prow, I don't think it is much to be feared. The unloading place for the land portage is a short distance up the mouth of the river Ribeirão, which comes into the big river a stone's throw below the fall on the right or Brazilian side, and we got safely into quiet water up the Ribeirão by about 1 p.m., overtaking two of the Bolivian patrons who had got ahead of me, and had already passed their canoes and cargoes over the portage.

The " arrastre," or portage, is not nearly so steep as at Theotonio or Girão, being, perhaps, an ascent of one in eight for about 100 yards over a pretty even bed of rock, then one in twelve over earth for another 200 yards, level for 200 more, and then sharp down to the river in about a further 100 yards, at the rate of about one in four.

We got our cargoes unloaded, two canoes being hauled over the portage before dark, my own being left for the following day. To drag the heavy canoes up the ascent taxed all the powers of the thirty men that we could get together for the work, but by dint of cachaça and shouting we got the craft over without assistance from the patrons who had preceded us.

The accompanying sketches of curious marks to be seen on rocks at three of the rapids, were made by Mr. Alan Grant-Dalton, who was my able and indefatigable assistant engineer during our stay at San Antonio. My ascent of the rapids having been made whilst the river was in flood, these marks were all under water, and I was consequently unable to inspect them; but I have been assured by many travellers that Mr. Grant-Dalton's sketches are exact and faithful copies of the inscriptions. Most probably they are the work of the Caripuna, or other wandering savages, for the Bolivian Indians ascending and descending the river are not likely to have wasted their time cutting these figures out of the hard rock.

At Trés Irmãos, 40 feet below highest flood water.

At Ribeirão, 35 feet below highest flood water.

At Madeira, 35 feet below highest flood water.

## CHAPTER XIII.

Bad arrangements of the Bolivian patrons for rationing their men—The rapid of Misericordia—Tradition attached thereto—Meeting with canoes from Bolivia—The Madeira rapids and the junction of the river Beni—Nomenclature of the river Madeira in its different sections—The rapids of Layes—Wild cocoa trees—The Falls of Pao Grande.

On the 23rd, in Ribeirão, we woke up all hands at daybreak, and got the last canoe over to the upper side. I would have liked to have stopped for the day at this fall, so as to give the men a few hours' leisure, that they might fish in the quiet water of the river Ribeirão, wash their clothes and rest a bit; but the Bolivian patrons were for going ahead, so we passed the cargo over and got ready for a start by about 2 p.m. We were to proceed that day as far as the next rapid, called Misericordia, and there delay while hunters were sent to try for some wild pigs or other fresh meat, as the stocks of that article remaining to the Bolivian patrons were getting rather low.

It appears to be the custom with Bolivian patrons to start with barely sufficient provisions for the time they expect the journey to take; they don't provide any surplus in case of delay. Then during the first days of the journey they give the men excessively large rations, in order that they may be well satisfied at starting, and so for the last two weeks of the run the men have to be put on half, or even less than half, rations. For instance, one of the Bolivian patrons advised me that the ration of rice should be half a pound daily, besides farinha; at this rate one could not carry enough rice for all the journey. And certainly the quantity is more than necessary; from three to four ounces per man daily being quite enough to thicken the "chupe," or soup, which is the stock dish of the Bolivian peon. This system is quite characteristic of Bolivians, both Indians and Carayanas (i.e., those having Spanish blood in their veins), for they cannot take anything by degrees; they must finish it all at once. Thus a bottle of wine or cachaça must be drunk at one sitting, and the next day they will go without. So also with their chicha-drinking; they will prepare a huge quantity, and get through it in one evening, then go without until another "fiesta" day or other suitable occasion calls for a fresh brew. At starting it was reckoned that we should do the journey up the rapids, and to the village of Exaltacion, in about five weeks; but a month has now passed, and we have at least another week's work to get through before we get out of the rapids. At this time I still had provisions in farinha and charqui for three weeks further, and had been able to spare four "alquieres" (bundles of 1 cwt. each) of farinha, and treat the men of the other canoes to cachaça every day for some time past. Charqui was somewhat scarcer, for we had counted upon game, but had only met with a few pavas, there being no time available for sending the men into the woods.

We got to Misericordia at 4 p.m., and unloaded half the cargoes, passing two canoes before dark up a creek on the right bank, at the end of which there was a very steep bit of rock, with very little water on it upon which to get the canoe over. This cachuela is especially dangerous, although at first sight it appears a mere corriente; but the river swirls over a point of rock and forms a succession of whirlpools from which, they say, a canoe, if once drawn in, can never escape. In ascending, this rapid must be passed by the creek on the right bank; but at low water it is said that the rapid does not offer much obstacle, although I am inclined to think that this information is very uncertain. The aforesaid channel on the right bank offers no obstacles that cannot be overcome by hard work in unloading or hauling, and is therefore preferable. The descent should be made almost in mid-channel, while, if anything, steering to the left rather than to the right bank. There is a tradition that the name of Misericordia was given to this rapid after a dreadful occurrence that is said to have happened in the early part of this century, when a party of Brazilian soldiers from the province of Mato Grosso descending the rapids, one of their canoes wrecked in mid-stream; some of the men succeeding in temporarily escaping to the rock, on which, their comrades being unable to afford them any help by ropes, or approach them with canoes, they were starved to death in sight of, but absolutely out of the reach of, their comrades. If this story be a true one, it is difficult to determine whose fate was the hardest; that of those who perished seeing their end approaching by slow but sure degrees, or that of their sorrowing comrades on the mainland, who were unable to afford any help to the sufferers on the dreadful rock. With this fearsome tale attached to the spot, well may the Bolivian Indian, on nearing the cachuela, fervently chant the solemn " Misericordia! Misericordia! livra nos siempre de todo mal."

On the 24th, we found that the canoes left the night before below the rapid had grounded from the fall of the river, and we had to take a little more cargo out so that they might float, when we got them hauled up the creek over the rocks, and reloaded by eight o'clock. Just as we were starting, we saw three canoes coming down the river from Bolivia, and got news that the country was in a state of revolution. This was a bad augury for the success of my journey through the Republic; but there was no help for it but to go ahead, and take things as they might be. We also learned that the Brazilian consul in the Beni provinces had recently been assassinated by one of his own Brazilian servants in his estancia, a few leagues below the village of Exaltacion. I was pleased to find that this outrage had not been committed by Bolivian Indians, who are, as a rule, much quieter and more tractable than the mixed races of Brazil. Proceeding onwards from Misericordia, our canoes kept on the right bank, arriving at nightfall at a good stopping-place, after having passed over four strong currents, and leaving the main part of the next cachuela to be passed on the following morning with the canoes half unloaded.

The whole of the 25th was occupied in passing

the principal fall of the Madeira Rapid and the currents above it. The junction of the river Beni occurs amongst the currents above the principal fall, and from this circumstance the fall has been named the " Cachuela de Madeira," as below the junction the Madeira River is said to commence. From the junction of the Beni to that of the Itenez, the river is by some called the Rio Grande, by others the Itenez, and it is only above the latter junction that the Mamoré reigns. Above the Madeira Fall, and in the neighbourhood of the junction of the Beni, the river is much broken up by islands, and consequently the navigation of this stretch is almost, if not quite, as bad as that of the " Rabo do Ribeirão." At the junction of the river Beni, the river appears as though it divided itself into two parts, and they seemed to me to be almost of equal width and volume of water. This day the south wind blew very strong and cold, and all the men complained greatly, as they had to be constantly in the water.

Early morning of the 26th the expedition continued the ascent of the river, arriving at the rapids of " Layes " about 11.30 a.m. These rapids are formed by two small falls with a current below them, and were passed with canoes half unloaded. Near the fall, but below it, is a wide stream on the right side of the river, and we halted for breakfast here, so as to allow the men time to fish ; but they had no luck in consequence of the south wind, which, it is said, hinders the fish from taking the baits. We got clear of the fall and canoes reloaded by about 4 p.m., and, though late, determined to endeavour to overtake the canoes that had got ahead of us, and which we saw up stream above us; but we were only able to get about a quarter of a mile or so when it got dark, and we had to pull up and make fast for the night. This cachuela gave us more trouble than was anticipated; but I fancy that it is better at low water, for the channels then would be better defined: now the channels are amongst rocks, and very difficult to find and to keep the canoes in. In this part of the river I noticed a great many wild cocoa trees, which, although growing almost universally on the banks of the Madeira and Mamoré, are hereabouts more thickly collected together. The fruit of these trees is of very superior quality, and it would require very little labour to organize an excellent plantation.

The 27th we started at daybreak, and got out of the last of the Layes currents by eight o'clock, and came in sight of the bluffs and highlands of the next cachuela, called "Pao Grande," at which we arrived by 9.30 a.m., pulling up in a capital little port with a good sandbank, but only room for about four canoes at a time. Here we overtook the other canoes that had got ahead, and had to unload all our cargoes, as the fall is impassable with loaded canoes at any season of the year. The channel we passed up is on the right or Brazilian side of the river, and to look at seems to be one of the worst passes amongst the rapids, having two "saltos," or jumps, each of about four feet in height, up which one would hardly fancy that canoes could be made to ascend. It was wonderful to see how well the Bolivian Indians managed to make the heavy canoes ascend these almost perpendicular falls. They would first seek out a part of the fall that, as well as having plenty of water going over it—say about eighteen inches in depth—should have a good supply of weeds growing on the rocks, as over these weeds the bottom of the canoe slides easily.  Then the bulk of the men are set to pull steadily on the two ropes that are attached to the bow, these ropes being spread out as much as possible on either side, so that a pull can be put on right or left as circumstances require.  A rope is also kept on the stern, but only requires the attention of a couple of good men, while in the canoe the captain at the helm directs all the workers, and two of the best men in the bows keep the canoe off the rocks as she answers to the pull of the men on shore.  In this manner three heavy canoes were passed up this fall in about a couple of hours.  On the land side of the channel the rocks stand up about twenty feet above the water, and it was rather an exciting scene to stand on one of these rocks and see the men pulling and shouting down below.  My canoe shipped a good deal of water by slewing round as it was being pulled up one of the jumps.  This was caused by one of the head ropes being allowed to slacken at this inopportune moment; but, as she was empty, it did not much matter.  The path over which the cargoes are carried is about a quarter of a mile in length, and goes over very rocky ground.  At dark we had nearly all our cargo over, so stopped work for the night.  Weather dull and cold, the wind being still southerly and chilly.  The men are, however, improving in health, slight attacks of fever with one or two of them being the only complaints.

## CHAPTER XIV.

The river Yata—Meeting with another party descending from Bolivia—The rapids of Bananeiras—Abandoned settlement—Variability of the Bolivian character—The cabeçeras of Bananeiras—The Sierra da Paca Nova—The rapids of Guajará Guasu and Merim—A few hints on leaving the last of the rapids.

THE next morning (the 28th) broke dull and cloudy, but warmer than the past two days, and by about 7.30 the sun came out to cheer us up. The river Yata, which we passed about this time, enters into the Madeira on its left or Bolivian bank, and appears to be a considerable stream, it being perhaps 100 yards in width at the junction. On the right or Brazilian side, opposite to the Yata, are rocks and a very stiff current, which by some travellers have been set down as a cachuela, but which are not now included in the existing nineteen.

Hereabouts we met a canoe descending the river from Bolivia, with about thirty men and four or five women going down to Bayetas, a rubber-gathering station already mentioned as being on the lower part of the Madeira. The men were all Cruzeños, and in charge of a capataz only, from whom I bought a small quantity of fresh Bolivian yuca flour, for which he charged me six hard dollars for about twenty-five pounds, worth at Exaltacion, in the Beni, about a dollar. This generous Bolivian was out of sugar, and begged me to let him have a few pounds. I had a good stock, so gave him five pounds, for which he allowed me a dollar out of the six he took from me for the yuca flour, although, if I had charged him according to his idea of the value of his food supplies in the cachuelas, I ought to have charged him about a dollar a pound. The whole of this day we paddled up the right or Brazilian bank until the first small current below the Bananeiras Falls was reached, when we crossed over to the Bolivian shore, where, about 5.30 p.m., we got stuck amongst a lot of driftwood, our hawsers getting entangled therein, so that we could not get up to the unloading place that night, but had to make fast and pass the night on a small mudbank as best we could.

On the 29th we got up to the port of the Bananeiras Falls by about six o'clock, and found the canoes that had preceded us, with their cargoes passed but the canoes still on this side. The channels for passing the canoes were full of rocks, and very dangerous, the one ours went up being very dry, and giving a great amount of work to the men. Some of the canoes went up a channel lower down stream than that I chose for mine, but had to encounter a drop in the water of about eight feet in as many yards, one of them filling and being saved with great difficulty. As we were detained the whole day at this fall, I took the opportunity of loading up a stock of cartridges for the journey, from the last rapid to the first village in Bolivia (Exaltacion), a journey of about ten days, during which very little time, if any, can be spared for stoppages.

At this fall, about eight or ten years ago, two Bolivians made a small settlement on the left or Bolivian side of the river, with the object of forming a rubber-gathering business. One of them, Don Miguel Cuellas, was returning to Bolivia, having made a small competency out of rubber on the Madeira River below San Antonio. He owned three of the largest canoes of the seven forming our expedition, his portion of the goods for sale in Bolivia going up with us being worth at least seven or eight thousand pounds. He told me that he and his partner lived at Bananeiras for about twelve months, but that they found the yield from the rubber trees to be very much less than that given by the trees below the falls of the Madeira; that their health had been uniformly good, and that they had not been molested by the savages, who seem in this part of the river to roam about on the Brazilian shore only.

Our cargoes were carried over the portage to the eastern side of the island which overlooks the fall, and we were ready to begin the struggle with the numerous currents which are found amongst the islands stretching above the main fall for nearly four miles of the river's course, and which are known as the "Cabeçeiras," or heads of the Bananeiras Falls; but the day was too far advanced to think of making any progress before nightfall.

Before leaving this cachuela, I had afforded me a convincing proof of the instability of character and the true selfishness of some Bolivians. There were three patrons in the expedition besides myself, and one of these, a certain Juan de Dios Molina, had arranged, before starting from San Antonio, that he would throughout the journey keep with my canoe, as my crew being known to be a very weak one, I was certain to require constant help at the rapids and currents. Besides having settled this, in the way of business, at San Antonio, this Molina had frequently during the journey assured me, as a friend, that he would not separate from me until we arrived at the townships of the Beni; but I discovered at Bananeiras that for some days past he had been complaining to the other two patrons of the great delays that I caused him, and had declared his intention of abandoning me to my own resources. This he took care not to do until we were almost out of the rapids, as he thought he would have no further need for the services of my small canoe, or montaria —which had been very serviceable to all the party, since the one belonging to Señor Morales was lost in Morinhos—and he also thought that he had obtained from me all the surplus cachaça and farinha that I had to spare, so that he could separate from me without much loss to himself. If Molina showed me the bad side of Bolivian character—and it was not much to be wondered at with him, seeing that he was almost a full-blooded Indian—I was fortunate in finding the good side in Don Miguel Cuellas, who volunteered to assist me, and waited for me amongst the difficult places in the rapids yet to be passed, and never lost sight of me until we reached Exaltacion, which we did two clear days before Molina, much to that worthy's chagrin. And thus it is with the Bolivians; you will find many crafty, mean, and

untruthful characters amongst them, but close by
this undesirable acquaintance you are sure to find
a generous, warm-hearted, and true friend such as I
found in Don Miguel Cuellas, without whose assistance I should certainly have come to grief amongst
the cabeçeiras of Bananeiras, or the wandering
savages of the upper waters of the Madeira. To
Don Miguel I am always bound to give sincere
thanks whenever I think of the latter end of my
journey on that river.

On the 30th we started, as usual, in good time,
and had to cross the openings of channels between
islands which appeared to me to be unpleasantly
dangerous, as the current ran fearfully strong down
them. We got over two of these safely, and then
saw Molina cross to an island in mid-stream, which
he barely succeeded in gaining. I liked the look of
this job much less than keeping to the mainland, for
I believe that if we had tried to follow, we should
certainly have missed the island, and have been
carried down stream right into the main body of the
cachuela, for my crew could never have made head-
way against the powerful current running in mid-
river; so, as I had the montaria, I kept to the mainland, and struggled on till about 10.30, when I
saw Don Miguel's three canoes ahead of me on the
same side, and unloading part of their cargoes in
order to get over a shallow current. On getting
up, Don Miguel offered me a pull by his men, which
I joyfully accepted, and got over the current well,
breakfasting above it, and starting again soon after
mid-day. I got on pretty well after this, being
generally able to keep at the tail of the largest of the

three canoes, called for distinction the "batelão."
These cabeçeiras of Bananeiras are as bad, if not
worse, than those of the Madeira Rapid, but not so
tiring as those of the Rabo of Ribeirão; we got
through the last of them by about half-past three,
and paddled on up the left bank till 5 p.m., when
we arrived at the stopping-place for the night. The
weather was again dull and cold, the morning
having been foggy, with small drizzling rain, and
as we had no sun, the men kept on their ponchos
all day. From where we stopped, one sees the high
range of hills called the "Sierra da Paca Nova,"
which form part of the Cordilheira Geral; they are
a considerable distance from the river, being apparently some thirty or forty miles inland.

The next morning, the 31st, was a very early
daybreak, and we started at 5 a.m., there being a
thick mist on the river till nearly nine o'clock, when
the sun came out warm and bright. When the fog
rose, all the seven canoes were almost in hail of one
another, and as we had been paddling all the morning without encountering any currents, I found that
I was able to keep my place in the file, behind the
batelão; so that Molina, who did not wait on the last
two mornings, as usual, for me to come up to his
"pascana," or stopping-place, will find it hard work
to abandon me to my own resources, as he intended.
After breakfasting about mid-day as usual, we arrived
at the next rapid of Guajará-guasu, where all the
seven canoes met together again, having to unload
half their cargoes before they could be hauled over
the shallow currents on the left or Bolivian side.
Over this cachuela I was assisted by Don Miguel's

men, who gladly accepted their " pinga," or tot of
cachaça, instead of Molina's men, who had heretofore
enjoyed this extra allowance. It was nightfall before we got all the canoes over the rapid, and as
hereabouts the men begin to have fears of the
" barbaros," or savages, we got our suppers over as
quickly as possible, and then re-embarked the cargoes
by moonlight, so as to be ready for an early start.

On June the 1st the day was fine, and the canoes
started by 5 a.m., but I had to wait whilst some of
my men fetched the montaria over the rapid ; however, we soon overtook the batelão, and in trying to
pass it at a corriente got foul of its rope, by which
the crew were hauling from shore. Fouling the
rope sent the batelão round on the rocks, and she
being a very heavy craft, deeply laden with iron and
other merchandise, gave a great deal of work to get
round again and afloat. About half a league above
the top current of Guajará-guasu, there is on the left
bank a very peculiar thin layer of rock, hollowed out
by a very strong and dangerous " remanso," or
return current ; the canoes run great risk of being
driven on to the bank, and as the layer of rock
jutted out about five feet above the water level, we
ran great danger from the sharp projections.

At about ten o'clock we came to Guajará Merim
(the word " Guasu " meaning " Great," and " Merim "
" Little," in the Lingua Geral of Northern Brazil),
which is the last of the nineteen rapids, and is at the
top end of a large island lying between the two
Guajarás. This rapid we passed on the left or
Brazilian shore, it being at this time of year little
more than a corriente, which we easily surmounted

by hauling for one rope's length, and so we passed above the region of the cachuelas, it being the thirty-ninth day since we left San Antonio.

The ascent of the cachuelas has been somewhat wearisome, as we have had to go through thirty-seven clear days of hard and constant labour, battling with the force of the many currents; but with a good crew and pleasant companions, both of which vital necessaries were wanting to me on my journey, I would not at all mind doing the rapids over again. To go with about three or four canoes well manned, and with a couple of montarias, would be much better than travelling with such a large number of canoes as seven; for the last of these has to wait such a long time at all the currents and cachuelas, where hauling by the rope is required before its turn comes. With a well-organized expedition I think the ascent, in this season of the year, might be accomplished in twenty-eight or thirty days. It may here be noted that a good hemp hawser an inch or an inch and a quarter in diameter, and about 200 feet in length, should be provided for each canoe. Piassava ropes do not answer, although from their lightness they are desirable; but they break so frequently, that they cannot be depended upon. Also each canoe should have a double and a single block to match the rope, as these are very useful at the land portages if from any cause the expedition should be short-handed. A good set of tools, a few nails, and some pitch tar and oakum should be provided, not forgetting a few sheets of tin for patching up holes that may be knocked into the canoes by obtrusive rocks.

# CHAPTER XV.

Start made up river above rapids with drums beating—The islands of Cavalho Marinho—A party of Baure Indians met with—Rate of progress calculated at two miles per hour—Otters, alligators, and monkeys shot—Steam navigation practicable on the river above the rapids—Stock taken of food-supplies left—Long hours worked.

HAVING got all the canoes over the last of the cachuelas, we started onwards with flags flying from the bows of the canoes, and with several " cajas," or drums, beating triumphal tattoos. The Indian boatmen always appear much delighted at having successfully surmounted the cachuelas, although they have to prepare for very long hours of hard paddling up the section of the river from the rapids to Exaltacion, as, owing to this length being much infested with savages on both shores, it is customary to stop as little as possible during the day.

The river above the falls is about half a mile in width, the country on either side being flat, and the banks covered with a very thick growth of " chuchia," a kind of wild cane that throws out a spear-like point fringed at the top with feathery seeds. From the straight tops of these canes the savages make their arrows, which are generally about five or six feet in length, looking almost more like spears or lances than arrows.

About half-past five in the evening we arrived at the islands called " Cavalho Marinho," and encamped for the night on one of them, it being always desirable to stop the night at an island if possible, as one is then perfectly secure from any attack by the savages, who in this part of the river do not seem to have any canoes.

The start was ordered very early the next morning, it being 2.30 a.m. only when all hands were called up, and we paddled on amongst the islands for some time before crossing over to the right bank. The islands are several in number, but have plenty of water in all the channels, so that there would be no obstruction to navigation by steamers, although with canoes one has to keep crossing from bank to bank in order to avoid the strong currents found at every bend of the stream. The country remains very flat and uninteresting, but the plague of marigueys, tavernas, and carapanas was something fearful, and much worse than anything I had experienced amongst the rapids. We kept on till 6.30 p.m., after fourteen and a half hours' work, allowing for the stoppages made for breakfast, etc., during which meal we were joined by a party descending from Bolivia, on their way to the Lower Madeira, on the usual speculation of rubber-gathering. The men were about thirty in number, and were all " Baures " or " Joaquinianos," and were a very fine set of fellows—indeed, as fine-looking a lot of Indians as one could put together in almost any quarter of the world.

The next start was earlier still, it being but half-past twelve at night when we recommenced our upward journey, by the light of a splendid full moon. The men got very little sleep and rose up very unwillingly, the long stretches of work being most trying, as at night one is sleepy, and by day the sun is very fatiguing.

I calculated to-day that our rate of progress is about two miles an hour. Each stroke of the paddle takes the canoe about a yard and a half, and we average forty-four strokes per minute; this gives sixty-six yards per minute, say about two miles per hour. Yesterday we paddled for fourteen and a half hours, and should therefore have done twenty-nine miles, and I fancy that was about the distance travelled.

To-day we stopped for breakfast at 10 a.m., after nine and a half hours' continuous paddle, and were off again at 11.30. I heard that Molina's men have now used up all their farinha, and have but little rice and charqui left; the effect of short commons being very visible with them, for they are generally the last of the file, and in trying to pass us this day they were easily beaten by my men.

In the afternoon I shot a " lontra," which I take to be an otter, as it has its cave in the roots of trees growing near the river bank. This fellow was of a dark dun colour, and about the size of my dog " Jack," who was a rather large and well-grown retriever. I had heard that the " lontra " was a beaver; but this was evidently an otter, with five-toed feet webbed, and with an otter-like head and tail, broad and flat, placed crosswise to the body, with the broad sides up and down. " Jack " was very near having a tussle with the otters—-for there were three altogether—and he jumped into the river after them, swimming after their heads as they bobbed up and down, and I was obliged to be careful with the rifle to be sure of not hitting "Jack" instead of the otters, of whom I fancy one more was killed besides the one we got into the canoe. At night we roasted the flesh, and I had a bit of the "lomo," or fillet, which was excellent, and much like fair juicy beef. I don't know whether otters are eaten at home, but on the river Madeira they are thought fair game, and in fact almost anything that can be killed is now eaten by the men. Don Miguel's men to-day shot three "caymanes" (alligators) and nine monkeys, all of which were roasted, the monkeys whole, good meals being made, and the joints remaining stored up for the next day. Monkey is good eating, but rather tough; cayman flesh I declined at present, the animals shot to-day being old and musky-flavoured. To-day we worked fifteen and a half hours altogether.

June 4th. The start was made at 1.30 a.m., and we kept up the left bank, the day being fine, and the sun not quite so hot as usual. I have paddled a good deal these last days, and this morning did so from 4.30 a.m. till 9.30, a fair stretch for one quite unaccustomed to such work; but I fancied that I helped the canoe along, for every extra paddle tells, and I got a spurt out of the men every now and again, by encouraging them with a timely "churka, churka!" My men were not in very good form, but what they would have been if, like the other crews, they had been obliged to be on short rations of farinha, charqui, and cachaça, I cannot conceive.

During the afternoon we passed a river coming in on the right or Brazilian bank, and then a long stretch of bank on the left side, falling into the river, causing a very strong current, with many trees sticking up, and greatly obstructing the navigation for canoes, which are always obliged to hug the shore. We got to the stopping-place, or "pascana," by about 7 p.m., finding Don Miguel and Señor Morales encamped there; but Molina is still behind—in fact, we have not seen him since early morning. At nightfall we passed a large "playa," or sandbank, on which there were a great many large cranes and other aquatic birds. We worked this day seventeen hours, as we only stopped half an hour for breakfast, the men eating cold otter and farinha. My bag to-day was four small cranes, which made a capital pot at night, and three pigeons, which I got at one shot, and with B B; these the boy roasted for cold luncheon to-morrow.

June 5th. The start was ordered at 1.30 a.m., a slight rain falling; we keep up the left bank, which appears to be the favourite one on this portion of the river, from the idea that the right or Brazilian side is a favourite hunting-ground of the savages. The river continues of a uniform width of about six or seven hundred yards, it being just a good shot for the Winchester rifle from one side to the other. Daybreak is generally a good time to get something for the pot, as one is able to get nearer to one's game than one can during the day, and this morning I got one very fine black duck (*pato royale*), and a couple of trumpeters or Orinoco geese (*marecas*). We christened these ducks "trumpeters," from the

H

trumpeting noise they make as they fly low over the water, giving one plenty of notice of their approach, in time to pick up the gun and be ready for them.

The river navigation for steamers would be excellent, so far as the depth of water is concerned, but the cutting of the wood fuel would be rather a difficult point to manage. There is, of course, plenty of wood on either bank; but the fear of attacks from the savages will render the establishment of wood-cutting stations a difficult question. The proper way will be for the Brazilian and Bolivian Governments to act jointly, and set up armed stockades on alternate sides of the river, say at distances of fifty miles apart, each one to be garrisoned by about forty or fifty men, who could organize wood-cutting parties, the sale of the fuel going a good way towards the payment of the expenses. In this way the forest would get thinned, and the savages would either make terms or retire further into the interior. The tribe that infests the right or Brazilian side are called " Sirionos," and those on the left or Bolivian bank are " Chacobos." These latter, it is said, are sometimes friendly, and have traded with the villagers of Exaltacion; but the former are a fierce and warlike tribe, that refuse to enter into **any** converse whatever with either the civilized Indians of Bolivia, or with the " Carayanas," as the Bolivians of Spanish extract are called.

We got up to the pascana for breakfast by about 11.30 a.m., and found that Don Miguel had kindly waited for us since about nine o'clock; however, we came up at the same time as the batelão did, so the delay was not altogether due to us.

Knowing that Don Miguel was short of farinha, I asked him how many days we should be in arriving at the village of Exaltacion, so that I might see if I had any stores to spare, as it would be better to reduce my rations than arrive at the pueblos with surplus food, while the other canoes were short. Molina's men are, I know, on very short commons; but, then, his canoes have stayed behind, so that I cannot share with them. Don Miguel calculated that we should be in Exaltacion by about the 14th, and that about a couple of days before that we should arrive at the "chacos," or plantations, where we could purchase plantains and other bread stuffs; so, as I have five alquieres of farinha left, and we require one in two days, with full rations of one pound and a half per man daily, I could spare at least one alquiere, which I passed over to Don Miguel, with an arroba of good wheaten flour.

After continuing the journey up the right bank, which is still preferred, as being freer from visits from savages, we saw, about 5.30 p.m., that Don Miguel had crossed over, to avoid a small corriente running pretty strongly round a rocky point; but as I saw that Señor Morales had kept to the same bank, and had stopped for the night about a mile and a half ahead, I managed to rope round the rock, and joined Señor Morales by about 7 p.m., after having had some little trouble in finding our way in the dark round a "playa," or sandbank.

On June the 6th we started at 2.45 a.m., and at daybreak saw an immense number of monkeys, pavas, and cranes, or "garças," on the banks and in the overhanging trees; but we were unable to do any shooting, as this morning we had got rather too far behind the other canoes. In this portion of the river there appears to be a great lagoon, not far from the left bank, and the muddy banks of a small " igarapé," or ravine, evidently running out of the lake were trodden up by the birds' feet just like a poultry-yard. We did not get up to-day to the breakfast pascana until 2 p.m., as we had a very hard and long morning's work, having had to cross the river several times to avoid strong running currents, and at one very large and shallow playa we had to pull with the rope, the men walking on the sandbank. We got up to the other canoes very late, and found that Don Miguel had very kindly waited for us as usual, and, to my disgust, I found that the batelão had arrived before us, having probably passed us before daybreak, or having started before us. I had to thank Don Miguel very much for having waited, as otherwise we should have paddled on without any breakfast; as it was, we were quite fagged and dismally hungry, having paddled for eleven hours without any stoppage. We could only give the men just time enough to cook and eat their chupe, and then off again after Don Miguel, who promised to stop at 4 p.m., so that we might get up to the sleeping-place in good time; but he must have gone much further than he intended, for it was 10 p.m. before we got up to him again. My men were much fagged, and it was too late for any cooking, so they had to put up with an extra ration of farinha and a " pinga " of cachaça, whilst my stand-by of sardines and farinha served me for a supper. To-day we paddled for eighteen hours, and it seemed that we were to have several days' hard work such as this before we get to Exaltacion, for the " barbaros " are said to be very bold hereabouts in the vicinity of the junction of the Itenez, where we now are.

# CHAPTER XVI.

Junction of the river Itenez—Short description of the Itenez or Guaporé
and its affluents—Fires at night prohibited on account of savages—A
capybara shot—Abundance of game above the rapids—False alarms
of attack by savages—Cooking-stove rigged up in the canoe—The
river Matocari—Hard work towing canoe—Open pampas—Strong
gale from the south hinders progress—Chocolotales of Exaltacion—
Falling banks—Estancia de Santiago—Value of oxen in the Estancias
of Mojos.

JUNE 7th. Starting at twenty minutes past midnight, we were soon left behind by the other canoes,
and at daybreak there was a thick mist on, which
cleared up by about seven o'clock; but no canoes
were in sight. On the left bank there are many
lagoons, for the number of ducks, cranes, and other
waterfowl hereabouts was very great. We passed
a long stretch of falling bank, with some trees overhanging, and looking, as we passed under them,
much as though they would fall on us. The current
underneath these falling banks is always very strong,
and gives great trouble to overcome, on account of
the large number of trees and dead wood at the foot
of the bank. The river began to widen considerably,
and as the wind blew strongly up stream, a very
considerable sea soon arose.

About 11 a.m. we got in sight of the junction
of a river on the right bank, and at first took it

for the Itenez; but it turned out only to be an arm of that river, for, proceeding onwards, we saw the other canoes encamped upon a large sandbank formed between the junction of the Itenez and the Mamoré. The river Itenez, whose waters are clear and dark-coloured, whilst the Mamoré's are muddy and whitish, is much wider than the Mamoré, which, however, gives its colour to the united waters below the junction, thus proving, probably, that the volume of its waters is greater than that of the Itenez. Both these rivers are exceedingly handsome at the junction, and so fine a " meeting of the waters " it would be difficult to match. This junction may be said to be the point of union of the extensive system of rivers that flow over the northern plain of Bolivia, and down part of the southern slope of the Cordilhera Geral, in the province of Mato Grosso in Brazil. The river Itenez in its higher portions is called the Guaporé, its head waters being separated from those of the river Paraguay by a land portage of but few miles in length. There are but few settlements or villages upon its right bank, or on the tributaries that empty themselves into it on that side, the town of Mato Grosso, near the source, being the one of most consequence, while the fort of Principe da Beira, about fifty miles from the junction, is simply a Brazilian outpost, at which, however, a considerable fortification has been erected. On the left bank there enter two rivers, called the Maddalena and the Baure, or Blanco, which are entirely in Bolivian territory; and on these rivers are some important villages, peopled by different tribes of civilized Indians, who were Christianized

by the Jesuit missionaries of the Beni, and are to-
day reckoned with that department.  On a branch
of the Baure River, near the abandoned missions of
San Simon and San Nicolas, gold quartz veins of
surpassing richness have, for some years, been known
to exist, and a Chilian society has lately been formed
to work these reefs.  With the river Itenez we have
nothing more to do ; the Mamoré, the sources of
which are all in Bolivian territory, being the river
up which the journey was prosecuted.

In this part of the journey the Bolivians talk a
great deal of the presence of " barbaros," and orders
were given that the canoes should not separate as
they had hitherto done ; but I had little hope that
the order would be carried out, for my men had
taken it into their heads to be sick again with fevers
and ague, so that my canoe was generally a long
way behind the others.

We left the junction of the rivers about 3 p.m.,
and at 5 p.m. stopped again for the evening meal,
starting again in about half an hour, and keeping on
till about nine, when we stopped at a large playa for
the night.  Here the Bolivian patrons gave a good
sample of the discipline they maintain with their
Indians.  The orders were that, as we were in territories supposed to be much roamed over by the
savages, we were to start early—as soon after midnight as possible—keep on till breakfast-time, about
8 or 9 a.m., then on again till dinner, about 5 or 6
p.m., when we were to shift quarters again ahead to
some convenient spot—a playa, if possible—where,
making fast the canoes quietly, we were to sleep till
midnight, and then start ahead again.  At this

sleeping-place no lights or loud talking to be allowed. Instead of this, when we got to this playa, one of the crews, who had some lumps of alligator flesh unroasted, lit fires and cooked the meat, and the patrons said nothing to them; and it appeared to me that the fear of losing the meat, although they had an enormous quantity already roasted, was greater than the fear of attack from the barbaros. Doubtless there are barbaros hereabouts, especially in the lands bordering on the Itenez, and higher up the Mamoré; there is also an igarapé below the junction of the two great rivers on the left bank, which leads up into districts bordering on the higher parts of the Beni, where the Chacobo barbaros are said to be in great numbers; but it is a chance that they should be *on* the great river, and my experience would go to prove that they will not attack even a single canoe, or else I was lucky enough to ascend the river when they were not on its banks, but up country.

June 8th. We started at 2 a.m., and kept up the right bank of the Mamoré, and having left the Madeira below the junction, we are now altogether in Bolivian territory. This morning I paddled from the start till breakfast-time, at 9 a.m., and kept the men sharp to their work, succeeding so well that we kept up with the other canoes, thus proving that when my men chose to work well there was no reason why we should be behindhand. When I work we have thirteen paddles going, and this number ought to and can send our canoe, which is not a large one, along right well; but if I take a short nap, or rest a time in the camarote, the men sleep at their paddles, and we then drop to the rear.

About 5.30 this morning, before it was fairly light, we passed an open pampa, with an igarapé running out at a sharp angle up stream into the river. It appeared as though it was a large drain cut by hand, for the slopes were just like canal banks, being covered with short grass, while the water running down was clear, and seemingly some three or four feet in depth.

Just above this igarapé I saw a large dark animal, the size of a large hog, moving slowly up the river bank, having, apparently, just emerged from its morning bath. In the dim light I could not be sure whether it was an animal or a savage, but as we were only about a dozen yards from the bank, I dropped my paddle, and taking up my gun, which was always ready to hand, let fly a charge of B B at the moving mass, which rolled down the bank into the river again. It proved to be a " capybara," or water-hog, and I was much pleased, as I had heard a great deal of this animal, and had never seen it or got a good description of it. The savages make ear ornaments of the front teeth of this rodent, and I have already stated that I was fortunate enough to get four of these from the Pacaguaras of the river Trés Irmãos. The capybara has the body of a pig, the hind quarters slightly humped and covered with long bristles ; the feet are three hoofed ; legs short and stumpy, but with plenty of flesh on them ; the head is almost exactly the shape of a rat's, with three upper and three lower teeth just like the incisors of a rat or rabbit. Its colour is a dark dun

all over. The teeth are very difficult to get out of
the head, more than three parts of their length being
set in the jaws. The only way is to hang the skull
up until it dries sufficiently to allow the teeth to
shake out, but this is an affair of some months.

This capybara gave us plenty of good fresh meat,
for I should think we got about four or five Bolivian
arrobas, say 1 or 1¼ cwt. from him; whole, he took
four of my strongest men to drag him along. The
meat greatly resembles the flesh of river turtles, but
it is not so tough; one can't compare it to any other
kind of animal flesh, it isn't like beef or pork, but is
something like rather tasteless veal. The fat cannot
be eaten, as it has a strong fishy taste. On arriving
at the breakfast place we cooked some steaks, which
were very palatable, and roughly roasted the joints,
that being the way in which the meat is kept when
time will not allow of its being properly made into
charqui, *i.e.* jerked or dried in the sun.

In the afternoon I shot a cayman for the men,
who had for some days been anxious to get one; this
fellow was about eight feet long, and was among the
reeds (capim) at the foot of the bank. A charge
of B B in his eye troubled him seriously, and backing
the canoe to him, we finished him with a bullet in
the same eye that was wounded by the shot. Hauling him on board, we put him in the bows of the
canoe in order that we might roast or "chapapear"
him at the first stopping-place. I also shot to-day a
large stork, called here a " cabeça seca," or dry head,
very much like, and probably identical with, the
" adjutant " of Calcutta. This fellow stands about a
couple of feet off the ground, body white with black

feathers in the wings, head fearfully ugly, with wattles all down the neck and bare head. In this part of the river every canoe is well stocked with meat, for everything seems eatable here. Birds of all kinds are eaten, except, of course, vultures and hawks, called here " souchus " and " gabilans ; " also a very common bird on these rivers, called a " cigana," and which is I think the " hoopoe ; " so, also, everything else, be it monkey, lizard, or alligator, is welcome to the men. This abundance of meat, whether fish, flesh, or fowl, justifies, in some measure, the practice of the Bolivian patrons, of trusting to the shooting above the rapids for meat, and giving all the Obidos charqui, etc., to the men amongst the cachuelas.

At 2 p.m. another halt was ordered for dinner, and then to row on till 10 p.m. for a short rest. About five o'clock we crossed from the right to the left bank, one of Don Miguel's canoes dropping behind to allow the large batelão and my own canoe to get into proper file, as Don Miguel had given orders to one of his mayordomos always to stop in the rear. Just as I pulled up into my place, I heard shouting, and saw the peons of the rearmost canoe, many of whom had gone on shore, come running down the bank and throw themselves into the river, shouting out " Los bougres! los bougres ! " The mayordomo mounted on the top of the camarote with his rifle, and I, concluding that the men had seen barbaros in the forest, ordered my crew to paddle out from under the bank, so that I might get a range for my rifle if necessary. The sun was, however, setting right in our faces, and prevented my seeing what was going on with the other canoe. The mayordomo fired three shots, and, when his peons had struggled into the canoe, paddled away as quickly as possible, shouting to the canoes that were on ahead, and to the crew of one, who, a short distance up stream, had landed on a sandbank, and were roasting alligator-flesh. When we all got together again, I found that the peons who went on shore, declared that they had seen two barbaros in the bush, and that the mayordomo had seen three on the bank some distance down stream. At these he fired, but, from the fact of the sun being in line, he could not be sure whether he hit them or not. Every one was much alarmed, as the savages hereabouts are said to be very bold; having at this spot, about three years ago, attacked a single canoe, killing a Brazilian, who was going to Bolivia as consul, and all his crew except one Indian, who managed to hide in the bush and then find his way by land to Exaltacion. We kept on until 7 p.m., when, crossing the river, we got to a large playa, at which we made fast for the night, no fires being allowed, and the night passed quietly.

June 9th. The start was made at 2 a.m., the canoes working up the right bank until daylight, when we were obliged to cross over to the other side, in order to avoid a strong current that we could not overcome with the paddles. I took a paddle till daylight, and then went on watch, rifle in hand, ready to do my best in case of a discharge of arrows from the bush; but my good fortune prevailed, and although we were, during the greater part of the day, far behind the other canoes, no attack was made upon us. There was a very cold wind from

the south beginning to blow to-day, the men seeming
to suffer much from it—one of them especially complaining greatly of the effect on his eyes, which
were almost closed up, and apparently giving him
great pain.

The usual halts for breakfast and dinner were
made during the day, and at nightfall we moved on
up the river, looking for a playa to pass the night
on. While paddling on in the dark, some of the
canoes being on either side of the river, we were
startled by hearing four shots fired from the canoes
on the opposite side to ourselves. It was impossible
to cross the river in the dark, and so we had to wait
in great anxiety to know what was occurring. The
firing ceasing, I kept on up stream, and overtook
Señor Morales, who was on the same side of the
river, from whence we heard the canoes opposite to
us proceeding on their way, and we accordingly
judged that there had been a false alarm. Soon
afterwards the moon rose, and Don Miguel's canoes
came over to our side, and we learned that they had
heard, while waiting for the large canoe that had
fallen somewhat in the rear, some suspicious noises
in the bush, sticks cracking, as though from being
trodden upon; so they discharged their guns in the
direction of the sounds, and soon afterwards crossed
over to the side where Señor Morales and I were.
The funk about barbaros was now at its height, and
every little noise in the bush, whether by night or
by day, is set down to barbaros following the canoes,
until a convenient spot, such as a point of land
commanding the canoes as they ascended near the
bank, should be chosen for the attack. Arriving at

a small playa, which afforded a clear space of about a score of yards to the forest, we made fast for the night, sleeping pretty soundly for a few hours, although we had no watch set or sentinels on guard.

June 10th. Started at 2.15 a.m., and by good luck I was able to keep my canoe somewhat ahead of the others, as towards daylight the other patrons and their mayordomos stopped about a good deal, shooting pavas, which were very numerous hereabouts. I did not get any, as to have tried to do so would have necessitated my stopping also to follow the birds into the bush, and I could not afford to lose the good place I had obtained to-day in the file of canoes.

To-day I rigged up a cooking-stove in the canoe, by filling a·large zinc basin that I had with sand, and thus I was able to get a cup of coffee or even some " chupe " for breakfast, prepared by my boy while the canoe was *en route*. This saved me a good deal of time, and enabled me to get something to eat at the hour most agreeable to me, and as the stoppages for breakfast and dinner were now made very early in the day, I found the invention a very good and useful one.

We had been travelling for the last three days through a very uniformly level country, but slightly raised above the highest flood line, but the forest still continues on either side of the river, the pampas passed as yet having been very small. The river keeps very good for navigation, although the many playas would give a pilot considerable trouble at night, the canoes often getting fast in the mud, and having to be guided into deep water by a man at the bow with a sounding-pole.

June 11th. We started very early at 1.15 a.m., and at 3 a.m. passed an igarapé, on the left bank, called the " Mayosa," which appears to be one of the few well-known points between the junction of the Itenez and the pueblo of Exaltacion. There was nothing special to record during the day, and about 6 p.m., as we came to a large playa, formed by a rocky formation, we concluded to stop for the night, and let the men get a little more sleep than they had lately been able to have allowed them.

June 12th. Started at 2 a.m., and at 8 a.m. we passed the river Matocari, emptying into the Mamoré on the right bank, its outlet being about fifty yards in width. This stream is said to be navigable as far as the villages of San Ramon and San Joaquin, which are distant from the Mamoré about two days' paddle during the rainy season. Goods for these villages may in that season be taken up this river, instead of being taken down to the junction of the Itenez, and passing the Fort of Principe da Beira, up the river Maddalena. During the afternoon we passed many pampas on either side of the river, which still keeps a fair breadth of about 500 or 600 yards. The pampas seem to be slightly raised above the highest river level, but sufficiently so to prevent their being flooded except in very high floods. At night we were unable to find any playa convenient for the night halt, so we made fast the canoes to a stump about fifteen yards from the shore.

June 13th. The morning was very cold and

chilly; we started at 1.30 a.m., crossing over to the left bank, following in rear of the big canoe, or batelão. Towards 4 a.m. a very strong and cold wind came up from the south, with a thick fog, and we made poor progress, crossing from one bank to another on account of strong currents, in one case having to send the men on shore to pull with the rope, which was very hard work, as the mud on the bank was very soft, making the men very cold, wet, and dirty, as they sank in it at every step up to their knees. When they came on board again, I served them with a ration of cachaça, and when the day broke we found that, notwithstanding all our mishaps, we were well up with the other canoes. The cold wind seemed to make the men very stupid and dull, and their rate of paddling got to be so bad, that, as I was determined not to lose the other canoes, I had to keep on without stopping to cook any breakfast, but made shift with what we had left over from the previous day.

About mid-day we came to large open pampas on either side of the river, which in this part of its course has some very severe bends, some of them being almost right angles. On the left bank is a grove of trees standing alone, and looking almost like young poplars, and as they are on the top of a cliff-like bank of yellow earth cut down by the current straight to the water, they form rather a remarkable landmark. In consequence of repeated crossings of the river to avoid shoals or currents, we made but slow progress, and this part of the river will require a good deal of study before steamers will be able to navigate easily, the playas especially being very numerous, and stretching out a great distance into the river.

We stopped for the night on the left bank, at a very large playa, which was so soft and muddy, that in trying to go after some ducks, I got thoroughly into it, and had to crawl out on hands and knees. Through this I spoiled a good pair of high boots; for my boy, who should have washed and dried them carefully, put them right into the fire for the second operation, and burnt the fronts completely off. During the night the south wind increased to almost a gale, and we were cold and miserable till morning.

June 14th. We did not start till 5.30 a.m., and made but poor progress on account of the gale which, blowing down on us, keeps us back. The men, also, are apparently quite unable to put out any power, and look more like a lot of blue-faced mummies than men, for it is curious how blue the Indians seem to turn when suffering intense cold, which certainly knocks them up much more than the hottest sun does. The country now appears more open, and extensive pampas are now very frequently occurring. This day we could only work about twelve hours, and at night the gale moderated.

June 15th. Started at 3.30 a.m., the day breaking cold and dull like the preceding ones, but the wind had somewhat moderated from that of yesterday, which might be termed half a gale.

The men still seemed in a numbed state, and it was impossible to get the least exertion out of them, for they paddle in an inert and wretched manner during the continuance of the cold. My thermometer had unfortunately got broken, but I should judge that the mercury would have stood very near, if not below, 50° Fahr.

At breakfast time to-day we found, on landing and passing through the fringe of forest on the bank, that we had arrived at the "chocolotales" of Exaltacion so that at last we had arrived near to some sort of civilization. These "chocolotales" appear to be very extensive and are found on both sides of the river, but to discover them it is necessary to go ashore and push one's way through the belt or fringe of chuchia and brushwood that has been left all along the river bank. These plantations of cocoa trees, or "chocolatales," as they are called, were made in the last century by the Mojos Indians of the department of the Beni, who were gathered together from their wandering habits, and formed into villages by the Jesuit missionaries of the Spanish South American dependencies of Peru and Bolivia. They are very extensive, and are now claimed as government properties, being farmed out, by the authorities of Exaltacion and Trinidad, to speculators who make good profits, as there is no labour, or very little, expended in clearing. At the proper season, which is during the months when the river is in flood, from February to March, the Cayubaba Indians from Exaltacion descend to these plantations, and collecting the cocoa pods which are then ripe, clear the trees somewhat of the dead leaves and rubbish that has fallen during the year, leaving the chocolotales to the savages and wild animals until the collecting time again comes round.

During the afternoon we passed a succession of these chocolatales, and also some small clearings, or "chacos," with plantains and other fruits growing in abundance. Each chaco has its hut, where the Cayubabas live during the few months in which they stay upon their plantations; but there were no inhabitants, the proper season for staying down the river having gone by. The absence of the proprietors did not, however, keep my fellow-travellers and the Indian boatmen from helping themselves to all the plantains and pumpkins that they could lay their hands on; and I was told that it was an understood custom that all travellers should help themselves as freely as they wished at these plantations, which are the first that parties ascending the rapids into Bolivia can arrive at.

Hereabouts we had to cross to the right bank to avoid a very strong current; and having to go under a very long stretch of falling bank, we very narrowly escaped being buried by a fall of many tons of earth. While paddling along, our captain saw ahead, small pieces of earth dropping down the straight wall of the bank, and just had time to sheer out into mid-river when down the mass came, very nearly bringing with it a lofty tree, which, had it fallen, would certainly have reached us with its topmost branches. Canoes ascending the river are much exposed to this danger, and in passing under these falling banks a constant watch must be kept.

To-day we found an arrow floating down the river, which the men declared to belong to the Chacobo tribe of savages that roam about in these districts; the arrow was of same size, form, and make as those used by the Caripunas and Pacaguaras of the Rapids.

At night we stopped opposite to the "Estancia de Santiago," the first of the cattle feeding-grounds of Bolivia that one arrives at in ascending the Mamoré. This was formerly the property of Don Barros Cardozo, Brazilian Consul in the Beni for some years, and who had been murdered by one of his Brazilian servants only a few weeks previously, as we had been informed by the canoes we met descending the river at the Misericordia Rapid. We now learned that the assassin had been hunted by the mayordomo, and other servants of the deceased consul, for some days, until he was discovered endeavouring to escape down the river in a small canoe ; and that, as he refused to surrender and menaced his pursuers with the same knife with which he had murdered his master, he was shot down and killed without waiting for process of law. This estancia is reported to have nearly 8000 head of cattle, and I was informed that, had the consul not lost his life, he had intended to drive a large number of his cattle by land from Guajará Merim to San Antonio. From the estancia to the first cachuela, the cattle would have been taken in canoes or on rafts—a comparatively easy work, as the navigation is entirely free from other obstacle than the playas or banks of sand which stretch out into the river at low water, leaving, however, in every case a channel deep enough and wide enough for craft that do not draw much water. Pasturage for the cattle would be easily found at night along the river banks, which are covered with "capim," a rough wild grass, or "chuchia," the wild cane, the succulent points of which are greedily eaten by the cattle. Oxen in the estancias of Mojos are worth from fifteen to twenty " pesos faibles," say about £2 10s. to £3 10s. a head, while at San Antonio and on the higher Madeira they are worth from eighty to one hundred milreis, or £8 to £10.

# CHAPTER XVII.

"El Cerrito"—Small steamer, the *Explorador*—"Taita Crusa"—The town of Exaltacion—The fifteen missions of the Beni and the tribes that belong to them—Some numerals and words in Mojeño, Cayubaba, Canichana, and Yuracaré—Education of the Indians.

JUNE 16th. We started at midnight in hopes of getting to the town of Exaltacion during the day, but did not get on very well till daybreak, for having to cross the river several times in the dark, we lost much way. At 9 a.m. we arrived at "El Cerrito," a chaco, and clearing with workshops for building canoes etc., belonging to the National Bolivian Navigation Company, the sister enterprise of the Railway of the Cachuelas. Here was a small steamer called the *Explorador*, which had in 1871 been taken entire up the rapids by Dr. Juan Francisco Velarde, the energetic agent of the navigation company. The taking of this small steamer over the rapids was certainly a most arduous task, and Dr. Velarde, and the American mechanics who accompanied him, deserve every credit for their pluck and steadfast determination to succeed in getting their craft over the nineteen cachuelas. The *Explorador* is a small steamer about forty feet in length, and was built by Messrs. Yarrow and Co. of Poplar, specially for the river Mamoré, her hull being made of the best Lowmoor iron, in order to resist the blows which she must have received in striking against the numerous rocks amongst the rapids, and when being hauled over the portages by the Indians, of whom there were about eighty employed. Her hull stood well, but her engines were not nearly strong enough, and broke down repeatedly in endeavouring to stem the currents. This little steamer is now quiet in the upper waters of the Mamoré, waiting for new engines, when she would be able to carry on a good business trading amongst the towns of the Beni, a department whose roads are laid out by nature in the stupendous network of riverine canals with which it is favoured, and upon which the villages are built.

El Cerrito is so called from its being the only hill that is to be found on this part of the river for many miles, and it is said to be the only spot that at exceptionally high floods remains above water. Here we got some fresh beef, eggs, and yucas, so we made a capital breakfast, that one did not require much coaxing to attack; for after fifty-three days since we started from San Antonio, during which time we had to get our meals when we could, and sometimes off what to many people would seem uneatable food, it will be believed that the sight of a piece of fresh beef was cheering indeed.

I started from El Cerrito about 1 p.m., having obtained the loan of five strong Cayubaba Indians to help my crew, who were glad of assistance; but just above the Cerrito the river runs straight for a considerable distance, and the current runs so strongly that I found we were quite unable to surmount it with paddles, so we had to put out a rope for towing, which was very difficult work as the bank was very muddy. At about 8 p.m. we stopped for the night at a hacienda, about five miles below Exaltacion, sleeping in the canoe, as it was too late to go up to the house and visit the " patron " that night.

The following morning I went up to the house, and introduced myself to the patron Señor José Aqurusa, or, as he is called by the Indians of the district, Taita (Father) Crusa. He was evidently an Indian, but of very good presence and manners, and being tall and grey-headed, he had rather a striking appearance. He is said to have great authority over the civilized Indians, being a " Cacique," or head man, of the Cayubabas, and it is supposed that even the wandering Chacobos respect him and his cattle ; while, during a time that he was corregidor of Exaltacion, they became friendly and visited the village for trading purposes. There were a good many Indians, mostly Cayubabas, about the house, and of women I think there must have been about five or six to each man, while children were running and rolling about in small droves. The house is of the usual South American up-country construction, open all round and with roof of palm leaves, of very great size in order to cover the sugar-mill, as well as certain great cupboard-like constructions which served as sleeping apartments for the women and children. Underneath this immense roof all the business of the day goes on, from the cutting up of the bullock to the cooking of the

" chupe," or soup, for breakfast or dinner, or the preparation of the national beverage of Bolivia, the " chicha," without which few Bolivians, be they Indians or of Spanish extraction, can exist: but of this chicha we shall have more hereafter. The sugar-mill was of primitive construction, but seemed to work well, and turned out sugar of an excellent quality. It was worked by a couple of very fine bullocks, the simple plan of ladling from the " trapiche," or mill, to the boilers being used instead of more complicated appliances. The working parts of the trapiche were all made of hard wood of excellent quality, the workmanship of the cogs and rollers speaking volumes for the ingenuity and skill of the Indian carpenters. There were a few bullocks in a corral, but they afforded a great contrast to the two fat oxen that worked the mill and that had evidently been stall-fed, and Señor Aqurusa set down the thin condition of those in the corral to the fact that during the past rainy season, in the early part of the year, the floods had been very high, and had consequently spoiled the greater portion of the pasturage.

Crossing over to the right bank, I called at the " chaco," or plantation, of Señor Francisco Ceballos, who received me very kindly, entertaining me very hospitably, and offering me free quarters in his house in Exaltacion, to which town, situated on the left bank of the Mamoré, we went about mid-day. The " puerto," or landing-place for the town, is situated at the apex of a large bend in the river, each arm being at least a league in length. The wind therefore, blowing up or down the river, exerts a great force on the craft made fast at the foot of the bank, which rises more than fifty feet above low water.

The town of Exaltacion is placed about a couple of miles inland from the river, the road to it being across a pampa, with a few isolated trees and a rough grass three or four feet in height, which at certain seasons is burnt, so that new grass fit for the cattle may spring up; the burning has to be done when the wind is quiet, and can be only done in patches, for if the fires were not kept under control, the villages and plantations would be greatly endangered. The town is built on this flat pampa, and consists of about a hundred houses, built of adobe walls, with tiled roofs, arranged in square blocks in the usual South American fashion. I had to stay in Exaltacion about ten days, as it was necessary to find a new crew, the men that I had brought with me from San Antonio being either from Exaltacion, or from the other villages on the Magdalena and Baures rivers; they consequently were very averse to continuing the journey up the river to Trinidad, and, as they sadly stood in need of rest, I determined to suffer the delay, and seek a new crew rather than oppress my old one by forcing them to take me on further.

The following is a list of the fifteen principal missions of the department of the Beni, which appears to have been one of the great fields of Jesuitical missionary effort in the sixteenth and seventeenth centuries.

Exaltacion, on the Mamoré, peopled by Cayubabas (1).

Santa Ana, on the Yacuma, an affluent of the Mamoré, peopled by Mobimas (2).

San Xavier, on the Mamoré, peopled by Mojeños (3).

San Ignacio, on the Tijamuchi, an affluent of the Mamoré, peopled by Mojeños (3).

Trinidad, on the Ybari, an affluent of the Mamoré, peopled by Mojeños (3).

Loreto, on the Ybari, an affluent of the Mamoré, peopled by Mojeños (3).

San Pedro, on the Machupa, an affluent of the Itenez, peopled by Canichanas (4).

San Joaquin, on the Machupa, an affluent of the Itenez, peopled by Itonamas or Machotos (5).

San Ramon, on the Machupa, an affluent of the Itenez, peopled by Itonamas or Machotos (5).

San Carlos, on the Itonama, an affluent of the Itenez, peopled by Baures (6).

Magdalena, on the Itonama, an affluent of the Itenez, peopled by Baures (6).

N. S. del Concepcion, on the Baures, or Blanco, an affluent of the Itencz, peopled by Baures (6).

N. S. del Carmen, on the Baures, or Blanco, an affluent of the Itencz, peopled by Baures (6).

Reyes, on the Beni, an affluent of the Mamoré, peopled by Maropas (7).

San Borja, on the Apiri, an affluent of the Mamoré, peopled by Maropas (7).

There are seven tribes of Indians in these fifteen villages, each tribe having a language of its own. There are also differences in the dialects of villages speaking the same mother tongue, such as Trinidad and San Xavier, or Magdalena and Nuestra Senora del Concepcion; but while these differences serve to render the Babel of tongues in the Beni still more confusing, one is only able to detect the seven leading languages as numbered in the list. There is another tribe (of whom more hereafter) that inhabit the lands on the highest waters of the Mamoré; this tribe is called the Yuracarés, but they are never reckoned amongst the Indians of the Beni.

Of the seven languages, the following numbers

and words are all that I had an opportunity of
obtaining :—

|  | Mojeño or Trinitario. | Cayubaba. | Canichana. |
|---|---|---|---|
| One | Etona | Carata | Merca |
| Two | Apina | Mitia | Calila |
| Three | Mopona | Curapa | Carajaca |
| Four |  | Chata |  |
| Five |  | Mitaru |  |
| Six |  | Tariduboi |  |

In endeavouring to follow the sound of these
words I have used the Spanish alphabet, that is
to say, *a* broad, *i* to be *e*, *e* a short *a*, *u* like *oo*,
*j* to be *h*, *c* hard before *a* and *o*, etc., etc. The
Mojeños and Canichanas do not appear to be able
to count beyond three; arriving at that, they commence again, and have to arrange all their calcula-
tions in sets of threes, which seems to be a most
complicated proceeding; thus, for a peso, or dollar,
that contains eight reales, they count "apina mo-
pona" and "apina," or two threes and two; how
they get on in the higher numbers I could not
understand, but as most of the Indians have learned
the Spanish numerals, I observed that they invariably counted the first three numbers in their
own language and then went off into cuatro, cinco,
etc. I managed to get the Cayubabas up to "tari-
duboi," or six, and then they would go on with
siete, ocho, nueve, etc. The Trinitarios have a
peculiarity with regard to their first numeral which
is worthy of mention; if they are counting they
will say "Etona," but if there is only one article
or thing to be spoken of, they say "Etonaricha,"
the addition of "icha" appearing to be a kind of

diminutive.   The following are a few words that
I noted.

| | Mojeño, or Trinitario. | Cayubaba. | Yuracaré. |
|---|---|---|---|
| Man | Jiro | Yasi | |
| Woman | Seni | Atoñanes | |
| People | Chani | | |
| Father | Ta'ta, or Pilla | Taita, or Apana | Atata |
| Mother | Meme | Apipi | Ameme |
| Son or Daughter | Chicha | Chiromi | |
| Wife | | Atoñanes | |
| Husband | | Até | |
| My | Ni | Ni and Ma | |
| Boy | | Miji | |
| Girl | | Mijiasi | |
| Sun | Sachi | Maca | Puyne |
| Moon | Cóje | Injani | Chuvi |
| Star | Reyje | | Pusichi |
| Day | Sachi | Carachu | |
| Night | Yoti | Garra (*g* soft) | |
| Fire | Yuco | Doré | Ayma |
| Water | Uni | Quita | Sama |
| Earth | Motaji | Datu | |
| Horse | Cuoyo | | |
| To eat | Pinica | Pañani | |
| Come and eat | Pi ana pinica | Aviro pañani | |
| To drink | Nero | Pacogucoi (*g* soft) | |
| Bring fire | Piuma yuco | Picha doré | Cuncayama |
| Bring water' | Piuma uni | Picha quita | Cuncayamsama |
| I go to drink water | Nero uni | | |
| Little | Paisarini | Irique | |
| Very little | Paisarichi | Padetai | |
| Go to sleep | Piana tinoca | | |
| Many people | Psinto poiachani | | |
| Let us go | Yánavori | | |
| Deep | Tupano | | |
| River | Cosará | | |
| Here | Pfjóca | | |
| Take hold | Anoca | | |
| There is not (no hay!) | Tajina | | |

The above words I have set down as near to the
sounds as I could.   It seems that many years ago

the Indians had a method of writing by short strokes, signs, and hieroglyphics; but that method is now almost entirely forgotten, and those who can write use the ordinary Roman letters. I have seen many excellent writers amongst them. All of them who had done service in the churches as sacristans and choristers are able to write; they also can read music, for which they use the ordinary five-line system. There are small schools in all the principal Indian villages in which reading, writing, and Catholic prayers are taught in the Castilian language; and I was rather surprised to see the amount of rudimentary knowledge that is drilled into the Indians, who, as a race, are not at all deficient in natural intellect, being, I believe, of a much higher grade than the Brazilian negroes of African descent.

# CHAPTER XVIII.

Festival of St. John the Baptist—Water-throwing—Morning mass—
Church of La Exaltacion de la Santa Cruz—" Macheteros," or Soldiers
of the Cross—Decrease of the Indians of the Beni—Suggestions for
the re-population of the department—A crew for Trinidad obtained
with difficulty—Desertion of an Indian lad—Landslip and dangers of
the port of Exaltacion—Changes in the courses of the rivers—Richness of the soil—Prices of provisions.

WHILE I was staying in Exaltacion the Festival of
St. John the Baptist occurred, on the 24th of
June, and the village was in fiesta, and no work
of any kind was done by the Indians. The chief
duty on this day appears to be to throw as much
water over each other as possible, this being a custom that has been introduced by the Bolivian patrons
or masters who are of Spanish origin. The great
object is to wet thoroughly the best-dressed man or
woman who shows on the street or at a window;
and possibly this is meant for a kind of baptism,
for as one cannot be made to go to the river as St.
John and his followers did, the river is brought, in
buckets and other vessels, to the unbeliever, who
must suffer the infliction of a good wetting with the
best grace he may; and thus he is at all events
made to practise the Christian virtues of patience
and long-suffering, for there is no escape from the
devout followers of the saint, the best plan being to

put on an old suit of clothing and provide one's self also with a bucket and squirt and set forth baptizing on one's own account.

Morning mass was held with great beating of drums and blowing of horns, the water play being abandoned for the nonce. The church is a very old edifice built of adobes, and was constructed by the Jesuits more than 200 years ago, the " cura " of the town informing me that there were ecclesiastical records belonging to it which vouched for its age. The façade facing on the central square of the village is highly ornamented with figures in cement handsomely painted; the columns are made in a twisted pattern, and there are, on either side of the principal door, images of a Christ and a Virgin, about eight feet in height, elaborately moulded and painted. The interior has been highly decorated with relievo ornamentation in mud cement, but has now become much decayed, all the pictures, of which there were a great many, having fallen out of their frames.

The service of the mass was of most barbarous character, and has evidently been adapted to the customs of the aborigines of these parts by the Jesuits. There were two Indians with head-dresses of macaw's feathers arranged so as to form a circle at the back of the head, and attached thereto is a long appendage, reaching to the ground and made of the breast feathers of the toucan, terminating with a real tiger's tail. These men have a species of bell-anklets to their feet, and a large wooden machete, or cutlass, in their right hands. Thus accoutred they execute dances in front of the altar and the

K

church door. These fellows are called " macheteros,"
and are intended to typify, I presume, the soldiers
of the Church fighting and conquering its enemies.
The interior of the church during mass presents a
good effect from the bright colours of the " tipoys "
of the Indian women, the two plaits of whose long

INDIAN GIRL OF EXALTACION.

glossy black hair are finished off with bright-coloured
ribbons called "ariches." The "tipoy" is made of
white or bright-coloured calico or print, and is a
long and straight garment which hangs in graceful
folds to the feet of the wearer, whose arms are
always bare from the shoulder. The bright colours

of these dresses made an effective contrast to the dark and sombre look of the church. The singing is of a squally character, the aim seeming to be to sing through the nose as much as possible; but every one seems to be thoroughly in earnest, and all cross themselves in proper fashion.

Most of these Indian women are, in their youth, comely and well featured, many of them being of very fair complexion, the darkest having skins of a burnished coppery hue. Some of them, however, adopt the barbarian's practice of filing or chipping their front teeth into sharp points, and this gives them a horrid look and reminds one of the dental arrangements of the alligators. This barbarous custom is also practised slightly, in some of the larger towns of the interior of Bolivia, and it strikes one as particularly painful to meet a señorita, blessed perhaps with pretty features and dressed in fashionable attire, and to observe when she opens her lips to smile that she discloses a set of teeth as sharp as any rattlesnake's.

The Indians of the Beni are, I fear, decreasing rapidly in numbers, and the deserted houses and lines of old streets now in ruins give a sad and desolate look to Exaltacion. The present population cannot be more than 1500, and I should judge that less than fifty years ago there must have been nearly 4000 Indians at the mission of " La Exaltacion de la Santa Cruz," or " The Raising of the Holy Cross."

The climate of Exaltacion is, I should judge, a very good one, except at times when the river overflows its banks, an occurrence which appears to occur with rather a remarkable regularity about once in seven years. The lands of Exaltacion are then flooded to a depth of perhaps six inches, and after the retirement of the waters, ague fever is epidemic, but at other times the air is pure and healthy. The reason for the decline of the Indian population is to be found, without doubt, in the baneful effects to Bolivia of the rubber-collecting trade of the Madeira and Purus rivers. This trade is the real cause that is rapidly depopulating, not only Exaltacion, but all the towns of the department of the Beni. To take the year 1873 as an example of the working of the emigration from Bolivia to the rubber districts of Northern Brazil. In that year forty-three canoes descended the rapids from Bolivia, with merchants on their way to Europe with ventures of " casca-rilla " (cinchona bark), or with speculators in the rubber estradas of the Madeira River, while in the same year thirteen canoes only ascended to Bolivia. We may average the Indians that leave Bolivia with these canoes at ten per canoe, and thus we have an exodus of 430 Indians from their country in twelve months, while only 130 return in the same period ; we thus have 300 Indians lost to Bolivia in 1873, and as the rubber-collecting fever has been decidedly on the decrease for the last four or five years, the year 1873 does not give a fifth of the number of Indians that have left in previous years. We may, I venture to think, estimate the drain of human life that the department of the Beni has suffered from the Northern Brazilian rubber trade at 1000 men per annum during the decade of 1862 to 1872. The worst feature of this emigration is, perhaps, the fact that rubber speculators and merchants descending the rapids will not allow the Indians to take any of the females of their families with them. This is done on account of avarice in some cases and necessity in others, which prompt the " patron " or owner of the descending craft to load his canoes as fully as he can with his merchandise, reserving as small a space as possible for provisions, which, on account of the quantity of farinha consumed, occupy so much space, that every mouth that requires to be filled, without its owner being able to assist in the propulsion of the craft, becomes a very serious consideration. Thus it arises that in every town of the Beni the females are in a majority of perhaps five to one over the males, and the populations are decreasing. According to the data given by a Portuguese exploring expedition, which travelled in 1749 from Pará to Matto Grosso *viâ* the river Madeira, an account of which has been published in a compilation, by Colonel George Earl Church, of the explorations that have been made in the valley of the river Madeira, there was then in the fifteen missions of the Beni, a total population of 26,000 Indians ; while at the present day, if all the Indians were collected together in these towns, it is probable that not more than 8000 would be found.

The only plan that is likely to succeed in restoring to these villages the Indian population, which is probably that which is best suited to the locality and climate, is that a treaty should be made by Bolivia with Brazil for the redemption of these Indians from the slavery in which they are held by their patrons the seringueiros, or rubber collectors.

It is true that the old form of slavery was abolished
in Bolivia when the Republic gained its independence; and in Brazil, in later years, every child of a
slave is born free, so that in the due course of events
slavery will be altogether abolished in the empire;
but on the Amazon, Madeira, and Purus rivers a far
worse form of slavery exists, for both Brazilian and
Bolivian patrons keep their Indians in their power
by means of debt and drink. At most of the barracas on the Madeira River where the seringueiros
live, the Sundays are passed in perfect orgies of
drunkenness, for it is on that day that the peon
delivers over to the patron the rubber that he has
collected during the week. The patron is also a
shopkeeper, and therefore treats his peon liberally to
white rum (called "cachaça" on the river), and, when
under the influence of this liquor, the poor peon is
induced to buy trinkets, calicoes, ribbons, and other
articles that he could do very well without. These
are charged to him at enormous prices, whilst his
rubber is credited to him at inversely corresponding
low ones, and thus he is kept under a heavy load of
debt, and cannot, under the Brazilian laws, leave his
patron until it is worked off, which happy event the
patron takes care shall not happen. A Bolivian
authority, aided by Brazilian officials, should visit
these unhappy exiles, and settle between patron and
peon the just state of the accounts; thus a thousand
Bolivian peons could with ease be gathered together
on the banks of the Madeira River. They could be
put to work on the railway of the rapids for two or
three years with advantage to themselves and to
their country, and return to their native villages at

the expiration of their agreements, with a small fund in hand. This would be the most expeditious method of repopulating the now half-deserted villages of the department of the Beni.

It was with difficulty that I obtained a crew of Indians in Exaltacion for the journey to Trinidad, for all the able-bodied men of the place were either at their plantations on the river or had gone with traders to the villages on the affluents of the Itenez. However, by overbidding one of the traders for a crew of Trinitarios, who, besides getting better pay from me, preferred to return to their own town rather than go with the trader to Reyes and other outlying towns, I was able to arrange for recommencing my journey on the 28th of June. On which day, after having taken my farewell of the principal men of the place, and having seen the last lot of baggage taken down to the puerto, I was ready to start by about 9 a.m., when, to my disgust, I found that my servant-boy named Trinidad, a young Indian that had been in my service for more than twelve months, and had accompanied me up over the rapids, had absconded and was missing. I sent back to the village for him, and lost several hours waiting in hopes that he would turn up, but without success. This is one of the most disagreeable features of travelling on the upper waters of the Mamoré, that at each successive village one is exposed to the loss of men; for the struggle for hands is very great amongst the traders, and the Bolivian Indian is easily tempted, besides being cunning enough to take advance money from two or three patrons at the same time, if he can get the chance of doing so. I tired of waiting for the runaway, and was fearful of losing some of the other men, who might, during the delay, change their minds as to going further up the river, and give me the slip also, so I started with nine paddlers and a captain—a fair crew, but one seat empty, which looked ugly.

The port of the town of Exaltacion must, if the town is ever to be served by steamer traffic, be moved higher up the river. While I was there an enormous mass of the bank at the port gave way and fell into the river, causing the loss of one man and a large canoe. This landslip measured more than 100 feet in length, the breadth of earth that fell being more than thirty feet at top, which was upwards of forty feet above the then water level. It is therefore evident that a more secure situation must be sought for the port, when any navigation of the Mamoré commences. On this part of the river, boats are much exposed to danger from the falling banks, which are called " tierras disbarrancandas." The Mamoré, and indeed all the rivers of the Beni valley, are for ever shifting their courses in many parts of the forests through which they flow. They undermine the banks on one side, which, falling away, form the numerous curves on the convex side of which the mud and sand brought down by the current is deposited, and playas and banks are formed, on which a forest grows in course of time. The river on the concave side of the curve is continually causing the trees of the *terra firma* to fall and obstruct the waterway, a barricade or " palisada " is formed, the river then returns in exceptionally high floods to its old course on the convex shore, bursting through the playas and sand-banks, and so the ever recurring changes of the river course continue. In illustration of this, I saw on the river Chapari a place where the current was breaking down a bank that was apparently *terra firma*, and had trees growing on it that were of great age. At the foot of this bank, and under some fifteen feet of earth, was a deposit of timber, blackened and, in fact, almost carbonized by time and pressure of the super-incumbent earth. From the manner in which these logs of timber were deposited, one above the other, it was evident that they formed part of a huge collection of drift-wood, such as may often be seen collected together in many parts of the rivers. On the Mamoré all " chacos," " barracas," and " pueblos " are placed some distance from the river, generally from half a mile to a mile, so that they may not be exposed to danger from the frequent changes of the river's course. In the cachuelas this feature of the river does not appear to exist, as there the formation of the country is of a more rocky nature.

At Exaltacion food-stuffs grown in the country are very cheap, the supply from the chacos being far greater than the wants of the sparse and scattered population. Cultivation, as is usual in all tropical countries, is carried on with a very small amount of labour, the rich soil requiring no digging or ploughing—sowing, only, being sufficient to give rich crops of maize, rice, yucas, yams, pumpkins, plantains, melons, tobacco, and all other kinds of tropical vegetation. The following are some of the prices of provisions in the Beni : " farinha de

yuca," or mandioca flour, twelve reales (4s. 10d.) per
Bolivian arroba of twenty-five pounds ; rice, six
reales the arroba in the husk—this only produces
about fifteen pounds when husked, thus the dressed
rice may be put at 2d. per pound. Sugar, brown, in
cakes, called " empanisadas," half a reale, say 2½d.
per pound; when partially refined and of a small and
white grain, it sells at one reale per pound. Ordinary
aguadiente, called cachaça below the rapids, and
white rum in English colonies, fetches eight reales
(3s. 2½d.) per frasqueira of three bottles, a stronger
and better sort of spirit, called " re-sacada," being
worth eight reales per bottle. Fresh meat sells at
one peso of eight reales (3s. 2½d.) per arroba of
twenty-five pounds; when preserved, by being salted
and dried in the sun, it is called " charqui," and
sells at three pesos (9s. 7½d.) per arroba, say 4⅗d. per
pound. Wheaten bread is very scarce, and when
obtainable costs half a reale, say 2½d., for a small
cake that may perhaps weigh a couple of ounces; the
reason for such a high price being that the flour has
to be brought all the way from Cochabamba, a town
in the interior of Bolivia that will be described hereafter. The tobacco grown in the Beni is of rough
appearance in the dried leaf. It is all used up in the
manufacture of very badly shaped cigars called
" puros," which sell for six reales, say 2s. 8d., per
100. In the absence of Havannahs or good smoking
mixture, a traveller will find them very acceptable.

## CHAPTER XIX.

Leave Exaltacion—Improvement in crew—Mobima Indians of Santa Ana
—"Mani" planted on sandbanks—The river Yacuma—Trading up
the Yacuma to Reyes, San Pablo, San Borja, etc.—Multitudes of
mosquitoes, etc.—Shoal of fish—Storks, ducks, flamingoes—Canichana
Indians—The river Apiri and the village of San Ignacio—Poling
over the shallows—The river Jamucheo—San Pedro—Traders haul
their canoes over a portage to San Pedro—Weather turns very cold—
The river Ybari—Arrival at Trinidad.

On the 28th of June I continued my journey up the
river Mamoré, starting from the puerto of Exaltacion about 1 p.m., and soon arriving at a landing-
place that is used when the river is full in the rainy
season. This appeared to me to be a much better
place for a permanent port, although it is further
away from the village than the lower one, but it has
the advantage that when the river is full it fills a
creek that runs to within a quarter of a mile of the
town, and up which canoes can then ascend, while,
in the dry season, it is not so subject to dangerous
landslips as the lower port is, for the banks are not
nearly so high.

We paddled on up stream till about 9 p.m., when
we stopped for the night at a playa, starting the
next morning at 5 a.m. with every prospect of a
good day's work, as the men are all strong and well,
and of a much better class than my old crew. I

have now eight Trinitarios and two Cruzeños, these last being much better paddlers than Cruzeños generally are, one of them also bidding fair to make me a very useful servant in place of the lad that decamped yesterday. The river continues to be about half a mile in width, and presents no features of special interest, large playas or sandbanks alternating with long stretches of falling banks. In the afternoon we saw a canoe with Mobima Indians from Santa Ana on the Yacuma River, who come to the large playas on the Mamoré in the dry season, to sow maize and various kinds of beans thereon. We halted at 9 p.m., the night being a very unpleasant one from the great number of mosquitoes, the camarota of the canoe being so full of traps that it was impossible to set up the "toldeta," or mosquito curtain, without letting in a lot of these bloodthirsty monsters ; and on day appearing, I found the curtain was a perfect hive of them, and that I had suffered a serious loss of vital fluid. We started early the next morning (June 30th), the men requiring very little urging. At daybreak I went ashore on a large playa, and found it planted with two sorts of "frijoles," or beans, and a kind of small pulse, called here "mani," which, from the description given me, appears to be much like East Indian "gram" (*i.e.* the large red class). This planting is carried on by the Santa Ana people, who come here in their narrow canoes or dug-outs, very long and very narrow, some being perhaps thirty feet long by sixteen or eighteen inches wide. This is the class of canoe used by the Cayubabas of Exaltacion, and by most of the Indian tribes of the Beni.

About half-past two in the afternoon we passed the mouth of the river Yacuma, on which is the pueblo of Santa Ana, the head-quarters of the Mobima Indians. From the breadth at its mouth, the river appears to be of considerable size; and the village is said to be " doce tornos," or twelve bends up river, this being the method by which the Indians describe a distance on these rivers. Probably the village is a good day's paddle from the junction of the Yacuma with the Mamoré. It is by this river that traders take goods for the pueblos of Reyes, San Pablo, San Borja, and Santa Cruz, all of which are peopled by the Maropa Indians, and from which villages a trade is carried to the towns of Apolobamba in Bolivian territory, and Sandia in Peruvian. The river Yacuma is said to be navigable all the year round for large canoes, and is free from savages; therefore a small steamer may be advantageously employed here, after the construction of the railway of the cachuelas. The Beni River is said to be known from its sources, near La Paz, down to Cavinas, where there is a small village and a mission; but below that point few persons, if any, have of late years navigated, for the savages, who infest the lands near the junction of the Beni and the Mamoré, at the Madeira Falls, are much dreaded. Doubtless these savages would be easily driven off when navigation commences in earnest on these waters, but it is just as well to have two lines of communication with the south-eastern towns of Peru. One of the merchants who accompanied me up the rapids, sold goods, to the value of £3400, in Exaltacion to a trader who sends canoes up the affluents of the

Mamoré or the Itenez to the various pueblos of the
department of the Beni, such as San Joaquin, San
Ramon, San Nicolas, and San Pedro on the Machupa
River, Magdalena on the Itonama, Concepcion de
Baures and El Carmen on the Baures or Blanco
River, the before-mentioned town of Reyes and
others on the Yacuma, and San Ignacio on the
Jamucheo. Considerable trade will doubtless be
opened up with these towns and villages, and work
will be found for two small steamers: one to run
on the affluents of the Mamoré, and the other on
those of the Itenez, the head-quarters of both being
at Exaltacion or El Cerrito, just below.

July 1st. Started at 5 a.m., having had better
luck with the mosquitoes last night, as I only had
about half a dozen under the curtain instead of
about a hundred, as I had the night before; but the
men, who slept on shore on a high sandbank, passed
a bad time and got no sleep at all, as the wind
continually lifted up the toldetas and allowed the
mosquitoes a free right of way. As soon as it was
light I had pretty good sport, getting a " cabeça
seca," three ducks, and a pava in a very short time.
There is always plenty of game to be had on this
part of the river—so much so that one need scarcely
provide any charqui, if it were not rather imprudent
to trust entirely to one's gun for the supply of a
canoe's crew of boatmen.

The country we pass through is very uniform,
" playas " and " tierras disbarrancandas," and bits
of pampa land, alternating with each other. There
are no " barbaros " hereabouts, and I should say
the lands from Exaltacion to Trinidad would be

very valuable for emigration ; climate splendid, land
of excellent quality for the production of crops of
sugar-cane, rice, maize, plantains, and every other
description of tropical produce, together with capital
pampas for cattle rearing. The bag to-day was
splendid—two cabeça secas, a very large stork, called
a "bata," four ducks, and a pava ; total eight. Also,
we got about a dozen good-sized fish, which the
men pulled out with their hands, there being a
shoal of them close inshore; and if we had had

THE BATA.

a net we could have got a canoe full with ease. The
" bata " is of the stork tribe ; it stands about five
feet high. Its wings, fully extended, cover eight feet
six inches ; colour white, head without feathers, but
deep black skin, with red bag or wattle on the
breast, where the body-feathers commence. The
beak is black, with a curious upward turn, and is
about twelve inches long. 'This fellow I shot with

the rifle at about 200 yards.    He had strength
left to make for the bush, but my young retriever
" Burro " bolted after him and kept him prisoner
amongst a heap of dead timber, until one of the
Indians got up to him and finished him off with
sundry blows on the head.    The flesh of these birds
is excellent eating, a steak off the breast, toasted over
the wood fire, being very tasty.    We saw a pair or
two of flamingoes, and also some spoonbills ; but
these birds seem very wary, and do not allow one
to get even within a rifle-shot of 200 or 300 yards.

July 2nd.    Started at 3.30. a.m.    This morning
we see but few ducks or other birds, the wind
perhaps driving them to cover, as it blows strong
from the north-east.    We have now passed the run of
the Santa Ana people, for we do not find the playas
sown with anything ; nor do we meet with canoes,
as we did yesterday, when we saw two or three
lots of these Santa Ana Indians.    This was a very
uneventful day, with no shooting to speak of.
Stopped for the night about 7 p.m.

July 3rd.    Started about 4.30 a.m., rather later
than usual, the men having overslept themselves ; for
we had intended to make the start about two instead
of after four o'clock.    Soon after sunrise we met a
canoe with Canichana Indians, going to some chaco
that they have near here, so we are now in the
San Pedro district.    We don't make the progress
I had hoped for, and it is clear that my canoe
is undermanned ; so I fear we shall take eight or
ten days from Exaltacion to Trinidad instead of the
usual six or seven.    I found to-day that we had
passed the river Apiri yesterday morning, about

breakfast-time. This river appears to be placed in the maps (Johnston's) too high up the Mamoré by about a day's journey—say fifteen or twenty miles. The pueblo of San Borja is on this river, but is a very small and insignificant place.

At 3 p.m. a heavy storm of rain, with thunder and lightning, came up with the wind, which has for the last two or three days been blowing from the north-east. About a third of an inch of rain fell. We stopped for the night about seven o'clock, and started the next morning, July 4th, shortly before 3 a.m., making a good early morning run. At day-break plenty of duck were about, and I got a couple of marrecas and five cuervos, the latter a kind of black teal that I consider to be very good eating. In the afternoon my captain, one Pedro Yche, a Trinitario Indian, left his steering for a time, and took a spell at the paddles. He is a remarkably fine Indian, and very strong, being far above the ordinary stamina of the Indians. On the journey up the rapids he was the moving spirit amongst Don Miguel's men, and whenever he put his shoulder to the canoes, in hauling them over the land portages, they **had** to go! To-day he started paddling with **such** good will that the paddle broke with the force he exerted in pulling it through the water. As we were short of paddles, he made the men cut a lot of long " chuchia " (wild cane) poles, from twelve to four-teen feet **in** length, and over the shallow waters of the playas we poled along, progressing very fairly. This is a favourite method with the Brazilians when travelling on the rivers, but the Bolivian Indians soon tire at it, **and** seem to prefer the monotonous work of paddling.  At night we stopped opposite to the mouth of the river Jamucheo or Tijamuchi, seven days' journey up which is the pueblo of San Ignacio.  To-day my total shooting was three ducks, eight cuervos, and a pava—a good bag, sufficient for a good " pot " and a grill for all hands.

July 5th. We started very early—at 3 a.m.—and about mid-day stopped for breakfast at the " puerto " or landing-place for the village of San Pedro, which is situated at the head of the river Machupa, which is an affluent of the Itenez.  This village is peopled by the Canichana tribe of the Beni Indians, and is about a couple of leagues from the eastern bank of the Mamoré.  There must be some slightly raised land, sufficiently elevated to form a watershed, a short distance from this bank of the great river, for the Machupa and other affluents of the Itenez run in a north-easterly direction, but the elevations are not of sufficient size to be seen as hills.  There are two ports for San Pedro, at the upper one of which we stayed for the night.  The sheds at these ports are large and well built, an Indian always living at them, who is termed the sentinel, and whose duty is to take care of the canoes of the villagers or traders, who leave their craft at the port while they visit the pueblo.  From the style of the work, the quality of the timber, and the tidiness of the place, my previous favourable opinion, obtained by the employment of a few Canichanas in San Antonio, was confirmed, to the effect that these Indians are the most desirable of any of the various tribes of the Beni.  They are excellent workmen with the axe, and are, I think, less addicted to the use of ardent spirits than the

Cayubabas or the Trinitarios. Traders going to San Pedro use the port on the Mamoré instead of going the round by the river Itenez. Their canoes are hauled up on land, and dragged by oxen across the two leagues of pampa between the Mamoré and the Machupa; and when steam navigation on the Mamoré commences, no doubt a corduroy road over this tract would be a great acquisition, so that the town of San Pedro may be accessible during all seasons from the Mamoré.

July 6th. We started again about 3 a.m., and at daybreak came to a playa where the current ran very strong; so tried the other side, but found the current worse, and the bank falling. We therefore returned to the playa, and dragged the canoe about a mile with a light rope, the men walking on the sand, and a couple of men in the canoe keeping her in a straight course with their chuchia poles. This morning the river was rising, and so the current was more rapid than usual, and the sandbanks were falling away as the water rose. In the afternoon we passed the port of the village of San Xavier, which is situated on a creek running into the Mamoré on its right bank, and at 5.30 p.m. stopped for the night at some " chacos " on the left bank of the river. During the night there was a little rain, and the wind changed from the north, where it had been for the last few days, round to the south, thus promising us some more cold nights.

July 7th. The south wind caused the day to break cold and dull, the thermometer going down to 66° Fahr., and not beginning to rise until past eight o'clock in the day; nevertheless, the men started early, because they hoped to get to the puerto of Trinidad, on the river Ybari, before nightfall. No shooting to-day, and very dull, unpleasant travelling on account of the cold; so I wrapped myself up in my Scotch maud, and read till twelve o'clock, when we stopped for breakfast. During the morning we were much delayed by the strong wind, which, being from the south, was right in our faces, and we were quite unable to make head against it in the shallow waters over the playas; we had, therefore, to keep under the banks in order to be somewhat sheltered from the wind, but as these banks were falling ones ("tierras disbarrancandas"), it was very unpleasant work. I had some sharp words with my captain, Pedro Yche, who is a good fellow, but very self-willed, and was far too fond of risking the canoe and our lives under these banks rather than brave the cold wind on the exposed playas. In couse-quence of all this trouble we did not make the progress we had hoped for, and at nightfall I ordered the canoe to the left bank of the river, where the banks were not falling, and where we could pass the night secure from the danger of being crushed by a heavy fall of earth; but we had a very bad night on account of the powerful wind, which many times during the night I fancied would cause the canoe to drag her moorings.

July 8th. The thermometer went down to 57°, and the night appeared to me to be about the coldest I had yet passed in the tropics; but perhaps above the cachuelas, when the south wind was blowing, it might have been as cold. I had not then a ther-mometer to register by, and was able to keep under the toldeta ; but last night this arrangement was quite useless, for the wind blew right through the camarota with a force so great as to render the fixing up of a curtain an utter impossibility. I think that Humboldt says that 21·8° Centigrade, equal to say 71° Fahrenheit, kept him from sleeping, so that our 57° may be considered as very trying indeed ; and so we found it.

We made a start about 5.30 a.m., as soon as daylight appeared—for there was no temptation to linger under our blankets, which were quite unable to keep out the searching wind—and about 7.30 we left the Mamoré, entering a river called Ybari, about 100 yards wide at its mouth. In this part of the Mamoré there are two rivers of the same name, " Ybari," and on one of these, the one now referred to, the town of Trinidad, the capital of the department of the Beni, is situated ; on the other, about a couple of days' journey southward, is the village of Loreto. This Ybari has plenty of water all the year round, and at present appears to be fairly navigable for small steamers, as it is perfectly free from dead wood or sandbanks, and the Indians tell me that even in the dry season there is water enough for large gariteas that draw, when loaded, four or five feet.

About mid-day we got to some chacos, or plantations, and stopped at one for breakfast, as it belonged to a " pariente," or relation, of my captain Pedro. The barracca was, however, empty, and the whole place seemed left to take care of itself. It was said that the people had gone to Cuatro Ojos, on the river Piray, the port for the town of Santa

Cruz de la Sierra, the most important place in the
north-east of Bolivia.   There was not much to lose
in the chaco, for the chocolotales have no fruit at this
season, and the " caña," or sugar-cane, was not ripe,
and the only edible things to be found in the clearing were pumpkins, called here " oquejos " (the
nearest spelling that I can get in Spanish, the " qu "
standing for " k," but " okehose " in English would
give the nearest pronunciation), and in Brazil
" jurumus " and " sapallos."   We helped ourselves
to some of these as an addition to our chupe, and
after our meal proceeded on our journey, the wind
blowing so cold and strong that we made very poor
progress.   At nightfall we were still a good way
from the puerto for Trinidad, so we stopped for
the night at another of the chacos, which are now
encountered pretty frequently on either side of the
Ybari.

July 9th.   The thermometer during the night
went down to 52½°, and from one's feelings it might
easily be thought that we were travelling in the
northern hemisphere instead of in the southern.
We arrived at the port of Trinidad about 9 a.m.,
and finding that the town was about two leagues
from the river, we prepared our breakfast and sent
messengers to the town for horses to ride there
on, and for bullock-carts for the baggage.   The
so-called port of Trinidad is like all the other
ports on the rivers, simply a place where, from the
depth of water, canoes can be moored to the bank, a
few steps being cut up the bank to the shed at the
top where the sentinel, whose duty it is to watch the
canoes, finds shelter.

# CHAPTER XX.

Pampas of Trinidad—Oxen of the Beni—Merchants of Trinidad—Carayanas—Cholos—Indios—Chicha, general drink in Bolivia—Baile and
Spanish dance—Bolivian drinking—Bolivian peculiarities—The old
maid's black cat—Smallpox amongst the Indians—Depopulation of
Trinidad—Wages of the peons—Drills, hammocks, shirts, and hats
made by Indians—Prices of provisions—Trade in Trinidad—Depreciated currency—Melgarejos.

In the afternoon I was agreeably surprised by the
arrival of Don Ignacio Bello, who very kindly rode
over from Trinidad to escort me to the town, where
he treated me in a most kind and hospitable manner.
Don Bello is the principal merchant of Trinidad, and
had, in 1872, made a journey down the rapids and
to Pará, returning from thence in 1873; and as I
had accompanied him from San Antonio to Pará, we
were old friends.

The road from the Ybari is over a flat pampa,
which stretches far beyond Trinidad, up to the
Itenez River, and which is covered with a species
of rough, tall grass that requires burning frequently.
These pampas are almost annually flooded, and are,
I think, more subject to these inundations than the
pampas on the opposite side of the Mamoré and near
Exaltacion. The inundations sometimes rise up to
the town of Trinidad, there being only one street
that is said to be left dry on these occasions. The

grazing lands generally have some slight eminences upon them, where the cattle find refuge during these floods. Upon the retirement of the waters, and when the sun has dried the rubbish, it is set fire to in as many places as possible and burnt up, after which the young grass springs up quickly with renewed vigour, and the cattle thrive excellently. The oxen of the department of the Beni are really handsome animals, being nearly twice as large as those of Brazil; indeed, I have seen many that would compare very favourably with our ordinary English bullocks. The heaviest of them are kept for hauling purposes, and are very well trained both for carts and for the " trapiches," or sugar-mills.

Trinidad is the capital of the department of the Beni, and is the seat of the prefecture. It is, however, but a small town, though larger than Exaltacion; the houses are many of them well built, of brick or adobe walls, and all have tiled roofs. There are a few merchants and storekeepers of considerable position and resources, whose principal trade appears to be the export of cocoa to Cochabamba and Santa Cruz, receiving in return flour and potatoes from Cochabamba, and dry goods from Santa Cruz, these latter being brought thither from the Brazilian town of Curumbá, on the river Paraguay. The merchants are all Bolivians of Spanish descent, but the bulk of the population is formed of Mojeño, or Trinitario Indians, who appear to me to be the most intelligent, as they certainly are the best-looking, of all the tribes of the Beni.

These Indians acknowledge the Bolivians as their patrons or employers only, and each tribe has its

SKETCHES OF TRINITARIO INDIANS.

" cacique," or headman, who seems to have authority over the whole tribe, and who is generally in the pay of the prefect or corregidor, as the case may be. The Bolivians of pure Spanish descent are called " Carayanas," whilst the mixed races are called " Cholos," and the pure Indians are termed " Indios."

The Trinitario Indians are a very good-looking race, but they are becoming so mixed with the carayanas, that complexions of all shades, from almost white to dusky red copper, are found amongst them. They are intelligent, and naturally active and hard working, but are much given to habits of drinking, which render them very uncertain and little to be depended upon. Their principal drink is " chicha," the national beverage of Bolivia, of which there are two kinds, " chicha cocida " and " chicha mascada," or boiled and chewed, the latter disgusting mode of preparation being the favourite.

The chicha cocida, or boiled chicha, is a simple preparation of maize corn, ground and boiled in any large vessel. The liquor being strained off and allowed to stand for a day to settle, forms, before fermentation sets in, a very pleasant drink, which is not intoxicating, but is very healthy and nutritious; indeed, I hardly know any drink that can be taken in hot climates with more impunity and with greater satisfaction. It is something like, but to my thinking much pleasanter than, the oatmeal and water drunk so largely by the stokers and others who have to stand the heat of the stoke-holes of ocean steamers.

Chicha mascada is a very different affair, and as this is *the* national beverage used in Bolivia, from the president down to the cholo, it is, although repugnant to civilized notions, necessary to describe it. The maize corn is first ground ready for a grand chicha brew, to which the owner of the chicha to be made invites as many old women as is thought needful. These hags are seated round empty flat tubs, called " bateas," and each one filling her mouth with the powdered corn, squirts it out into the batea after having mumbled it well with her often toothless jaws. When a sufficient quantity of this odious mess is collected, water is added in accordance with the idea of the quantity of liquor to be disposed of at the coming festival, or sufficient for a day or two's sale; the brew is then agitated well with a stick, and, having been boiled for a short time, is left to cool, when it is put by for use. After keeping for two or three days, it ferments, and becomes almost equal in intoxicating effects to good home-brewed ale. The Indians prepare large quantities of this chicha mascada whenever they wish to have a drinking bout, or whenever any festival of the Church or village takes place. On these occasions enormous quantities are drunk, and the bout never terminates until the supply is out, by which time the drinkers are all thoroughly tipsy.

So general is the use of this filthy drink throughout the republic, that all European travellers must be careful, when accepting a drink of chicha, to be sure that they know how it has been prepared. To my mind, the Bolivians will never be a people that merit respect until they do away with the numerous chicha mascada shops that are to be found in every town and village, and on every road, throughout the republic. The very idea of the horrid thing is

enough to demoralize any people, and how a custom
derived from savages can have taken such firm hold
upon a people of Spanish descent, is hard to imagine.
I must, however, at the same time say that there
are numerous Bolivian families amongst the higher
classes in which the chicha mascada is never
allowed to be seen or used.

While in Trinidad I was honoured by a " baile,"
or ball, at which, as I had the privilege of supplying
the drinks, chicha mascada was rigidly tabooed.
At this dance all the respectable families of the town
attended, and the affair was a very ceremonious one.
We had a full wind and string band of Indians, who
played some very fair polka and quadrille music, in
which the bass accompaniment of the " bajones " was
very prominent.    This " bajo " is like an enormous
Pan-pipe, or like half a dozen organ tubes, made of
bamboo.    The first of these tubes is about six feet
in length, and the last about half that.    The player
rests the foot of the longest one on the ground,
and, holding the instrument in a sloping position,
blows through the rough mouthpieces fitted in the
top of the tubes, producing a rumbling sort of bass
accompaniment, which appeared to me to entirely
spoil the effect of the violins and fifes, which dis-
coursed some very fair dance music.    Another noisy
accompaniment was afforded by the " caja," or drum,
made of a small section of a tree hollowed out, and
having a hide stretched tightly over either end,
which was vigorously beaten by rough short sticks
about nine inches in length.

I now saw for the first time what is probably
the real Spanish dance ; for although polkas and

quadrilles have found their way even to the centre of South America, still the " baile suelto," or loose dance, as it is called, is the favourite. There is a good deal of grace and good dancing in this affair, in which a couple occupy in their turn all the floor of the room, while the company beat time to the music with a loud clapping of hands. This beating time is to give the dancers encouragement to good and lively dancing, and it is a pleasant sight to see a stately old don pirouette round his fair (dare we say dusky?) partner, with a dexterous flourish of the handkerchief which both performers use throughout the dance. As the custom is that any one of the company seated around who is detected neglecting to join in beating time should be immediately con- demned to " take a drink," I had occasion several times to thank my luck that the national drink was not necessarily an accompaniment of the national dance. As, however, a good strong brandy or white rum (aguadiente) punch was the favourite article of consumption, it was just as well not to be " fined in a drink " too often. I must say that the company, " el bello sexo " included, were very good hands at re- freshing themselves with the punch—so much so that it became, long ere the close of the ball, hard to tell whether the " baile borracho " was simulated or real. This baile borracho, or drunken dance, is another Bolivian custom, which consists in reeling through a quadrille as though one were unable to dance straight, the most highly applauded performer being the " he " or " she " who can best simulate in- toxication.

It is often said—and perhaps it is a just reproach

—that we English people are a hard-drinking set, but I think that the Bolivians beat us hollow; and certainly, in my few travels, east and west, I never came across any people that could at all compare with the Bolivians in downright hard drinking, and I don't suppose that any other country can boast of such an institution as the baile borracho, which is occasionally danced in the best society of Bolivia.

While taking note of some peculiarities of Bolivian character in the way of eating and drinking, I am reminded of a custom that I think is decidedly, among civilized people, confined to Bolivians (for we can, perhaps, hardly count the Chinese as within the pale of civilization, although they call us barbarians). I allude to the liking that Bolivians have for eating cats, which are much esteemed in Bolivia, where they are fattened up for the table. I have tasted monkey, lizard, and indeed almost every kind of living thing that can be shot in the forests, but it has not yet been my lot to eat cat knowingly; so I can't say whether the flesh of Bolivian cats is superior to that of specimens of the feline race in other parts of the world, or whether it is equal to Ostend rabbit. But the Bolivian cat looks much like his relations in other countries, so probably the explanation is that the Bolivians are a peculiar people, and that their liking for cats and chicha mascada is one of their peculiarities. During my stay in Trinidad I was most hospitably entertained at the table of Don Ignacio Bello, where, fortunately for me, cats and chicha mascada were not on the *menu*; but good fresh beef in abundance formed the staple food, varied with mutton now and then, and fish almost every day. As Don Bello had no spare sleeping-quarters to offer me, I was accommodated with a couple of rooms in the house of an amiable aged and virgin member of the " bello sexo" of Trinidad, and during my stay there her favourite cat was missed. The old lady was disconsolate, and a general search was ordered, at which I assisted; and chancing to look into the round brick oven in the back yard, I espied a black cat therein, which refused to be aroused by sundry prods and blows from a thick stick. Discovering that it had departed this life, I delicately informed its sorrowing owner that she might console herself by dining off her pet, which, doubtless feeling its last end approaching, had gone into the oven to bake itself, so that its mistress might be saved the trouble and pain of preparing it for the table. However, the old lady averred that she could not eat a pet that she had possessed, I think she said, for some twenty years or more; but my belief was that she thought it would be too tough, being of such great age. Anyhow, it is certain that in many Bolivian families the cats are petted, and, when fat and in good condition, slain and devoured.

At the time of my visit the town did not display a very animated appearance, for smallpox was very prevalent at the time, and numbers of people, both old and young, appeared to have suffered greatly. This disease almost decimates the Indians at frequently recurring intervals, for the authorities have no idea of isolating the sick, and vaccination is but partially enforced; the Indians, in ignorance of its benefits, being naturally averse to it. At San

Antonio, the doctors of the railway staff had, however, very little difficulty in persuading the Indians to submit themselves to the operation, which was so successful, that out of upwards of 100 Indians who were on the station when the smallpox broke out amongst us, only four, I think, died; notwithstanding that very few, if any, of them had been vaccinated in their own country, and that the disease, operating upon Indian blood, seems to be specially virulent.

The people also complained bitterly of the great emigration to the rubber-grounds of Brazil, and spoke of Trinidad as depopulated, many houses appearing to be left altogether empty and uncared for. Nevertheless, there seems to be a good deal of business done in the place, and the principal merchants appear to be very well off; but the construction of the Madeira and Mamoré Railway, which would cause an entire change in the route of trade with Bolivia, is the only event that can save the once flourishing department of the Beni from becoming again the hunting-grounds of the savage Siriono and the haunt of the wild beasts of the forests. The opening up of the route past the rapids would arrest entirely the decay of these fertile provinces, by affording a ready means of transit to a good market for the chocolate, sugar, tobacco, oxen, hides, tallow, skins, and other produce, for which the inhabitants are now only able to realize but a small amount in value compared with what they will be able to when the route is open, and some of the Bolivian peons in exile in Brazil have been brought back to their homes.

In consequence of the scarcity of hands, the peons now get thirty to forty per cent. more for their journeys than they did a couple of years ago; thus, from Trinidad to Coni, they now get eight pesos for the up river voyage, and two for bringing back the canoes, while formerly the price was six to seven pesos for the round trip. The monthly rate of pay does not, however, seem to have altered much, as it is still about five pesos (16s.) per month.

The Indians of Trinidad, Santa Cruz, and other towns of the department of the Beni, though, like most men of Indian race, fond of the *dolce far niente*, " swing in a hammock," " smoke cigarette " kind of existence, are very clever in their specialities. Some of the produce of their hand-looms will compare very favourably with the fabrics of civilized countries, if not for texture, at least for strength and durability, and a wearer of their " macanas," or linen drill, can be certain that there is no shoddy or size in the material. So, also, the hammocks they weave from the native cotton are handsome and strong, whilst the " cascaras," or bark shirts, that they beat out of the inner skin of several trees, are marvels of patience and ingenuity, and the hats they weave from the young and tender leaves of a low-growing palm tree are quite equal to the much-vaunted hats of Panamá. A straw hat worth about three or four dollars in the Beni, the collection of the straws for which has occupied an Indian for months, would be equal to one costing twenty or thirty in Panamá.

Prices of provisions are much the same as those current in Exaltacion. I observed, however, that Manchester goods, such as calicoes, longcloths,

M

ribbons, etc., are brought to Trinidad from Curumbá,
*viâ* Santa Cruz, at prices far below those at which
they can be brought at present from Pará, *viâ* the
cachuelas, and it is evident that when the trade in
these goods is carried up the Amazon and over the
railway, the merchants of Pará must be contented
with smaller profits than those they now obtain.
Pará on the Amazon, and Curumbá on the Paraguay,
are both Brazilian ports, and I presume that the
same tariff of customs rules alike at both places;
nevertheless, calicoes bought in Pará, that cannot be
sold in the river Madeira for less than 250 or 300
ries (say 1*s.* to 1*s.* 2½*d.*) per yard, can be bought in
Trinidad at two reales, or 9½*d.*; also longcloths
on the Madeira sell at 200 to 300 reis (9½*d.* to
1*s.* 2½*d.*) per yard, and are only worth one and
a half to two and a half reales (say 7¼*d.* to 1*s.*)
per yard in Trinidad.  It must, however, be noted
that only very low quality goods are brought
from Curumbá, and that the secret of business in
Trinidad seems to be to sell at a low price without
regard to quality.  The articles that leave the best
profit when taken up the cachuelas are iron pots,
enamelled saucepans, and other general ironware for
house use; also claret of a low class—for any stuff
called "wine" and sold in bottles, with pretty
etiquettes, fetches eight reales (3*s.* 2½*d.*) per bottle—
and no Bolivian in the Beni would pay more, even
for "Chateau Margaux" or "Chambertin."  Gun-
powder in one-pound tins fetches twenty reales, or
about 8*s.* 6*d.*

As I found that Don Bello was on the point of
making a journey to Cochabamba by the rivers

Chapari and Coni, I decided to proceed in his company, **and** give up any idea of visiting Santa Cruz, more especially as I was informed that the river Piray was very dry, and the Siriono savages, who dwell on its banks, were very active, having attacked several canoes during the months immediately prior to my arrival in Trinidad.

Before leaving Trinidad, it is the best plan to change any Brazilian paper money that one may have, for it is perfectly useless in the interior of Bolivia; and one must be careful to examine well the dollars given in exchange, as there is an immense amount of bad money in the Beni, where the worst of the extremely depreciated currency of Bolivia seems to have collected. The fact is, that when any of the traders get hold of any good silver dollars, they immediately inter them in some safe spot, as it is thus only that they can keep any funds they may have over what they need for their ordinary trade requirements, which they keep going by the use of the depreciated coins. To get properly acquainted with the money of Bolivia takes considerable time and trouble. The best coinage is the new one struck during recent years at the mint at Potosí, namely, the dollar of 500 grains, equal in value **and** quality to the Peruvian sole. Half-dollar pieces, reales, and medios are also coined of equally good quality. The old money from Spanish times, and the dollars bearing a tree on the reverse, are all of good silver, but for the last twenty years or so a succession of presidents have enriched themselves at the expense of the country by the issue of an inferior coinage, culminating with the scandalous production issued by Melgarejo and his minister Muñoz. These pesos, or "Melgarejos," as they are called, are nominally worth eight reales, or about 3s. 2½d., but intrinsically they may be worth about 2s. They are also called "moneda de dos caras," or the "money with two faces," as they bear the profiles of the president and his minister, who have, unwittingly, held themselves up to the derision and hatred of their countrymen, by putting the legend "Honor y Talento" ("Honour and Talent") on the infamous robbery they perpetrated. The Melgarejos have been largely imitated by clever coiners in various parts of the republic, so that the diversity of impressions has become exceedingly great, and in some towns the coins that have faces with long beards are most acceptable, while in others the short-bearded ones only will pass. I found it a good plan to keep about half long beards and half short beards in my stock, and then, on arriving at a town, one soon finds out what style is most in fashion, and can act accordingly.

The Government was making some faint endeavours to get some of this vile money out of circulation, and many were the projects put forward for the purpose by the members of the Congress of 1874; but revolution, which appears to be the normal condition of Bolivia, broke out towards the end of the year, and then the question became, not what were the infirmities from which the country suffered, but who should be doctor or president, and consequently the depreciated currency still remains a curse to the country.

# CHAPTER XXI.

Start from Trinidad with convoy of nine canoes—Hacienda de San Antonio—Shifting of the river's course—The river Securé—Bella Vista, the port of Loreto—Siriono savages—State and ceremony in preparation of meals—Excellent character of Bolivian chocolate—Junction of the river Grande—River Piray—The Mamoré left, and the Chapari entered—The Chimoré route to Coni preferable to that of the Chapari—Class of steamers suitable for the upper Mamoré—Difficulties of navigation in the Chapari—Scarcity of game—Number of Indians available in Trinidad for navigation of the upper rivers—The raya fish—Jaguars—Mountain ranges approached—Bamboo trees seen—The river Coni.

WHEN one is dependent upon Bolivian Indians for means of locomotion, it is impossible to secure punctuality in starting, and although the men were ordered for the 15th of the month (July, 1874), it was the 19th before they were ready. The 16th was the feast of the " Virgen del Carmen," and of course the men could not leave on the eve of a holy festival; which being over, they required a couple of days at least to sleep off the effects of the heavy drinking which seems to be the sole end and aim of these frequently recurring " dias de fiesta."

On the 19th, my canoe, a light one, joined a convoy of nine, with an aggregate number of 100 Indians in the crews, that then left Trinidad for the port of Cochabamba, at the head of the river Coni, which falls into the Chapari, one of the principal

affluents of the river Mamoré.    All these canoes
were laden with cocoa in the bean, or " pepita " as it
is called, a few tiger skins and tamarinds being the
only other articles that were taken up for sale in the
interior of Bolivia.

Canoes ascending the Mamoré from Trinidad do
not have to return by the river Ybari, as there is a
lagoon, about a league from the town, from which
a creek, or " curiche," gives egress to the principal
river, which above Trinidad still preserves a bold
and wide course, with free facilities for navigation,
and has many plantations and sugar estates on its
banks.

The first night we bivouacked on the Mamoré, a
short distance only above the junction of the creek
just mentioned, and on the 20th we made good
progress, as the light canoes, or " montarias," travel
rapidly.    In the afternoon we stopped for a couple
of hours at the " trapiche " of Don Mariano Vargas,
the " Intendente " of Police for Trinidad.    This
gentleman, a native of Cochabamba, or a " Colla,"
as those born in the hilly interior of Bolivia are
termed by the Bolivians of the plains of the Beni,
treated us very hospitably, and showed me great
kindness, supplying me gratis with a new rudder
for my canoe, which, after starting from Trinidad,
had proved too small for its work.    The sugar-cane
plantations (" cañaverales ") on this estate were of
considerable extent, and there were also large
tobacco, coffee, and cocoa plantations.

The river hereabouts, as elsewhere above Exaltacion, appears to be continually changing its course,
for behind Don Mariano's establishment is a channel,

now dry, that has evidently been the course in past years, and the river again shows signs at this point of making back for its old track. The want of any knowledge amongst the settlers as to how to keep the river within bounds must at times lead to serious losses. Although the river overflows its banks frequently on this part of its course, there is no doubt that rough groynes run at an angle, covering the weak places, so as to prevent the banks being destroyed and falling, would tend to keep the river more in one course; for behind the groynes silt would soon be deposited, and the bank would not be exposed to so much scour, as the force of the stream would be diverted more into mid-channel.

We left Don Mariano's about 5 p.m., and at nightfall stopped at a sand playa after an hour and a half's good work, and, having had a quiet night, started again on the 21st, at daybreak. The climate on this part of the river seems to be excellent, and the temperatures, I noted, in the shade of my cabin, which was covered with palm leaves and a bullock's hide, varied from 62° Fahr. at night to 88° at mid-day. We passed some large lagoons on the right bank of the river, and on the left bank saw the mouth of the river Securé, on the sand-bar of which were congregated together a larger number of alligators, basking in the sun, than I saw on any other part of the Mamoré. It was no use shooting any of them, as we had plenty of beef in the canoes, and although the Indians are very glad to eat cayman flesh when amongst the rapids, they scorn the idea when in their own country of the Beni, where the term " cayman-eater " (" come caiman ") is a common term of abuse in their villages. The river Securé has its rise in the mountains of the northern part of the province of Cochabamba, and though broad and wide for a great portion of its course, is very shallow, and entirely unnavigable from the driftwood and timber collected therein. An expedition, sent up by the Prefect of the Beni from Trinidad, shortly before my arrival there, returned with the only result of the impracticability for any kind of navigation. At mid-day we stopped on the right bank, at the mouth of a small but rapid stream running through mudbanks, where it was expected that we should be able to get some plantains and yams, etc.; but the banks were too soft to enable us to go to the chacos close by, belonging to the villagers of Loreto, and the stream was too shallow for the canoes. About 4 p.m. we got to Bella Vista, the port of Loreto, where we stayed while Don Bello went about a quarter of a mile inland to a hacienda, for some tamarinds to add to his merchandise for Cochabamba. Here is a trapiche, and many large and well-kept cane-fields and plantations, but the land is much cut up by old river-courses, called " madres," or mothers, and must be almost entirely inundated in exceptionally high floods, such as those caused by the rains of 1872 and 1873, which were two very wet years. The town of Loreto is about a couple of leagues from the river, and is inhabited by Indians of the Trinitario family. As we were leaving, one Señor Nasario Buitraga came down the river from Cochabamba and the river Chapari, his arrival delaying us till nightfall, as Don Bello and he had some little business and a great deal of talk to get through. Buitraga's account of the state of politics in Bolivia was not very encouraging to the prospeets of my journey, as there was fear of a *coup d'état* by President Frias and his party, who, being in a minority, were supposed to entertain the idea of dismissing the Congress forcibly, as they had the troops at their disposal. Chatting over these things with Buitraga detained us till 7.30 p.m., when the men were ordered to their paddles, and the journey was continued until midnight, when a suitable resting-place was found on a playa.

The next two days, the 22nd and 23rd, had nothing of importance worthy record, except that we made good progress, the journey being continued steadfastly and pleasantly. Above Bella Vista, it is said that the right bank is subject to visitation by the Siriono savages, a fierce and thoroughly intractable tribe, that infest the banks of the river Piray. It is, therefore, advisable for canoes to keep on the left bank, on which, a short distance in the interior, are plantations of cocoa belonging to the Government. On this part of the river I had frequent opportunities of adding something fresh to the supper-table, either in the way of a duck or pava, or perhaps a stork that had fallen to a long shot from my Winchester. Remembering these suppers brings vividly to my mind the amount of state that a Bolivian patron observes at his meals when *en voyage*. Immediately the canoes touch land, whether for the midday or for the evening meal, the first thing the captain of the crews must see to is to put on some of his men to clear a space in the bush for the patron; then, while others seek dry firewood, some are despatched to the canoes for the patron's camp-table, chair, and hammock, in which last luxurious resting-place, swinging from tree to tree, the patron smokes the everlasting " cigarito de maiz " (cigarette rolled in husks of the Indian corn), whilst his body-servant prepares the repast. Then, while the cooking goes on, the camp-table is covered with a small cloth, the cleanliness of which does not appear to be so much an object as that it should have as much embroidery or lace attached to it as possible. In fact, I have seen many table-cloths, with about a square yard of cloth in the centre, having from two to three feet of embroidery on every side.   Next, the much-coveted deep silver dish that every Bolivian of any pretensions to decency must have, even though he has not a clean shirt in his portmanteau, is pro-duced and placed in due state on the embroidered cloth. This dish, or " fuente," as it is termed, having been filled with " chupe " (a kind of watery stew, composed of whatever meat or fish is in the larder for the day, with rice, onions, garlic, "ahi," or strong chillies, and any vegetable added), a plateful of farinha is also placed on the table, together with as many different kinds of bread or biscuit as possible; and the patron, guests, and confidential dependents having taken their seats, all state and ceremony is at an end, for each one being armed with a spoon, a simultaneous attack upon the silver fuente, or fount, is at once commenced, and he who is most dexterous with his weapon secures not only the major portion of the savoury mess, but, if he be a successful fisher, the most solid and substantial morsels.

The meal is not, however, considered complete without a cup of chocolate, made from the excellent cocoa growing on the banks of the Mamoré River, near Exaltacion and Trinidad. This chocolate is, in my opinion, quite equal, if not superior, to the well-known Maravilla or Caracas cocoa, so largely sold at the present day, and may be exported in large quantities from Bolivia when the railway of the rapids is complete. At present each trader to Pará takes a full cargo of cocoa in hide seroons, a ready sale being sure to be met with there, as the quality is so much superior to that grown in Brazil itself.

On the 24th, the sixth day after leaving Trinidad, we arrived at the " Junta de los Rios," being the junction of the Rio Grande with the Mamoré. The Rio Grande takes its rise on the southern slopes of the mountains near the town of Cochabamba, from whence it flows in a southerly direction until it is turned towards the west by the mountains near Sucre, when it takes a magnificent curve round to the north, and flows on to join the Mamoré; and although it has the longest course of the rivers of Bolivia, it is so shallow that it is quite useless for purposes of navigation. Although the whole of its course is laid down on most maps, I should be inclined to think that probably it has never been fully explored, for the Siriono savages have made their last stand in the strip of land through which it flows, between the Piray and the Itonama or Magdalena.

About forty leagues from the Junta de los

Rios, the river Piray runs into the Rio Grande on its left bank, and from this point the Rio Grande receives the name of Sará until it joins the Mamoré. The Piray, of the navigation of which I can only speak from hearsay, flows from the district of Santa Cruz, and is said to be free from all obstacle for at least eight months of the year; but for the remaining four I should think it would be closed to steamers, as even canoes have to be unloaded and dragged over the shallows, which, I was told, are of frequent occurrence. The Rio Grande at its mouth appeared to be very dry, while the Mamoré had plenty of water, and was about 500 yards in width.

About 9 a.m. on the 25th, we entered the river Chapari, leaving the Mamoré, or as it is called from the junction upwards, the Chimoré, on our left. I was only able to ascend the Chimoré a short distance, just to get some slight idea of its capabilities for navigation purposes, and it seemed to me to be a far superior river in volume of water to the Chapari, which is barely 200 yards wide at its junction with the Mamoré, and brings down beautifully clear water, that soon becomes lost in the muddy waters of the larger river. I was much disappointed that Don Bello did not arrange to ascend the Chimoré to its port of the same name, instead of taking the Chapari, which, as will hereafter be seen, is full of obstructions to the progress of the canoes. I suppose the reason why the Chapari route is the one in general use, is that it allows the canoes to ascend right up to the (so-called) port of Coni, or the landing-place and depôt for the city of Cochabamba; while the port of the Chimoré is about two leagues distant therefrom. A good road might easily be made across from Chimoré to Coni, and I should think that the ascent of the Chimoré could be done in about half the time required for that of the Chapari, as I have been credibly informed that there are no rapids, and but few shallows, on the Chimoré.

Throughout the day the Chapari kept of a uniform width of about 150 yards, and though every turn of the river caused the usual playa, or sand-bank, there was always a fair channel for the canoes.

Steamers for the upper waters of the Mamoré —that is, above the rapids—should be about 80 or 100 tons burthen, and stern-wheel boats would probably be the best for the purpose, as they would be of lighter draft than screw-propellers. Eighteen inches to two feet should be the limit of draft, although the channels would generally admit of deeper vessels being used—indeed, some of the canoes draw three and three feet six inches ; but the danger of grounding on the playa is so constant, that only flat-bottomed craft would be always sure of making fair progress. At present the practice is, when it is found impossible to haul the canoes, with their loads, over the shallows, to unload them and drag the packages through the shallow water, in hides doubled up so as to form rough and water-tight boxes, termed " pelotos," and frequently the cargoes are thus drawn along for two or three days successively.

When steam navigation is commenced on these upper waters of the Mamoré, a station should be set up opposite to the Junta de los Rios, that is, on the left bank of the Mamoré. It would serve as a depository for canoes and goods from or for Santa Cruz, and would be free from attacks of the Siriono savages, who are on the opposite shore, and do not seem to use canoes at all. As we proceed with the journey, we shall see what the capabilities of the Chapari are for navigation ; but rapids and strong currents (" cachuelas " and " corrientes ") are spoken of as existing higher up, and also " barbaros," or savages, called Yuracarés ; but they are " manso," or tame, being called barbaros simply because they refuse to be baptized into the Roman Catholic Church.

During the day we were frequently much delayed by getting into false channels amongst the sand-banks ; these often obliged us to return a considerable distance before we got into the right course, as they do not connect with each other, but end abruptly in a most inexplicable manner.

There is very little, if anything, to shoot on the river Chapari, for the Yuracarés are such good hunters that game of all kinds has become very scarce in their district. Fish is said to be very abundant, but as we worked long hours by day, the men were too tired to sit up fishing at night, and consequently we had no time to test the resources of the river in this respect.

On the 26th we paddled, nearly the whole of the day, through a succession of snags and dead trees that had collected across the river, and formed an almost complete barricade. These obstructions might be removed by hauling them down stream with a steam-tug, but the operation would be a long and difficult one. In the afternoon, being about ten minutes behind the other canoes, I took up a channel on the right bank, and kept on round a large island formed in a big bend of the river, the channel being very dry, and in places very full of snags. It is, however, much shorter than the main course of the river, which we got into again before nightfall.

July 27th. Throughout the day's journey the river was wider than the part travelled over yesterday, and there were fewer snags and less fallen timber to delay the canoes. To-day we overtake two large cargo canoes, or gariteas, belonging to Don Bello, and there are four others ahead, all laden with cocoa for sale in Cochabamba. Thus there are nine canoes altogether in our party, and this would seem to give proof that there are a good many men always to be had in Trinidad, although to look at the place one would fancy it deserted ; and such was the impression that I gathered from my visit there. However, when one thinks of the number of canoes always in movement on the upper rivers, it is clear that there must be a considerable population. To-day I counted up the " tripulaciones," or crews, with us and the four canoes ahead, and made the number of men to be exactly 100, exclusive of servants. Most of these are from Trinidad, and there are other canoes on the Piray for Cuatro Ojos, and down the Mamoré to Santa Ana, Exaltacion, and the other villages. During the afternoon we passed a station called the " Cruz," being simply a rough cross set up to mark the half distance from the mouth of the river to the port of Coni.

The next day (28th) the morning was very cold,

the thermometer going down to 60°, through the
continuance of a strong south wind which has been
blowing for the last few days. The river this day
was bordered with groves of chuchia, which one
of the Bolivian patrons chose to set on fire. The
canes being very dry, the fire took large propor-
tions with great rapidity, and the wind blowing
straight down stream, our canoes passed a bad
time from the quantity of ashes that were blown
over us.

During the afternoon, Don Bello being a short
distance ahead of my canoe, I saw him take aim at
something near him on the bank; but his gun missed
fire, and he beckoned to me. However, before I
could get fairly up, a fine deer ran down the bank
and rapidly up again. Having my double barrel in
hand, I fired with B B, but was out of range. The
deer was as large as a good-sized English sheep, and
I much regretted that we did not manage between
us to secure him. During the evening I consoled
myself by making the best rifle-shot I ever made, or
probably ever shall make, killing a pava from the
opposite side of the river, the bird being at the top
of a tree probably 100 feet high, and the river
being more than 150 yards in width. Certainly
the Winchester rifles do make extraordinary good
shooting; but such a shot as this was, of course,
a chance that will never occur again to one.

On the 29th the river, which during the last
three days had been very fairly favourable for
navigation, again appeared full of old timber and
snags; we therefore made very slow progress, having
to make many delays on account of the heavy cargo

canoes, which drew from two to four feet of water, requiring to be partially unloaded in many parts of the course travelled over to-day. Our lighter passenger canoes, or montarias, could have got far in advance of the cargo craft, but we should not have gained time by doing so, for the probable result would have been that we should have been kept waiting an unconscionable time for the cargoes at the Coni, while the crews were fishing and otherwise delaying, as they invariably do when out of the sight of their patrons. Upon one occasion, when they overtook us, we found that one of the men had just been stung by a "raya" fish, the wound being in the heel. The man was suffering a good deal of pain—about as much, I judged, as that caused by a scorpion's sting. I gave him a glass of cachaça, with about thirty drops of chlorodyne, to dull the pain; and as we had no ammonia available at the moment, I advised him to bathe his leg and foot freely with urine. The raya of these rivers appears to be much smaller than that of the coasts of Venezuela, where I have seen them nearly two feet square; while these are rarely more than six or eight inches square. The bite or sting is here, consequently, not so much to be dreaded as that of the rayas of Venezuela, which cause a wound that might be thought to have been caused by a severe cut from a jagged knife; while on these rivers the wound is invariably a punctured one only. In Venezuela the wound is considered to be very dangerous, and people rarely recover from it, while here it appears not to have much more effect than the sting of a scorpion or centipede; but that is bad enough, and painful in the extreme. The offensive weapon of the raya is placed at the root of the tail, and is, perhaps, three or four inches in length, by about a quarter of an inch in width. The sides are serrated, the points of the teeth being set at an angle, with its apex towards the end of the sting, and thus, when this probe is driven into whatever the fish is attacking, it enters readily; but when it is withdrawn, the teeth scratch and tear the sides of the wound, doubtless depositing at this time the poison, which is probably injected through small channels along these teeth in the same way as the rattlesnake and the cobra di capella inject their poison down a groove in the under side of their fangs. As the fish is flat and of a dark brown colour, it is at all times difficult to detect; but it is more especially so on the stony beds of the upper rivers, where the men, who have to wade barefooted over the shallows, are always in danger, the rayas being in great abundance. A good stout pair of thigh boots is, however, a perfect preservative from the attack of this venomous fish.

On the next two days, the 30th and 31st of July, our toilsome journey was continued in a constant battle with the shallow water and stockades of dead wood. During a mid-day halt, one of the Bolivian merchants, who had a number of tiger skins as part of his cargo, opened the packages and spread the skins out on the sandbanks, to have the dust and insects beaten out of them, as well as to air them—an operation that is very necessary, as the skins, being fresh, are soon damaged if left packed for any length of time. The trade in these skins seems to be a favourite one, the best sale for them being in La Paz, where the Quichuan Indians pay a long price for them for use on their feast-days. When dressed in these skins, and their heads adorned with macaw feathers, they are supposed to represent the wild animals of their country's forests. These tigers or jaguars are of good size, and must be splendid beasts when alive, as some of the skins are fully five and six feet from the root of the tail to the tip of the nose, with dark and lustrous spots that give them a very handsome appearance. From the large trade in these skins, it would seem that these animals are very numerous in the forests and on the pampas of the Beni, and it seems strange that throughout the journey we did not meet with any of them, although their footprints were always met with wherever we landed.

August 1st. The river appears to be wider than ever, being at least 500 yards in width, and running very strongly. We are now six days on this river, and instead of its decreasing it grows wider, but it is also much shallower—so much so that, what with the shallows and dead wood, it would be quite impossible to take up any kind of steamer. At mid-day we saw four large otters (" lobos "), and I sent a ball amongst them from about 500 yards distance. It seemed as though one had been hit, for there was a great commotion amongst them, and only three were seen afterwards, though the body of the wounded one did not turn up, probably being carried away by the strong current; the other three made for the shore and were lost in the bush. In the afternoon my montaria was very nearly upset; for we were pulling hard against a strong current, when it mounted a sunken pole, and, swinging round, the rudder broke clear away. Drifting down stream, we managed to get hold of a stump, and, passing a rope on shore, hauled up to the bank to effect repairs. In any little accident such as this, the principal danger seems to be caused by the men themselves, who, instead of sitting perfectly still, get excited and rise from their seats, and as the canoe sways about, they disturb the equilibrium, and one is fortunate indeed if an upset does not occur; therefore, the first thing for the patron to do in any accident is to shout at the men to keep their seats, and, if necessary, enforce his orders by any means at his command. To-day the "marigueys," "carapanas," and mosquitoes made their appearance again, the lower part of this river having been very free from these pests; but as the nights have got much warmer, owing to the cessation of the south wind, the increased temperature may have brought them out.

August 2nd. The morning start is now obliged to be deferred until full daylight, as the numerous shallows and other obstructions render it impossible to travel in the dark. Just as we were starting we saw a small canoe pass rapidly by us on the opposite side of the river. There were three men in it, who were the first of the Yucararé Indians that we had seen. We called to them, but they would not answer or come over to us. These Indians do not use bark canoes like the Caripunas and Pacaguaras of the rapids, but dug-outs of a very narrow and long description, much similar to those used by the Cayubabas of Exaltacion.

High mountains in the south now made their appearance, being probably the ridge shown on the maps as running from the Chapari towards the Chilon and the Rio Grande. The tops of these hills were in sight yesterday afternoon, but this morning whole ranges come into view, following one another far into the interior, the summits of those farthest off being lost in the cloudy atmosphere.

On the banks of this upper part of the river, the large kind of bamboo grows in abundance. This very useful tree is here called " taquarembo," while in Venezuela I recollect it is called " wacwa," and this difference of names given to things in Spanish-speaking countries causes great confusion of ideas to travellers. Bamboo is not found on the Amazon or on the Madeira, as it seems to require a dryer and higher land.

Soon after starting we arrived at the mouth of the river Coni, which enters the Chapari on its right bank. The port of Coni, where we finally leave our canoes and take to the road for Cochabamba, is about six leagues from the junction of the Coni with the Chapari, which changes its name above the junction to San Matéo. The Coni is a small river about 100 yards in width at its outlet, and so shallow that we had to drag the canoes over the bar, which we had no sooner overcome than fresh shallows obstructed our progress. Indeed, so unsuitable for any navigation is this river, that the whole of this day and the two following ones, the 3rd and 4th of August, were occupied in one incessant struggle with the shallows, so that the six leagues (eighteen miles) from the mouth of the river to the port occupied us for three entire days. These shallows are dignified by the name of the " cachuelas," or falls, of the Coni, but they are properly speaking " corrientes," or rapids, running over long banks covered with loose stones brought down from the mountains during the floods ; and as the whole course of this river is one constant succession of these rapids, it is surprising that it has been selected by the Bolivian traders instead of the Chimoré, to arrive at which the road from Cocha-bamba would only have been some four leagues longer.

# THROUGH BOLIVIA AND PERU.

# CHAPTER XXII.

CONI is distant about forty-five leagues from Cochabamba, and is only a small clearing in the jungle, with a few huts, where the mule-drivers and traders from Cochabamba remain while waiting in the dry season for the arrival of the canoes from Trinidad. At this place I found a corregidor and a few traders who had come down from Cochabamba, the corregidor to receive the departmental tolls on the traffic, and the traders their cargoes of cocoa, as well as to ship the return loads of wheaten flour, salt, and potatoes.

The salt is made up in bricks weighing probably ten or twelve pounds each, and is brought from the "salitreras," or salinas of Central and Western Bolivia. A brick, or "pan" as it is called, is worth three pesos, or about 9s. 6d., in Trinidad. The trade in this article is a very important one to the civilized Indians of the Beni, as that department is entirely without any salt deposits; but the savages of the Madeira, such as the Caripunas and Pacaguaras, do not seem to have acquired a taste for the luxury, as, although they will eat salted provisions when given to them, they do not ask for salt or care to accept it.

There were about 200 mules in all waiting at Coni, the cargo for each one being eight Bolivian arrobas, or about two hundredweight. During the five or six months that this trade is open, more than 1000 cargoes of eight arrobas each are received from Cochabamba in salt or flour, while a similar quantity of cocoa, dressed hides, and tiger skins is returned; and this trade is carried on under every possible difficulty of miserable roads and defective means of navigation. As the mule-drivers only come to Coni when they expect to get a freight, intending travellers must make arrangements to have animals ready for their arrival, or they will probably have to foot it over very bad roads. The hire of a mule from Coni to Cochabamba, or *vice versâ*, is fourteen pesos (about £2 5s.).

Coni is about 950 feet above sea-level, and has a delightful climate, the vegetation not being of that dense and rank nature found on the Amazon and Madeira Rivers. There are consequently fewer insect plagues, such as mosquitoes, etc., and fever and ague are very little if at all known. When the Amazonian route for the commerce of Bolivia begins to be fairly opened up, the present location of the port of Coni must be abandoned, and a clearing and port made on the Chimoré, at the small Indian village of the same name on that river.

The district is the home of the Yuracaré Indians,

who are called savages, but are very friendly and well disposed. They are nomads in so far as that they only live in one clearing for perhaps two or three years, until they are tired of the spot, or fancy that the chaco does not yield so well as it did at first; while possibly another reason for the move is that, as they are very smart hunters, the game has got scarce within reasonable walking distance. They then shift to another part of their district, which extends from the higher waters of the Chapari to the foot of the hills of San Antonio and Espiritu Santo on the road to Cochabamba.

The day after our arrival at Coni, two of the headmen came to pay us a visit, accompanied by half a dozen of their women, who were laden with burdens of plantains and yams, which they carried in nets, supported on their backs by a band which passed across their foreheads. These people are very much like the ordinary Mojos Indians and the Pacaguaras of the river Trés Irmãos, but are much more civilized than the latter tribe, as they do not all wear their hair in the usual savage style, cut close over the eyes and hanging down behind, while they always have some sort of clothing, either a bark shirt or some articles purchased from the traders. Many of them understand Spanish very fairly, and they all were very well behaved; indeed, it was wonderful to see what self-restraint they exercised, controlling their curiosity in a marvellous manner, and not asking for everything that took their fancy, as do the Pacaguaras and Caripunas of the rapids; and I rewarded their patience accordingly by presents of cigars, sugar, biscuits, and a " pinga " or small drink of Hollands apiece, which latter they seemed to approve of highly. The men are fairly formed and of good stature, but the women are undersized, and appear to be rather ill-treated, as is customary among savage tribes.

They use but few adornments, a necklace of wooden beads or of seeds being the general orna-

NECKLACE OF BRIGHT RED BEANS.

ment amongst them. Their bark shirts are the finest that are made anywhere in the Beni. Those made by the Mojos Indians are all of a dark-brown colour, and of coarse, rough texture; but the Yuracarés make theirs from a tree that gives a fine white bark, which, when beaten out to the proper thinness, is painted in very bright colours. Some of the patterns thus painted on the shirts are of great merit, and all the colours are extracted from the various dye-yielding trees or earths of the forests. A good cascara can be bought from them for about two pesos. The chief, or cacique of the tribe, on state occasions wears a curious appendage or pigtail, composed of bright feathers from macaws and toucans, backs of bright-coloured beetles, and shells of nuts, etc. All the tribe paint small black stripes and rings on their arms and legs, whilst the women have a smear of red or black paint on their cheeks. I was fortunate enough to secure three very fine specimens of these bark shirts, one of the cacique's pigtails, some of their necklaces, and a set of their musical instruments, which, as may be sur-

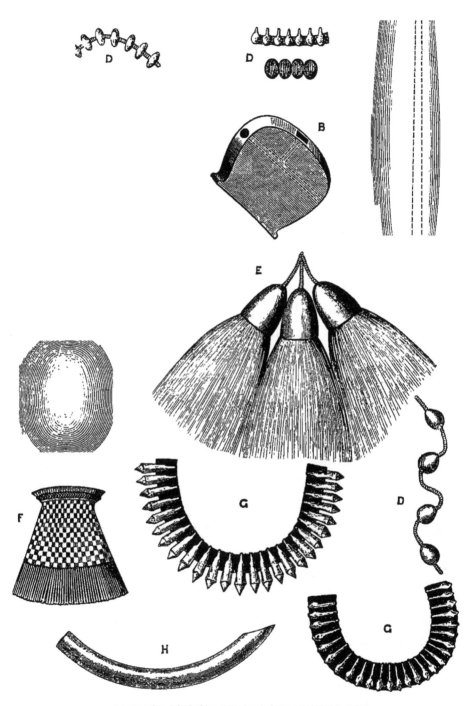

GROUP OF BOLIVIAN MUSICAL INSTRUMENTS, ETC.

A, Flute, made of hard wood; B B B, Whistles, made of hard wood; C, Flutes, made of leg-bones of a stork; D D D, Necklaces, made of seeds and beads; E, Ornaments, made of nut-shells and toucan breast feathers; F, Small comb, made of hard wood; G G, Necklaces of monkey's teeth; H, Tooth of Capybara, used as ear ornament by Caripunas.

mised, are of a most primitive character. They are of various shapes, producing at most three or four notes, and are generally made of some hard kind of wood ; but a monkey's thigh-bone or the leg-bone of a stork is often pressed into the service, as, being hollow, these bones are easily made into a rough kind of flute or whistle. I could not discover much melody in the concerts which these Indians favoured us with, the principal object seeming to be the production of as much noise as possible; the custom being for as many performers as there are instruments, to seat themselves in a ring, and each one to produce any note he pleases without the slightest reference to his neighbour's efforts. The effect is therefore more startling than pleasant, especially as the fifers are accompanied by a drummer, whose business seems to be to overcome, if possible, with his own horrible instrument, the effect of the ear-piercing whistles.

These Indians produce a very fair kind of cloth or drill from the wild cotton which is found in abundance on their territory, and as they are very clever in extracting dyes of different colours from the forest, they make up some very good hammock-cloths, sashes, and other articles. They probably have been taught this art of weaving by the civilized Indians of the Beni, who, as I have before mentioned, make some very excellent and durable material called macanas.

The corregidor says that altogether there are about 500 or 600 men in the tribe, and they appear to be fairly under his orders. As I was travelling on public business and had taken charge of

despatches for the Government at Chuquisaca from the prefect of the Beni, the corregidor offered me a guard of these Indians for the journey to Cochabamba, and appointed the cacique and five young Indians to accompany me. The cacique's name was Gregorio Frias, and he seemed to have an idea that he was a relative of the then president of the republic, Don Tomas Frias; and perhaps he was not far wrong, as I was told that a few years ago a brother of his excellency lived in the district for some time, and had many of these Indians at work on his chaco and coffee plantations, some trees of which are still to be seen at the Coni, bearing excellent fruit. The other Indians were young men, named Juan Baptista, Amadeo, Carlos, Roman, and Donato, who were all pleasant-looking young fellows that I was glad to have as companions of my march to Cochabamba.

The Yuracarés have evidently been under the tutelage of the Jesuit missionaries in bygone years, as they preserve a few traditions in proof thereof. It is supposed that some unscrupulous servant of the Church made use of the ascendancy gained by the Jesuits over these Indians for his own purposes, and oppressed them until they turned against him and his religion. I observed that the oldest of those who travelled with me always took off their hats when passing a church, as though they had some idea of paying respect to it; but the same men told me that they considered the priests to be very bad men, and that they would not allow them to visit or remain in their villages.

I translate the following account of one of their

traditions from a journal published in Cochabamba in October, 1872, in which is given a short account of the sources of the river Mamoré. The paper says, that " a little distance above the junction of the rivers Sacta and Vio, three large stones are met with, placed one above the other in the form of a column about thirty yards in height, dividing the river into two channels, and offering a gigantic and imposing spectacle to the observer. According to the tradition of the Yuracarés, the human species sprang from the union of the tiger with these stones, the offspring being called Mamoré, which, in their tongue, is equivalent for Eve. This Eve had two sons : one, a son of crime and perversity, became the progenitor of the Carais, as the Yuracarés call the Bolivians and other strangers who pass through their territory ; the other, full of goodness, virtue, and blessings, was the ancestor of the Yuracarés. This tradition, which parodies the characters of Cain and Abel, serves to prove that these Indians preserve some notions of the Book of Genesis, which had probably been taught them by the missionaries that had been amongst them." Here is a confusion of ideas, one of the most curious of which seems to me to be the placing the tiger as the deity, or first cause, as this would seem to have some analogy with the tiger-worship prevailing amongst certain tribes of the jungles of Hindostan.

At Coni I was first struck with the great difference between the Bolivian Indians of the interior of the republic and the Indians of the plains of the Beni. The former, who are all styled " Collas " (meaning dwellers in the Cordilleras) by those who inhabit the plains, are at first sight seen to be of an entirely different race, evidently dwellers in a cold climate, whilst the Indians of the plains are only able to live in warm tropical places. The Colla Indian is hardly ever seen without his poncho on, and muffler, or "bufanda," round his neck. At a glance you see that he has an aversion to the cleansing effect of water, whilst the Indian of the plains only wears his poncho at nights or on very cold days, and will, if he is allowed, spend half his time in bathing. The Yuracarés who accompanied me continually stopped for a bath every time we crossed the river.

Through the kindness of Don Ignacio Bello, to whom nearly all the animals then at the Coni were contracted, I was able to arrange for mules for my journey to Cochabamba; and on the 9th of August I started, accompanied by an arriero, or mule-driver, and my servant-boy, the Cruzeño that I had been fortunate enough to secure in Exaltacion, who, instead of going from Trinidad to Santa Cruz, his native place, had decided to follow me to Sucre on the understanding that I should send him home from that town—a promise that I readily agreed to, for he had become very useful and trustworthy, but which he, poor boy, never saw carried out, as he died of small-pox in Cochabamba. The Cacique of the Yuracarés and the five boys of the tribe also accompanied me, and proved very useful on the road, as they generally managed during the day to shoot with their bows and arrows either fish from the river or game from the forest, a welcome addition to the repasts at the nightly halts. These

Indians always volunteer to accompany a traveller of any position, and as it was desirable that they should be especially well disposed towards the navigation and railway enterprises, I took considerable pains to conciliate them, and believe that when operations are resumed for opening up the Bolivian commerce they will be found very useful allies. As labourers will have to be taken to the works from the interior of the republic, the Yuracarés can be made very useful in clearing ground at the Chimoré port, and in navigating the canoes that take the labourers as far as Trinidad, or perhaps as far as the first of the rapids, Guajará Merim, from whence the labourers could march to the various points on the railway where their services are required. They could also be made use of as guards against the few hostile tribes of the Mamoré, such as the Sirionos and the Chacobos; while, under proper management, it might be possible to induce a hundred or two of them to locate themselves at the wooding stations which will be required above the rapids when steam navigation is organized. As these Indians are more expert with their bows and arrows than any other tribe of the Mamoré, their presence would effectually check the incursions of those savages that refuse to approach civilization in the slightest degree. They are also reputed to be the bravest of all the tribes of the Beni, as proof of which I was told that the many marks and scars on their bodies are caused by the practice that prevails amongst the young braves of the tribe of slashing their bodies in sport, to show how well they can bear pain ; and if a quarrel arises amongst them, the custom is for the whole of the tribe to turn out in the chaco, or some other open spot, where the belligerents are set opposite each other at about 100 paces, when, each being armed with bow and arrows, a regular duel ensues, the tribe encouraging the combatants to continue the fight until one of them is mortally wounded or sinks exhausted from loss of blood.

The road from the Coni leads in a south-west direction, and is simply a path cut through the forest of sufficient width for a mule and its cargo. After about four hours' ride we arrived at Pachimoco, a single house, where lives the Intendente of the Yuracarés, José Tiflis by name, and next in authority to the cacique. We were received very kindly, the supplies of the chaco, such as yucas, maize, and plantains, being freely offered to us. Here I noticed that many of these Indians suffer from skin diseases, amongst them being a leper. Their women are dirty and uncombed, and, after the usual manner of savages, have to do all the hard work of wood and water carrying, while the men hunt, fish, and plant in the chacos. From the Coni to Pachimoco is reckoned as five leagues, but it cannot be more than four, if so much, as we were travelling barely four hours and did not do more than about a league an hour, as the road was very bad, being full of pot-holes of mud and slush. The "naturales," as the Yuracarés are generally termed by the Bolivians, are splendid walkers, and on the few good parts of the road I had to keep my mule well at work in order to be up with the cacique, who led the way on foot ahead, carrying my gun, and a very fair-sized burden slung at his back. Just as we got to the clearing a heavy shower of rain fell, so I decided not to go any further that night, but accepted the invitation of the intendente, who had the centre of the hut cleared for my camp-bed. A number of the Trinitario boatmen, who had walked over from the Coni to visit the Yuracarés, slept just outside the hut, and kept up a continuous chatter till far on into the night.

The next morning (10th August) the mules were caught and cargoes up by about half-past seven, and, bidding adieu to the intendente and his family, we took the road, refreshed by a few hours' good sleep. A couple of hours' riding brought us to the river San Antonio, an affluent of the San Matéo, which river runs into the Chapari. The San Antonio, where we first crossed it, is about a mile in width, forming, at this dry season, an immense playa of water-worn stones, through which the river finds its way in shallow channels, whilst during the rains the whole width is covered with a very turbulent and rapid stream, perfectly impassable by man or beast. The eastern bank of this river was a succession of high cliffs. One which we passed under I judged to be 130 to 150 feet sheer perpendicular height, being cut straight down—the rock, a rotten sandstone of reddish brown colour, having been cut down by the river, which is continually wearing it away at its base. Other cliffs, as high and yellower in colour, appeared on ahead, glistening brightly in the glare of the sun. Amongst the stones in the bed of the river were limestones, sandstones, and conglomerates of all colours, many being splotched with a bright red lichen that grows on the rocks and stones that are under water. The limestones were almost all veined with a clear opaque quartz, and I observed a fine class of serpentine, the base of a dark olive green, with veins of whitish colour.

Having crossed the river, the track leaves the plains of the Mamoré and the Chapari, and soon commences to enter upon the mountainous districts called the Yungas of Espiritu Santo. The track so far is but a path cut through the forest, and is in wet weather quite impassable, from the depth of mud and the numerous holes in which mule and rider may easily come to grief. Over the hilly lands it has in former days been roughly paved in parts, after the fashion of old Spanish roads. Where this rough paving is absent the paths are much worn by the trampling of the mules, and by the drainage of the rains which hollows them out, so that at times one seems to be riding between two walls of earth.

After about seven hours' ride, we arrived at a " pascana," or stopping-place, in the Yungas, near the same river that we had crossed early in the morning; and the spot being convenient for a resting-place, we halted for the night, turning the mules loose to graze on the river-banks. This practice of loosing the mules at night causes great delay in starting on the following morning, but it is unavoidable until clearings are made in the forest, as the animals must be free to wander at will in the forest in search of the softer leaves, succulent plants, and small patches of grass, which is all they get after their day's work, for the arrieros will not carry any corn with them, as it would occupy the place of a cargo, and so deprive them of so much freight.

On this part of the journey, a small tent that I had with me came in exceedingly useful, as without it I should have had to sleep at night exposed to the dews, which are very heavy, to say nothing of the rains, which fell frequently. A small ridge-shaped tent of striped cloth is easily carried on such a journey, as it requires two poles only, which should be jointed and form one package together with the pegs and ropes, whilst the cloth folds into another. The two packages just fit nicely between two portmanteaus, and complete one mule-burden. The tent-cloth should by all means be double, as the heavy rains soon soak through, and drip from a single cloth.

August 11th. We could not start till half-past seven in the morning, having had considerable trouble to get the mules together. The road keeps up the course of the San Antonio, into which it descends frequently, and these ascents and descents, or "cuestas," as they are called, gave us some of the roughest riding I have ever had. When the hill to be surmounted is · very high and steep, the path is cut in zig-zags, which were so short and of such sharp turns that when one mule was in the bend of one angle the next one in the file was immediately below, while the preceding one would be just overhead. However, I managed to ride the whole way, although it is the usual practice to climb these cuestas on foot, and drive one's mule on ahead, after having made fast the bridle to the saddle; but I had to dismount once in crossing the river, when the mule had mounted a large stone in mid-stream, and was in danger of slipping ; so I got down, and having coaxed her to descend into the stream again, was able to remount and complete the passage.   The day was passed in this kind of rough work, and towards afternoon we came to patches of cleared lands and scattered houses in the district known as Espiritu Santo.   Our third halt was made at one of these clearings, called " Cristal Maio," situated at an elevation of 1920 feet above sea-level.   These settlements are made by Bolivians of the type found throughout the interior of the republic, such as Cochabambinos, Pazeños, etc., as they are called according to the town or district from which they come.   It is, however, only the Bolivians with any tinge of Spanish blood that are known by these names, as the pure Indians are all either Quichuans or Aymarás.

The principal proprietor of the district is a Señor Prado of Totora near Cochabamba, and by permission of his mayordomo, or head man, I put up for the night in one of his houses ; and as I had during the day shot a fine large black monkey, we had a good supper for all hands.   This mayordomo was at first inclined to refuse us permission to stay for the night on the lands under his care, and ordered us off, even going so far as to fetch a rusty old musket out, and threaten to shoot our mules, which my arriero had very imprudently let loose into a clearing of grass without permission ; but upon my ordering the mules to be caught and tied up, he was pacified, and a little quiet persuasion, accompanied by a cigar and a " pinga " of " re-sacada " or nip of extra strong aguadiente from my travelling flask, together with the prospect of a share of our supper of roast monkey, procured us leave to hang up our hammocks in the house and turn the mules into the regular "largadero," or grazing ground, along the river-bank.

Before night closed in I had a splended bath in the torrent near at hand, and as all mosquitoes, marigueys, and other venomous flies have been left behind, it was highly enjoyable. Amongst the rocks in the bed of the torrent was a soft kind of marble, quite white and crystalline; there was also a slaty sort of limestone of an earthy nature, with thin white veins or bands of quartz; and there was evidence in the rusty look of many boulders that iron enters into the composition of many of the formations of the district, even if true ironstone is not to be found. A stone was given to me here which had bands of a soft black substance that seemed to me to be an inferior kind of plumbago, and I was told that there was a large deposit of this mineral in the neighbourhood.

Rain is said to be almost perpetual in this district, the months of August and September alone being blessed with a few fine days. The houses, in view of this constant rain, are built with roofs of very steep pitch, with an angle of sixty degrees perhaps; whilst the settlers who can afford the heavy cost have covered their houses with sheets of tin or zinc, brought at great expense from Cochabamba and the Pacific coast. The timbers used are extraordinarily heavy, in order that the violence of the wind in the frequent storms may not overturn the houses. A foundation wall of dry stone, raised about eighteen inches from the ground, is first placed, and on that a bed-plate of hard timber dressed with the axe to twelve or fourteen inches square, then the uprights and wall-plates to match complete a most solid framing. In many cases side walls are altogether absent, the only closed-up part being in the tall sloping roof. The wind has thus free passage through the lower part, and the house is not so easily overturned—a catastrophe which I was told frequently happens to houses with closed side walls.

The chief agriculture of the district is that of "coca," the "cocales" or plantations of which seem to be the principal wealth of the settlers, as the best districts for the production of this valuable plant appear to be the eastern slopes of the northern hills of Bolivia. A very large trade in the article is carried on at most of the towns of the republic, but Totora appears to be the principal depôt. The plant is a small tree, allowed to grow to four or five feet in height, and planted in rows about eighteen inches apart, which are kept in excellent order. The leaves, which are narrow and about two or three inches in length, are collected carefully, dried in the sun on a prepared earthen or cement floor, and then, when pressed into "seroons," are ready for dispatch to Totora, where they fetch from eleven to sixteen pesos the "sesta" of twenty-two pounds, say 1s. 7d. to 2s. 4d. per pound.

The use of coca is almost unknown to, and certainly not practised by the Indians of the plains of the Mamoré, but the Quichuan and Aymará Indians appear to be unable to exist without this stimulant, for it serves them in place of food and drink when driving their mules or llamas on the long journeys which separate the towns of the interior of the republic. These Indians carry, attached to their belts or waistbands, a small pouch with two compartments: in the larger the coca leaves are kept; whilst the other has a store of wood-ashes, a pinch of which is put into the mouth along with two or three of the leaves. The use of wood-ashes put me in mind of the East Indies, where a small quantity of lime or ashes is used along with the betel leaves and areca palm nut, the whole together forming the luxury for masticating called "Pan." I heard some wonderful tales of the pedestrian powers of the Indians, and observed that the arrieros and others with whom I travelled always provided a store of coca amongst the first articles, when preparing for a journey. Any of these Indians will think nothing of keeping on the run all day behind the baggage-mules, and doing thirty or forty miles daily for weeks together. I cannot speak from personal experience of the beneficial effects of "coca-chewing" in staving off hunger, as on my journeys I have always been fortunate enough to have sufficient provision for the day's requirements in my saddle-bags; and I must say that I always preferred even a hard biscuit, to say nothing of a hard-boiled egg or a snack of cold meat, to a chew of coca; so perhaps the few experiments I made were not sufficiently persevered in. There is very little if any taste in the coca leaf, the only flavour being such as well washed-out tea leaves would be likely to afford.

The night passed quietly under the roof placed at our disposition by our irate friend the mayor-domo, and the following day, the 12th August, we started about 8 a.m., after the usual trouble and delay in catching the mules. This fourth day's ride continued to be over very rough ground, the whole of the distance done being over a succession of cuestas, which, in places, were actual staircases. At one moment the rider would ascend to 3000 feet elevation, and then quickly down to 2500 and even 2000, the road being dug out of the side of the rock, just wide enough to allow of the passage of one mule with its burden.

At a place called Minas Maio there is a tradition that gold has been found in the sands of the ravine, and at a river called the "Tuy," in Espiritu Santo, the river-bed was full of quartz stones, from which I selected a few that have since been declared by a geological authority to have come from gold-bearing reefs. There is also much shaly ironstone in some of the ravines, while copper pyrites abound in some of the quartz stones in the rivers; and there is no doubt that the region is highly metalliferous, and will well repay explorers when improved navigation on the Mamoré and the projected railway round the rapids of the Madeira shall have caused the ameliora-tion of the present bad roads of the district.

There are a good many houses on the slopes of the hills surrounding the broader part of the valley of the Tuy, which appears to be still on the water-shed of the Mamoré. Several of these houses are roofed with sheets of tin, and the clearings, though small, are many in number, thus making up a good acreage of cleared land. Towards dusk we stopped at a place called " El Chaco," and occupied a corner of a hut; but whose it was, or by whose permission we took up our quarters therein, I failed to dis-cover. There were one or two miserable-looking Indians about, but they said nothing to us as we appropriated the space we required; and it seems to be the custom in these parts for travellers to enter any house they please, and take possession of what-ever part of it suits their fancy best. I observed, however, that this custom only holds good when the traveller, from his appearance and belongings in baggage, animals, servants, etc., seems likely to be able to pay for the shelter he seeks. In consequence of the many clearings, it is now necessary to tie up the mules at night, and they are given a grass called " saracachi," which appears to be grown especially for them. This grass, which is rough and coarse, but much liked by the animals, is peculiar to the district, and grows in low stunted bunches, which are cut off at the ground, leaving the roots, which soon afford another growth. Coffee of a very superior class grows here, but does not appear to be cultivated largely, owing, doubtless, to the greater profits yielded by the coca. Cotton also is some-what general, and the trees appeared to be of very fine growth, but as they were only in flower, I could not judge of the quality. Cultivating the coca for trade, and plantains for food, appear to be the sole occupation of the wretched-looking Collas and Quichuan Indians, who all seem, in this district at least, to be a most morose set of fellows. They work in regular gangs in the coca plantations, about a

dozen Quichuan Indians, or peons, at work, cleaning
between the rows, being overlooked by a colla
" sobre-estante," or foreman.   The settlers are in-
hospitable in the extreme, but perhaps this may be
because they only produce sufficient provisions for
their own use.   I found it impossible to purchase even
a fowl, or a few eggs, at any price ; so that, had I not
had with me a small supply of good " charqui " from
Trinidad, and a few tinned meats, I should have
passed a bad time on this part of the road.   The
people about here appear to understand but little
Spanish, their ordinary language being Quichuan ;
and they appear to be in the utmost poverty,
although I was told that the peons earn four reales
per day (about 1s. 7d.), and are found in rations
of yucas and plantains.   They are, as a rule, dirty
and uncombed, being clothed in rags of all colours—
that is, if one can apply the word " colour " to the
different dingy hues that prevail in their extraordinary apparel.

   The mountains at El Chaco rise, on either
side of the river, to a height of probably 6000 or
7000 feet, their tops, generally in the clouds, being
clothed with forest.   Rain fell heavily during the
night, and the following morning (the 13th) was
also wet, so we waited till 8 a.m., when, there being
no sign of a break in the downpour, we made up our
minds to brave the worst and continue our journey.
The road soon became terribly bad, being much
softened by the heavy rain ; and on one cuesta,
where there had been a great landslip during the
past wet season, the riding became very dangerous
—so much so that we were forced to dismount and

drive the mules on ahead. This landslip was of such extent that it seemed as though the whole side of the hill had fallen away, the path being covered up for more than a mile in length, a distance that had to be traversed in drenching rain over the *débris* of the mountain-side; and as at every step one sank in the soft earth nearly up to one's knees, both men and animals were glad to get on to the track again. The summit of this range, called the " Cuesta del Lina Tambo," took us up to about 6150 feet above sea-level. Towards afternoon the rain ceased, but the forest was very wet and the mists very thick.

At about 5000 feet elevation, I noticed that the lowland vegetation of palms of all classes ceased, and tree-ferns became very numerous, whilst mosses and ferns in endless varieties were most luxuriant. The trees, which were now less lofty, were all thickly covered with moss.

After passing the summit of Lina Tambo, we crossed a river, called the San Jacinto, over a bridge of rough timbers, spanning perhaps sixty feet, and built with abutments of dry stone (*i.e.* without mortar). From these abutments large balks of timber projected on either side about twelve feet, and were joined together by a centre span of about thirty-five, the whole forming a substantial, though strange-looking structure. When crossing this river, one would be led to think that the main watershed of the district had been passed, as the San Jacinto apparently flows in a contrary direction to that of the San Mateo and San Antonio; but this must be caused by a great bend of the ravine which

forms its course, for it is also an affluent of the
Chapari and Chimoré system, the highest Cordillera
being still two days' ride further on. Owing to
the time occupied in trudging across the landslip,
the night overtook us before we could reach the next
houses, called Los Jocotales, and we therefore made
the fifth night's halt at a "pascana," or resting-
place, by the roadside, setting up the tent, and
hobbling the mules to prevent their straying; but
notwithstanding our care in this respect, we found
next morning that one of them was missing, and
from her tracks we found that she, having probably
slipped her hobbles, had wandered onwards on her
own account, thinking, doubtless, that as the roads
were so bad she would get on better without a
burden. We had to divide her cargo amongst the
others, and after following her up for about a
couple of hours, we found her, grazing by the way-
side, and were again able to make her perform her
share of the work; and soon after we came to Los
Jocotales, where we had hoped to have passed the
previous night. At this place tolls are taken, two
reales, or 9½d., being charged for each cargo of
merchandise carried by mules or donkeys; but luggage, or any articles not intended for sale, are
allowed to go free. The traders complain bitterly
of having to pay tolls upon a road that is so little
cared for as this is; and certainly their complaints
are just ones, for no repairs are ever done to the
road unless a landslip takes place, which, as it
totally destroys the road, renders a reconstruction
imperatively necessary. This toll is farmed out by
the municipality of Cochabamba, and the farmer

being supposed to maintain the road out of the tolls he collects, of course he does not spend more in repairs than he is positively obliged to.

Towards mid-day we ascended a very high ridge of hills, on the summit of which the aneroid marked nearly 8000 feet above sea-level. Here my arriero knocked up with a bad foot, from having, at Pachi-moco, trodden upon an arrow, which entered the sole of his foot. The wound being but a slight one, he did not pay proper attention to it, but now, from the walking, it has become so painful as to necessitate his taking some rest; so, although it was only about two o'clock in the afternoon, as soon as we had passed the hill we made for the first houses that were to be seen. These were a few small huts where live the Indians in charge of the cattle grazing on the coarse and rough grass on the hill-sides. These huts are called Inca Corral, and are pitched in a wide valley, running nearly north and south at an elevation of 7715 feet above sea-level. The wind blew down this valley with searching force, the thermometer at night sinking to $39\frac{1}{2}°$ Fahr. The Quichuan Indians build their huts so small and so low in height, that I was at first much averse to sleeping in any of them, especially as they are generally black with smoke and dirt from the fire burning in an earthen pan on the floor, the smoke from which has to find its way through sundry holes and crevices in the walls and roof. At this place I set up my tent, but the wind blew so keenly that the canvas was quite unable to keep it out; and although I had plenty of blankets, I passed a miserable night, from the intense cold caused by the searching gusts, which seemed to pass right through all the wraps I could heap on the camp-bed. After this night's experience I was never too particular as to the size or the condition of the hut offered me as a sleeping-place, for in these high altitudes, four walls with a roof of mud, or of any other solid material, are much preferable to canvas.

The country has now become much more open, the tropical forests having been left behind and below us. The ferns of all kinds are now lost, and the few trees are quite stunted and covered with mosses and lichens, which, being mostly of a whitish colour, give an appearance of age and decay to the prospect. Maize of a very large size and very sweet is grown here, also barley and potatoes. A so-called fruit, but which is really a root, in appearance and taste much like a small yellow carrot, is eaten raw in large quantities, and esteemed a great delicacy by the cotters; its name, as nearly as I could make out, is " Yacunes."

On the next day, August 15th, when daylight broke, the grass was covered with hoar-frost, and as the thermometer only registered 39°, the cold seemed intense—at least, to our party, who had just come from the tropical plains of the Mamoré. The morning was, however, clear, and therefore, as soon as the sun shone over the hills, the temperature rose rapidly. Proceeding up the valley or raised plateau of Inca Corral, we soon began the ascent of the Cuesta de Malaga, the highest on the road between Coni and Cochabamba. This hill is really the dividing ridge of the watersheds of the Mamoré and Rio Grande systems. On this ascent I noticed that all trees stopped at about 10,800 feet elevation. Some high peaks near the pass had snow in their crevices, and I was told that in 1873 a snow-storm in August filled up the pass, and an arriero and his " recua," or drove of mules, perished in the drift. A cross set up by the wayside attests the catastrophe. Here we met a party of the Yuracaré Indians on their way back from Cochabamba, where they had been sent by the Corregidor of Coni as escort to a lady relation of his returning thither. The poor fellows seemed to feel the cold terribly, as the only wraps they had were their bark shirts and a few strips of linen cloth. Their blue faces and swollen fingers told a tale of so great suffering, that the few reales they gained by their journey were indeed well earned. Seeing how the cold affected these Indians, I asked the party with me if they would not rather return ; but the younger ones, who had never been to Cochabamba, were anxious to see the city, and therefore elected to go. Fortunately, I had a few spare blankets, and at nights, when they were huddled together, they were able to keep fairly warm.

The summit of the pass I made to be 12,550 feet, and soon after crossing it we came to cultivated lands and a few isolated huts.

# CHAPTER XXIII.

Total change in the appearance of nature—Cochi-jancbi—Barley and
potatoes—Chuño—Road to Coni by Bandiola—Sacába—Approach to
Cochabamba—Tambos—Apartments—The city and people—Luxuriously furnished houses—Fruits, flowers, and grain crops—Douche
baths—Alaméda, or public garden—Sweets and ices—Tertulias and
rocking-chairs — Commercial firms and their trade — Cascarilla, or
cinchona bark—Hospitality of foreign residents and others—Moonlight ride—Climate—Want of sanitary arrangements—Mineral wealth
of the district.

FROM the top of the cuesta of Malaga onwards into
Bolivia the face of nature is so changed, that one
seems to have suddenly arrived in another land.  To
the north of this hill, the mountains are covered
with trees, and the plains bear their luxuriant wealth
of tropical vegetation, but on the south the aspect
is very different.  On this side, the rocky mountain
ranges of the Andes seem to produce nothing but
crops of stones, which lie so thickly upon all the
level plains that cultivation can only be carried on
after the most laborious work.  This rocky and stony
nature of the soil gives the country a very dreary
look, which is only relieved by trees and foliage,
wherever a river has afforded opportunities of
irrigation.

On the uplands and slopes of the hills barley
and potatoes are grown, while on the uncultivated

lands a rough and long grass grows in tufts, and affords fair grazing for sheep and oxen.

About 5 p.m. we arrived at Cochi-janchi, at 10,950 feet above sea-level. This village has a particularly melancholy look, as there is not a vestige of a tree to be seen ; the houses, which are very small in size, being built with walls and roofs of mud, or adobe, placed in enclosures made by walls of the same material. There is a small church built with mud, like the houses, and there are altogether about fifty or sixty farms scattered over the hillside. The people must be very industrious, as the hills are much cultivated, some up to their summits, of pro-bably 12,500 or 13,000 feet elevation. The district supplies Cochabamba with potatoes, and there appears to be a large trade done in them, both fresh and preserved. In the latter state they are called " chuño," which is really nothing more than a frozen potato, and a most horrid substitute for the real article. The process of preserving seems to be that the potatoes are cut into slices and then into cubes, about the size of ordinary dice ; these are exposed to the almost nightly frosts until they present a dry, corky appearance, in which state they will keep for any length of time, and form the staple article of food with the Quichuan Indians ; indeed, throughout the interior of the republic, the chuño is met with at every table. I cannot say that I discovered its excellencies, for it seemed to me to taste just as it looks, like cork ; but it is nevertheless a favourite component part of the chupé, which forms the first course both at breakfast and dinner. And certainly it appears to me to be the easiest method by which potatoes can be preserved; no tins or air-tight cases being required—a dry floor or sack serving all purposes for storage.

The mules are now fed with barley, given to them in the straw and unthreshed. This fodder seems to suit both mules and horses admirably, but requires to be varied now and then with grass food when the animal is not on a journey. It costs, near Cochabamba, about two pesos, or 6s. 2d., the quintal of 100 lbs. weight, about sufficient for four animals' nightly rations.

From Cochi-janchi there is another track that leads to Coni, by passing through a district called Bandiola, to the east of Espiritu Santo; but that track also has to pass the ridge of Malaga, and I was credibly informed that the cuestas in that direction are far more severe than those over which I travelled; and as my Yuracaré Indians refused to return to their homes by the Bandiola road, I think it may be agreed that it is not a practicable one. The Malaga cuesta, although rising to a great height, was not very steep, the ascent and descent being so gradual that I did not once have to dismount from my mule in going over it.

Next day, August 16th, the thermometer stood at 45° at six o'clock, which was quite cold enough to be pleasant, but not so sharp as the previous night at Inca Corral. I tried to get my arriero started early, but as he had many visits to make in the pueblo, and much chicha to drink at each house, it was past ten o'clock before we got on the road again. We soon began another ascent, which was very laborious, as the mules show signs of tiring more and more every day. The top of this hill was 600 feet lower than the cuesta of Malaga.

After passing several small and insignificant villages, we came to the town of Sacába, a very considerable place. The day was market day, and the "plazas," or squares, were full of the country people, who wear ponchos and shawls of the brightest colours, so that the scene was most picturesque. These markets are held in the open air, and almost everything that can be named is to be bought. Bread, meat, general provisions and stores, drugs, dyes, woollens, calicoes, and other stuffs of all kinds, pots, pans, and household implements, the stalls being all mixed up together, so that the market has a look as though the tradesmen of the town had emptied the contents of their shops out into the plaza. There are, however, no public horse or cattle fairs in Bolivia, the trade in animals being carried on quietly between the owners of the flocks of sheep and droves of oxen that one sees on the hills, and the butchers. The beasts are always killed, and their carcases dressed and cut up at public abattoirs outside the town, the meat being sold in the plazas or market-places, there being no butchers' shops in any of the streets. The houses of Sacába are decently built in regular streets, but as the town is situated in a stony plain, the dust was very trying when a strong north wind was blowing. Our ride up to and through the town was done during a perfect dust-storm—so thick that it was necessary to tie our handkerchiefs over our faces, or we should, I think, have been suffocated. As for the people in the open plaza, they must have suffered severely, and their goods of a perishable nature must have been almost spoiled by the clouds of dust that passed over the town.

Leaving Sacába, our shortest route lay across a ridge of mountains that stretch out into the plain, and behind which the city of Cochabamba is situated; but, as the mules were very tired and footsore, we kept to the plain, and went round the end of the ridge. The approach to Cochabamba was up a stream, now dry, with what appeared to be country residences on either side, many having considerable pretensions to comfort, and all having good, well-stocked gardens. These country houses are called " quintas," and the owners mostly have town residences as well. A bridge for the road had been built over the river, but one of the piers had fallen, from the simple fact that the foundations were not on rock, but on sand and small stones. We entered the city about half-past six in the evening, crossing the principal plaza just as it was getting dark, putting up at the " tambo," where, with difficulty, I succeeded in getting a small and dark room, which was quite destitute of any bedding or furniture. There was nothing to be had to eat or drink in the tambo, and I could only get a plate of greasily cooked beef-steak, which my boy managed to buy somewhere outside; but, notwithstanding the poverty of the accommodation, having had supper, I managed to pass a very good night, as I had my camp-bed, and was therefore independent of hotel fittings, being always able to sleep well, provided that I could get under a water-tight roof.

The tambo is an old Spanish institution that is fast giving way to the hotel, or "posada,"and probably

Bolivia is the only South American republic where the tambo can be seen in its old-fashioned style. The tambo of Bolivia is not so well managed as the travelling bungalow of India, where the wayfarer not only finds a room, but also finds the necessary articles of furniture, such as a cot and washing apparatus, while there is always an attendant who can prepare a repast if the traveller has no servant of his own. In Cochabamba the tambo, as a building, outwardly is all well enough, but the rooms are small, dark, and badly ventilated, and in place of furniture a brick or mud shelf, of a width sufficient for sleeping on, is built up in one corner, or right across the end of the room. Sometimes this sleeping-bank takes the form of a daïs, raised only about a foot above the ordinary floor of the room, and the arrangement is in Bolivia not confined to tambos, but found also in many middle-class houses in use instead of bedsteads. Most travellers carry a mattress and pillows with their baggage; and in Bolivia a very useful mattress is made, specially for travelling, not too thick, and with one side covered with leather, so that when rolled up there is no danger of the stuff side getting wet, and when in use the leather side, being below, helps to keep the damp from the sleeper. Bolivians seem to be able to sleep soundly on this table or shelf arrangement; but European travellers should be careful to have their own cots with them, as, if they try the tables, they will soon find that sleep is out of the question, the mud or bricks being tenanted by armies of active insects, to whom the arrival of a stranger in the land affords an opportunity for varying their nightly rations of Bolivian vitality that they are not at all slack in availing themselves of. Materials for washing seem to be quite superfluities in Bolivian tambos, and it becomes, therefore, necessary to carry a metal basin on one's travels. However, the daily charge for a room is not at all extravagant, being a couple of reales, or about ninepence; but probably the proprietors of the tambos think that as the tribes of insects, that may be said to be joint owners of the hostelry, are sure to take a good contribution for themselves out of the unlucky traveller, it would be but justice to let off his pocket as lightly as possible. Fortunately for me, I was not destined to remain long in the tambo of Cochabamba, for on the following day I presented my letters of introduction, and soon had several kind offers of hospitality from various friends. Probably the reason why tambos are so badly furnished and attended to, is that it is the custom for travellers in Bolivia to quarter themselves on friends, and therefore there is not sufficient custom for good hotels. Had I arrived earlier in the day, I should have gone straight to the friends to whom I had been recommended; but, after all, I found that I had so many offers that, as I could not divide my time fairly amongst all the hospitable people who were willing to house me, I decided the difficulty by taking apartments, and secured a first floor in one of the best streets leading out of the principal square. My drawing-room was very large and lofty, and, being furnished in the usual South American style, with chairs, sofas, and a very small pedestal table, had quite a diplomatic look about it. The rent was also

in diplomatic style, being sixty pesos faibles, or
about £10 per month—quite enough, considering
that no attendance or cooking was required, as I
invariably took my meals with one or other of my
acquaintances, and my boy prepared my morning
coffee and attended to the rooms. More moderate
apartments may be had in the city, but one cannot
reckon upon getting a couple of decent rooms for

VIEW OF COCHABAMBA.  (*From a photograph.*)

less than thirty or forty pesos per month—say £5
to £8.

Cochabamba, probably the most important town
of the republic of Bolivia, is situated in a plain
8450 feet above sea-level, overlooked by the rugged
snow-clad heights of Tunari and Larati, whose giant
tops rise fully 10,000 feet above the city. The town

is well built, with regular streets, which all lead to the usual central plaza, in which are the government and municipal offices, and a cathedral that occupies nearly the whole of one side of the square. The public offices have a handsome colonnade extending over the foot pavement and running round two sides of the plaza, forming a promenade with good shelter either from sun or rain. There are in the city about 50,000 people, and amongst the upper classes are found many descendants of old Spanish families, but the bulk of the population are Indians of Quichuan or Aymará extraction. The language of society and commerce is Castilian, and the Indians of the town, who amongst themselves use their own tongue, whether Quichuan or Aymará, nearly all speak or understand Spanish; in the outlying villages and farms very few have been sufficiently educated to know any but their own language, and it therefore becomes necessary to have an interpreter for the journey from one town to another. These Indians present many features of interest, but their character and peculiarities are seen to greater advantage in their little homesteads on the mountains, and we shall have frequent opportunities of meeting with them outside the cities.

After many weeks of rough travelling, one of the greatest pleasures of arriving at Cochabamba is to meet with a well, nay, highly educated society, the fairer portion of which especially attract observation; for, apart from the natural charms with which " el bello sexo " of Spanish descent are largely endowed, the ladies of Cochabamba are generally accomplished musicians, while many are also good linguists, French and Italian being more in favour than English or German. But the "bello sexo" of Sucre, or Chuquisaca, as it is otherwise called, are generally considered to be more graceful and elegant than those of Cochabamba; so I must not part with all my praises for "las bellas Cochabambinas," but reserve some for the fair Sucrenses, or Chuquisa-queñas. Many of the best houses are luxuriously furnished, and as all the furniture and appointments are either of American or European manufacture, the cost of an establishment must be very excessive, as everything has to be brought on mules or donkeys over the Andes from the ports of the Pacific coast. I saw several drawing-rooms in the city that had as much plate-glass and as many orna-ments as are to be seen in a tastefully furnished house in London, and most houses of any pretensions have good pianos, which, costing perhaps £60 or £80 in Europe, are worth about £200 by the time they get to Cochabamba. At this rate, one can easily see that it must take a small fortune to furnish a house decently in the interior of the republic of Bolivia.

The chief wealth of the department appears to be in agriculture, for Cochabamba may certainly claim to be the agricultural capital of Bolivia, La Paz, Potosi, and Oruro being the chief mineral centres, whilst the true capital of the republic, Sucre, is the political and educational centre. Cochabamba is the storehouse for the crops of wheat, maize, barley, and potatoes that are grown on the plains on which the city is built. There are many large gardens in the outskirts of the town, which produce fruits of all kinds, such as grapes, oranges, apples, pears, peaches, apricots, and strawberries. Roses, carnations, camelias, and most European flowers are also grown, so that a visitor may easily fancy himself in the south of France, or even in a well-stocked garden at home, only that the latter idea must be of one of the finest summer days of England for the comparison to hold good at all, for it is almost impossible otherwise to compare the blue sky and fine clear atmosphere of Cochabamba with our own murky and cloudy skies. Nearly all the quintas, or country houses, are furnished with bathing arrangements, and have good gardens attached to them ; but the one that took my fancy most was named " Maiorina," a most valuable possession, or "finca," as they are called. This finca not only has the largest and best stock of fruit and flowers, but it also has a really splendid douche bath. The house is built on a steep hillside, and a small mountain stream of clear cold water is led by an aqueduct into the bath-house, which is dug out to a depth of perhaps twelve feet, and well lined with marble. The fall of water is about twenty feet, and as the stream enters the bath-house with a volume of about six inches deep by twelve inches in width, the blow received by the bather at the bottom is so severe that great caution is required to avoid exposing one's head to the full force of the water. The stream has its rise in the snow that almost continually lies on the top of Tunari, and the water is therefore intensely cold—so much so, that to descend into the well of the bath nearly takes one's breath away. The first effect of the cold upon me was to give an intense pain at the back of the head below the ears. I was therefore very cautious at first to keep clear of the big douche, and, holding my hands over my head, and bending forward somewhat in a diving attitude, receive the spray only, diverted from the main stream by the hands. I was told that several incautious bathers had been knocked down by the fall, and as the attendant does not remain in the bath-room, such an occurrence may easily end fatally. Notwithstanding the intense coldness of the water, and the fact that the bath is about three miles from the city, it is well frequented, and I saw many young ladies go with great regularity, although I should have thought the cold would have deterred them from bathing. The bath is the property of the owner of the Finca Maiorina, but he kindly allows the public to use it on payment of a reale each, or about $4\frac{1}{2}d.$, a payment which can only suffice to keep an attendant. The cost of construction and the repairs must be altogether at the expense of the proprietor, to whom all visitors to Cochabamba should be very grateful, for the bath is certainly a splendid luxury.

Cochabamba, like the generality of South American towns, has its " alaméda," or place of public resort. To call these alamédas parks, would be misleading, for they are generally too small to be dignified with such a title, being more like some of the small parks or gardens that have of late years been made in the suburbs of London, on spots that were previously howling wastes, tenanted only by brickbats, dead cats, and street arabs. Certainly London has somewhat improved latterly in the matter of public enclosures, but still we could take a lesson in this respect from South America, where, when a town is commenced, almost the first thing projected is a plaza, or public square, and then an alaméda, or public garden; so that the town, as it grows, is sure of having some open breathing-places left unbuilt upon. Such a course might be adopted with great advantage in each of the rapidly built up suburban districts of London, where street is built close upon street, and terrace upon terrace, so that to get a breath of fresh air one is obliged to travel long distances to one of our noble parks, or right into the country. The alaméda of Cochabamba is just outside the town, and easily accessible on an evening or early morning stroll; it consists of four avenues made by poplar trees. But one cannot speak highly of the care bestowed on its preservation, for the walks are covered with a thick dust, which rises in clouds upon the slightest provocation. The entrance is through a gate or façade of considerable size, built of rough stonework, covered with plaster, on which, painted in bright and glaring colours, are representations, by a native artist, of some of the battles fought during the War of Independence, that ended in the break up of the empire of Spain in South America into the republics of the present day. Art in Bolivia does not appear to have risen to any great height, and therefore the frescoes and paintings by native artists that are to be seen in public places are not of a very high order of merit, and remind one forcibly of the cheap and highly coloured scenes sold at home for children's portable theatres. The rules of perspective also appear to be about as much known in Bolivia as they apparently are in China or Japan; so that the paintings have a mediæval or Byzantine look about them, which might perhaps be highly appreciated in certain high art circles of the present day.

The city is fairly furnished with shops, which do not, however, make any great show in the windows, the goods being laid out in large stores or warehouses. A few fondas and billiard-rooms have inferior *table d'hôtes*, where the ordinary meals of the country can be procured, but the cuisine is of very third-rate character, and such places are therefore to be avoided if possible. Chocolate, sweets, and confectionery are plentiful and good, but the splendid ices that are to be had all through the year are the greatest luxury of Cochabamba. These are both cheap and good, and are made, it is said, from the snow always lying in the crevices of the heights of Tunari, from whence it is brought down by Indians for the ice-makers, who turn it into cream, vanilla, lemon, or strawberry ices, which meet with a ready sale during the heat of the midday and afternoon hours.

At the "tertulias," or evening parties, which are quite an institution in Cochabamba, ices play an important part, along with tea, coffee, cigarettes, and small-talk. These tertulias are, to my mind, about the most dreary performances that a human being can be forced to assist at. It is the custom after dinner for the ladies of the house to take up their positions in rocking-chairs, a number of which are placed in a circle, generally near the open windows, except on the few occasions when the

Q

weather is unfavourable. Gentlemen friends are then expected to drop in promiscuously and, occupying the vacant chairs, provide the ladies with a feast of small-talk and scandal, which seems to be as much admired in the west of the world as it is in the east. Frequently these meetings take a political turn—and, indeed, one may almost say that they always do—for it is very rare to find more than one of the various parties of the day represented at a tertulia, as party spirit runs so high in the gloriously free republics, that it is not at all safe to differ in opinion with your neighbour at what would appear to be a friendly reunion. A stranger, of course, is not supposed to take any side in politics, but it is difficult to avoid being thought to be of the same party as one's host; and it is therefore sometimes necessary to shift your opinions with every visit that you make during the course of the evening, as you are not expected to stay at any one house more than half an hour at the most, unless you are on very intimate terms with the family. To see a circle of say ten or a dozen people rocking away, some vigorously and others lackadaisically, while endeavouring to keep up a conversation, has a very funny look; but the motion of the chairs is so pleasant, that one soon falls in with the custom, and rocks as hard as any of the natives, though not able to join always in the chatting. The same kind of dreary visiting is practised on Sunday afternoons, from about two until four or five, during which hours polite and proper young men are to be seen hastening from house to house, got up in most elaborate style, and evidently making a most serious business of a social duty that, if taken more leisurely, would be a pleasure. A peculiarity I noticed particularly at these tertulias was, that each of the ladies present was addressed by the title of " señorita." Whatever her age or position in life, married or single, rich or poor, all are señoritas in Bolivia. It used to sound excessively funny to hear an old lady, perhaps a grandmamma, called " señorita," whilst the same term was used for her granddaughters; but, as in Rome one must do as Romans do, so, in Bolivia, a traveller who wishes to be thought polite and cultivated must be careful to address all Bolivianas by the style and title of " señorita."

There are many commercial firms of considerable standing, the principal being three German houses, who make very large importations of European manufactures. All these goods have to be brought on mules' backs from the ports of the Pacific coast over the Andes, and are therefore greatly enhanced in value by the time they get to be exposed for sale in the merchant's store, the freight from the port of Arica to the interior of the republic varying from £40 to £80 per ton of twenty quintals of 100 Spanish pounds each, according to the season or the class of goods. A ton would be about eight mule-loads, and taking beer or wine as an example, we find that the cost of the freight of a case of any liquor from the Pacific coast would be £1 5s., and at times £2 10s., while the first cost at home of a case of beer would not perhaps be more than 10s. or 12s.

In consequence of this excessively high cost of

freighting, the exports of Bolivia are limited almost entirely to the richest portions of the minerals with which the interior of the country abounds, and to " cascarilla," or the bark of the cinchona tree. Bolivia enjoys an almost total monopoly of this latter valuable product, which received the name of Peruvian bark, because Bolivia itself was called Alto Peru before the War of Independence ; but, at the present time, I think it may safely be asserted that all the Peruvian bark that is exported from Peru is collected in the forests of the province of Caupolican in Bolivia.* Indeed, so localized is the cinchona tree, being only found over, comparatively speaking, a small tract of country, that it may be feared that in a few years it will become almost extinct, as the tree dies after the bark has been stripped from it. The government of Bolivia—that is to say, whenever there is any central power worth calling a government—is always satisfied with collecting the export duties on the " cascarilla," and takes no steps whatever to ensure the replanting of the forests, but seems to be satisfied with prohibiting the export of plants or seeds, and thinks thus to keep the valuable trade to the country, ignoring totally the fact that the day is fast approaching when all the cinchona trees will have been killed, and a trade that might, with very little care, have been a continuous source of revenue, will be entirely lost. But this short-sighted policy is pursued in Bolivia in every branch of revenue. Even the sums

.* The average yearly shipments of Peruvian bark from Arica amount to 9611 cwts., of 100 lbs. each, having a cash value at the port of about £118,300. (See Appendix, p. 400.)

received from farming the tolls on the roads, such as they are, have to be sent to the provincial or central treasuries, and not a cent is spent in repairs until the road gets into a totally impassable condition, when a few spasmodic efforts are made, and the smallest amount possible is laid out, in order that the cash shall only be diverted from the public treasury for as short a time as may be.

Notwithstanding the difficulties under which trade is carried on in Bolivia, the merchants appear to do a flourishing business, and some of the best firms keep up princely establishments, and generally have branches in all the chief towns of the republic. The foreigners resident in Bolivia are somewhat exclusive in their social life, and although on friendly terms with the townspeople, it is only on certain occasions that one sees a mixed company of Bolivians and Europeans. But I noticed that this exclusiveness only referred to dinner-parties— a class of entertainment for which the European residents evidently do not think the Bolivians sufficiently well educated. There is, it must be allowed, good reason for thinking so, as the manners and customs of a Bolivian dinner-table differ in many essential points from a European one. For instance, salt-cellars are not often provided with salt-spoons; one's own knife being thought to be all that is wanted for carving the joint, serving vegetables, and helping one's self to salt, pepper, or mustard. Similarly, table or gravy spoons are almost unknown, as every one helps himself to soup or gravy with his own spoon. These little peculiarities, doubtless, account for the almost general absence of European guests at Bolivian tables, **and** *vice versâ*. At balls or soirées it is, of course, absolutely necessary that ladies should be, if not in a majority, at least well represented; and as there are not sufficient European ladies in any town even for a quadrille, it is upon these occasions that one gets a chance of seeing the ladies of the country to the greatest advantage. The German merchants do not seem to admire the " bello sexo " of Bolivia sufficiently to be often caught in the matrimonial net, and any bold adventurer who falls captive to the charms of a fair Boliviana, and accepts her for better or worse, is by his fellow-countrymen rather thought to have made a mistake. Frequently the balls and parties are got up in an impromptu manner, and then they are really delightful. I remember one of these, at which, after dancing till nearly midnight, a moonlight ride was proposed, and immediately put into execution. There was no lack of horses, and, through the kindness of one of my German friends, I was excellently well mounted; and away we started, about half a dozen ladies and a dozen cavaliers. Through the quiet town we rode at a good pace, and out across the plain to a lagoon, then entirely dry, where we ran races by the bright moonlight, and let off some rockets and crackers that one of the Germans had brought with him. We passed our pocket-flasks round, the ladies also not disdaining a small nip to keep them from catching cold with the night air, and then back to town, having thoroughly enjoyed the ride.

The foreign residents in Cochabamba always

receive travellers with the greatest kindness and hospitality, and for my part I shall always retain the liveliest memories of the good time I spent with them. By one of the principal German firms I was received quite as a friend, although I was not provided with letters of introduction to the house. The establishment I refer to was throughout kept up on a most magnificent scale, and the arrangements of the various rooms, such as dining, billiard, and smoking and reading rooms, were as complete and as well ordered as many a club at home. An American firm of contractors for public works, and owners of the coaches that run from Cochabamba to Arani through the valley of Cliza, have a fine house and workshops just on the outskirts of the city, and are, far and away, the most hospitable men it has ever been my lot to meet with; indeed, I do not call to mind ever having seen such an open house kept up anywhere else. So truly hospitable are these worthy Americans, that they expect every English-speaking traveller who passes through Cochabamba to go direct to their house, and just take up his quarters there, as though he were an old friend of years' standing. I was an entire stranger to them, and did not know of this excellent custom of theirs, and so I fear that I involuntarily offended them by going to the tambo instead of to their establishment; however, I did my best afterwards to make up for lost time, by eating as many breakfasts and dinners with them as possible, for they certainly kept the best cook in Cochabamba. Every day these good fellows have meals prepared for at least half a dozen more people than they have staying with

them at the moment, so that they are always prepared to receive casual droppers-in, and on Sundays
I have seen a score or so of self-invited guests sit
down to a first-rate breakfast, excellent in character
and quality, both in eatables and drinkables, and the
meal has gone on just as though it had been specially
prepared for the occasion. Long life to these hospitable Yankees, say I, and may their shadow never
be less! and I am sure that every one who knows
them personally will echo my wish for their prosperity and success.

While praising the hospitality of the foreigners
resident in Cochabamba, I must not forget that
shown me by many of the native families of the
town, lest it should be thought that the Bolivians
are behind their European friends in this respect.
By all the Bolivians with whom I came in contact, I
was received with the greatest cordiality, and by
one family, to the head of which I had been specially
recommended by Don Ignacio Bello of Trinidad,
I was received quite as one of the family circle,
which I take to be about the greatest compliment
that can be paid to a stranger. My host, in this
case, was a travelled and highly educated man, while
his charming señora was of one of the best families
of La Paz, and they had evidently improved greatly
upon the general manners and customs of the
country, for their table was always well appointed,
and bountifully supplied with good things.

Cochabamba has a small theatre, but there is no
regular company, and travelling ones seldom visit
the town, as it is out of the principal routes of
travel. During my stay, there was an amateur per-

formance by young men, who took both male and female parts; but their acting was childish and nonsensical in the extreme, and the townsfolk seemed to be of the same opinion, for the amateurs played to empty benches.

The climate of Cochabamba may, in my opinion, be classed amongst the finest of the world, as it enjoys an almost perpetual summer, whilst the nights are pleasantly cool, and therefore invigorating to constitutions depressed by the humid heat of the Madeira and Amazon valleys. There seems to be but little difference all the year round. Certain months have more rain than others, the wettest months being November to January, but even then the rain only falls in the shape of good heavy showers, lasting, perhaps, an hour or so, when the sun breaks out again. A thoroughly wet day, with rain falling from morn till night, is a great rarity in Cochabamba, although at higher and lower altitudes, in the same parallel of latitude, such days are of frequent occurrence, while the central plains of Bolivia seem to have just a desirable amount of rainfall and no more.

Few towns could be mentioned that are more advantageously situated, from a hygienic point of view; indeed, I should say that a " City of Health " might be established at Cochabamba with very good results. Fever and ague are quite unknown, and if sanitary matters were attended to, it might soon be said that the place was quite free from diseases of any kind; but unfortunately, at present, such sicknesses as small-pox and scarlet fever are got rid of with difficulty, owing to the filthy habits of at

least four-fifths of the natives of the place, who seem
to be quite without any notions of public cleanliness.
There are no sewers or drains of any kind whatever,
and consequently the state of the whole city, with
the exception of a few of the principal squares and
main thoroughfares, which are swept every day by a
gang of prisoners from the town jail, can be easier
imagined than described. Vaccination also is much
neglected, and consequently, when an outbreak of
this dreadful scourge occurs, it rapidly takes vast
dimensions, and great numbers suffer and die, for the
Indian blood seems to cause the disease to take its
most virulent form.

A town like this offers a most favourable opportunity for showing clearly the advantages afforded
by a dry earth system of sewage to cities destitute of
a plentiful supply of water. A president who would
introduce this beneficent system into Bolivia would,
in my opinion, confer a far greater favour on his
country than any of its rulers have hitherto succeeded in doing. It will, perhaps, scarcely be
credited, that even in the best establishments there
are no closets or other receptacles for house refuse ;
indeed, in my experience throughout the country,
such a convenience never came to my notice, excepting in the houses of the foreign residents. There is
a back yard to most houses, which I can only
describe as a dreadful *cloaca maxima*, and this horrid
place is frequented by all the members of the family,
without distinction of age or sex. The house refuse
is thrown in this yard, and although pigs, dogs,
mules, and any other animals that may be on the
establishment are turned loose therein, the hot sun

seems left to do the work of a disinfectant, except that an occasional sweeping takes place, when the rubbish that remains is set fire to, and burned to ashes.

When one sees such a dreadful want of the commonest knowledge of sanitary matters amongst a society otherwise sufficiently cultivated, one is almost tempted to think that there must be something fundamentally wrong in the educational system of the country; and certainly it must be set down as a great blot upon the teachings of the Roman Catholic clergy of South America, that they have not taught their flocks the elementary principle that "cleanliness is next to godliness." The people are, however, so apathetic, and so thoroughly wedded to their customs, that probably a revolution might be threatened to any president who should endeavour to make a law of common decency obligatory in the republic. Perhaps, however, it has been thought that sewers are beyond the financial resources of the towns; and there may be another good reason, namely, that an abundant supply of water is not to be depended upon all the year round. But dry earth is always at hand, and therefore it seems at once apparent that Moule's system would confer great blessings upon all the communities, if it were thoroughly carried out.

Very little has been done in mining in the immediate neighbourhood of Cochabamba, as from its great distance from the coast the carriage of any but the richest silver ores would be too expensive to leave any profit for the miner. There is, however, without doubt, immense wealth in minerals in all the hills encircling the plain in which the city stands, and, in proof of this, I was shown many specimens of manganese, silver, and lead ores that had been taken from the outcrop of the lodes in the district. These minerals must remain unexplored until the railway and navigation of the Madeira valley shall have opened up Eastern Bolivia, and caused good roads to be made from the headwaters of the Madeira and Amazon to the interior of the republic.

The people of Cochabamba, of all classes and shades of public opinion, are resolved to do all that lies in their power to assist this enterprise to completion, for they see in it their only hope of emancipating themselves from the heavy costs and charges levied upon all their European necessities by the merchants of La Paz and the Peruvian ports on the Pacific coast, as also their only hope of securing an outlet for those abundant agricultural products that are now lost for want of customers.

# CHAPTER XXIV.

FROM Cochabamba, the shortest route across the republic to the Pacific coast, is to go by Oruro to Tacna and Arica, and the road is a regularly travelled one, with posting-houses, which I have been told are the best in Bolivia. My business obliged me to visit Sucre, and I determined to make a round by Totora and Misque, in order to see a new cart-road that was in course of construction from Arani to Totora, at which place I hoped to obtain some information as to the practicability of a road from thence to the Chimoré, the proposed new port for the navigation enterprise of the Madeira River.

The only means of travelling in the interior of Bolivia is by mules; so I bargained with an arriero for the necessary animals for the journey to Sucre, at the rate of fifteen pesos, about £2 8*s*., for each animal, the arriero having to provide forage at his own expense. This is the best bargain to make, but the arrieros prefer getting the traveller to buy the forage, so that, acting in collusion with the villagers or posting-house keepers, they may be able to defraud the unfortunate traveller daily. The usual charge per mule from Cochabamba to Sucre is about twelve or thirteen pesos, say £2, inclusive of expenses for forage, etc.; but the route by Totora is longer than the route mostly used, which goes by San Pedro, so I had to pay a higher price. As some parts of the road are said to be infested by foot-pads, it is not advisable to travel alone; and as it would be difficult to find an honest arriero who would do so, it is just as well to make some inquiries about the arriero that offers his services, and secure one that is known to the merchants or respectable people. The gentry who in Bolivia practise the profession of mule-drivers, are not as a rule to be trusted with untold gold, but the " gay muleteer " seems all over the world to have rather a shady reputation; however, if a traveller secures an arriero that is well known to the merchants, he and his belongings will be perfectly safe.

On the 31st of August, I despatched my arriero ahead with my baggage and saddle-mules, and settled to leave Cochabamba in Messrs. Haviland and Keay's coach about mid-day, the proprietors, my worthy American friends, having given me a free ride to Arani. We ought to have left at mid-day, but the prefect was behindhand with his despatches to the central government at Sucre, so we were detained for nearly an hour beyond the proper time of starting. The coaches are big, lumbering affairs, looking like a cross between a Spanish diligence and a French char-à-banc, but they are, by their weight and strength of springs and wheels, well suited to the extremely rough roads that have to be travelled over. They are drawn by six horses, driven in our case by an American coachman with a wooden leg, he having had his leg broken in one of the frequent upsets that the conveyances meet with. A Bolivian who travelled in my company to Totora, and who was contractor for the new road that I was going to see, was lame from the same cause; so when I took my seat, and said farewell to the friends who came to see me off, I must say I had serious misgivings as to whether I should reach the journey's end in safety, and would far rather have mounted my mule, instead of accepting the seat in the coach.

The roads were frightfully loose, the six horses raising fearful clouds of dust; consequently the driver and native passengers required frequent and copious draughts of their national drinks at every chicha-shop we passed, these libations being varied by repeated applications to bottles of "pisco," or white rum, during the runs between the "chicherias." I don't think that I could conscientiously say that this heavy drinking was entirely caused by the dust, as all the passengers seemed to have provided themselves with bottles of pisco quite as part of their travelling impedimenta. The result was that the driver soon got so intoxicated that he was quite unable to keep his team on the track which was dignified with the name of a road. How he managed to keep himself on the box was a marvel; but I fancy that he was able to jam the end of his wooden leg into a crack in the foot-board, and so, getting a purchase, he was able to retain his seat notwithstanding his condition, and the severe lurches that the coach took at frequent intervals. As for the passengers, the frequent drinks took effect in different ways; the men were mostly hilarious and noisy, but the females of the party, and some of the younger males, were very ill. Certainly the movements of the coach, as it swayed and rolled over the ruts and channels in the track, were almost as bad as those of a small Liverpool liner " in the Bay of Biscay O ! " but if so much pisco and chicha had not been consumed *en route*, I think we should have been spared some of the very distressing scenes that occurred on the road.

Leaving Cochabamba, we were soon on the pampas, and as August is one of the dry months, the fields were bare and dusty, but in the spring and showery seasons large crops of barley, wheat, and maize are raised. The pampas are dotted over with the dome-shaped huts and houses of the Quichuan Indians, and from their being built in mud and stones, the country presents features similar to many of the plains of Central India, with their stone and mud walled villages. We passed through the towns of Tarata and Cliza, both populous and flourishing places, built on the flat pampas, and at each of these towns we had to stop while politics were discussed, and vast quantities of pisco and chicha consumed; indeed, these stoppages were so frequent and of such lengthy duration, that it was quite dark before we arrived at Punata, where my Bolivian friends had determined to put up for the night; considering the bad state of the roads, the condition of our Jehu, the frequent jibbing of the horses, who, whenever the coach got into an extra deep rut, scattered all over the road and stood head to head, refusing either to pull, or even to move out of the way and allow the passengers to push the coach themselves, a performance that we had to go through several times, until the horses seemed to be ashamed of themselves, and suddenly started off at full gallop again.

The arriero, with the mules and luggage, got to Punata shortly before we arrived there, and were waiting for us on the plaza. My Bolivian friend would not allow me to go to the public tambo, but took me to the house of a friend of his, Señor Manuel Arauco, who received me most kindly, and gave me both house-room and entertainment. My host is one of the most influential persons of Punata, and a most remarkable man. On entering his house I was much struck with the dignity of his appearance, he being perhaps six feet three or four inches, and of a frame suitable to such a height; but when he did me the honour of introducing me to his family, and I beheld a tall and stately lady in the prime of life, with, three queenly daughters, all up to six feet at least, and of most handsome and pleasing features, I thought it would be hard to match such a bevy of graces anywhere else in the world. My first impressions almost inclined me to believe that some one of the numerous accidents of the journey from Cochabamba had been fatal in its effects, and that I, a second Gulliver, had awakened in Brobdignagia,

R

but the kind and pleasing manners of my host and hostess soon convinced me that though my entertainers were giants they were also mortals. The evening passed away quickly, in the usual rocking-chair and desultory chit-chat style, and the following morning I was ready for the road by 7 a.m.; but my Bolivian friend was not to the fore, heavy drinking not being compatible with early rising. I therefore sent my baggage mules ahead with the arriero and servant boy, giving them orders to wait for me at Vacas, the village where we intended to make the next halt, the distance from Punata being about thirty miles.

While waiting for my Bolivian friend to sleep off the effects of yesterday's chicha and pisco, I strolled through the streets of Punata, which I found to be a town of about 16,000 inhabitants, with the usual central plaza, and roughly paved, but well laid-out streets. The chief trade seemed to be in wheat, barley, and potatoes, which were to be bought either wholesale or retail in almost every store. Clothing for the Indian population seems to be made in the town; ponchos and a kind of rough cloth being made from vicunha and other wools. Felt hats are also a staple industry of the place, and, being of excellent quality, are much sought for throughout the republic. The best and softest are made from vicunha wool, and are worth from twelve to fifteen pesos bolivianos—say £2 10s. to £3 ; but one of sheep's wool can be bought for any price, from half a dollar upwards. The makers of these hats use a rough frame, on which a cloth is stretched to receive the wool; under this is suspended a kind of bow, the cord of which passes about an inch or two over the cloth; the wool is then beaten by the cord being pulled smartly, the effect of the process being to beat the wool into a very fine fluff, which is wetted and pressed into the required shape with the addition of sufficient size to give the necessary stiffness. The delay in starting also gave me the opportunity of becoming better acquainted with my host, Señor Arauco, whom I found to be a most worthy and intelligent man. He possesses a very interesting museum of animals, birds, insects, and general products of the province, and although he is of independent circumstances, he is by no means an idle man. He told me that his amusements consisted of the " arts and sciences," and that he made what discoveries he could, and instructed young men of the town in any that proved to be useful. Indeed, the whole family seemed to be occupied in teaching something, for the young ladies taught artificial-flower making and lace-making gratuitously, they having learned these useful accomplishments from books. Señor Arauco's labours included photographing, bird-stuffing, and preserving skins of animals, cabinet-making, tanning, and wood-staining; and he showed me some excellently tanned specimens of leather of different colours and qualities; also various dyestuffs and drugs collected in the forests of the hills which border on the plains of the Beni. Amongst other articles, I noticed and brought away samples of brasiletto wood, campeachy, and a root which might be utilized as a purple dye instead of orchella weed; also turmeric, collected near Santa Cruz, and called " coorcama " in the district. This article commands a large sale in Europe at about £30 per ton, and as it is to be found in large quantities on the slope of all the hills bordering the plains of the Beni, it might, with great advantage, be made an article of export when the railway of the rapids has been constructed. Señor Arauco, spoke with great enthusiasm of the benefits to accrue to the eastern provinces of Bolivia from the completion of the railway and navigation schemes.

Towards mid-day my Bolivian companion pulled himself together, and we started from Punata about 1 p.m., and, after a couple of hours' ride, passed through Arani, a small town at the end of the pampa, remarkable only for its extremely narrow and ill-paved streets. We then began to ascend the hills by the new road, for which my Bolivian companion was the contractor. The road is worked in zigzag grades up the mountain sides, the inclination being probably 1 in 8 and 1 in 10, and seeming to me to be too steep for any kind of coach, including American ones with wooden-legged drivers. The scenery in these parts is wild and gloomy, the hills being almost denuded of any kind of vegetation except a long rough grass, which seems to give good pasturage to the cattle, roaming about apparently quite untended or watched by any one. The view from the hills looking across the pampas of Arani and Cliza would have been very fine had it not been much obscured by clouds of dust, and by the mirage left by the intense heat of the mid-day sun.

We had to ride pretty sharply, as travelling after dark on such roads is not at all a pleasant business, for one could easily miss the road, and find one's self rolling down the mountain side; but we had better luck, and got to Vacas about seven o'clock, just as night was falling in. Near Vacas are the lagoons from which it is proposed to take water for the irrigation of the pampas of the Cliza and Arani valley. These lakes are three in number, the largest being about one and a half leagues in length, by half a league in breadth. The works, which have been carried out by Messrs. Haviland and Keay, of Cochabamba, for account of Mr. Henry Meiggs, of Lima, are now in abeyance, and it was supposed that they would be abandoned, as it was surmised that if the channels cut from the lagoons to the pampas were opened, the lagoons would drain dry in about four years, and therefore no return for the capital spent (about £50,000) would be obtained. I think it may be considered that these lagoons are only drainage deposits from the surrounding hills, which attain altitudes of 14,000 and 15,000 feet, the lakes themselves being about 9500 feet above sea level, while the pampas to be irrigated are at an altitude of nearly 9000 feet. There are no rivers to empty themselves into the lagoons, and there is only the drainage of the hills to depend upon, and as this drainage is probably in excess of the yearly evaporation, the level of the water is kept up; but some authorities think that the lakes are decreasing yearly in size, while others say that the level is kept up by a supply from springs below the ordinary surface level. These lakes are probably parallels, on a small scale, of Lake Titicaca, in the north-western corner of Bolivia, or of the Lake of Valencia in Venezuela, lakes that are known to be decreasing rapidly from extended agriculture, aided, in the case of Lake Valencia, by denudation of forests. If irrigation could be taken to the pampa lands of the Cliza valley, they would perhaps become the richest agricultural plains in the world, as their climate, owing to the considerable elevation, is suitable for the production of almost any cereal; and it seems somewhat strange that proper statistics of the rainfall of the district have not been taken, in order to determine whether the yearly supply received into the lakes would be equal to the demand.

Vacas is a small Indian village, of no other interest than that it is said that from thence exists a path that leads to the Chimoré and Coni, and its position on the map would lead to the belief that it is favourably situated for explorations to those rivers. As we arrived after dark, we found the posta locked up and deserted, but, after some little trouble, the man in charge was hunted up by our arriero, and a fowl and some potatoes having been purchased, we set our boys to make a " chupe ; " for we had been provident enough to put up a small bag of onions, chillies, and other condiments, not for. getting the ever necessary garlic, before we left Cochabamba. We therefore managed to make a very excellent pot, which provided us with a capital supper, after which my camp-bed was put together for me, and my Bolivian friend contented himself with a shake-down on the mud bench, which, with a rough table, forms the only furniture of the postas, whilst the arriero and the boys slept on the hides and mats that we carried for covering the cargoes of baggage, and for protecting the animals' backs from the pack-saddles.

The next morning, the 2nd of September, we were up betimes, having our mules saddled and cargoes up by 6 a.m., when we left Vacas, intending to make the day's journey end at Totora, distant about twelve leagues. The greater part of the route lay over the new road from Arani to Totora, which has been made without any engineering help, the grades, consequently, being very uncertain. The sites chosen for the road might also in many cases have been much improved upon. In one instance, part of the road, about two leagues before arriving at Pocona, a small and unimportant village about midway between Arani and Totora, has been taken over a ridge, the descent from which is accomplished by a zigzag of three inclines of possibly 1 in 6 at least, while a far preferable route up a ravine near by was available, in which the abrupt descent might have been avoided by a continuous grade of about 1 in 25. However, considerable work has been undertaken in the construction of this road, some of the cuts being of great depth, one point of rock being cut down fifty feet at least. Altogether, the work reflects the greatest credit on the contractor, Señor Demetrio Jordan, of Cochabamba, it being the first piece of road construction undertaken in the republic by a Bolivian contractor. The tools in use by the peons were of the most miserable description, and of native manufacture, and, considering this, it is clear that the Quichuan Indians may be made very fair navvies. The daily wages they earned were, I was given to understand, about four reales, or 1s. 7d., without provisions.

Pocona merits no other mention, than that its

beautiful site, at the head of a splendid valley, will attract a population when the interior of the republic enjoys the facilities of improved ways of communication.

At dusk we arrived at Totora, the approach to which reminded me very much of a ride in the Black Country of home, for the numerous chicherias on the outskirts of the town were belching forth many-tongued flames of fire into the gathering darkness. Totora is a place of considerable trade, and contains about 15,000 inhabitants. It is the chief emporium in Eastern Bolivia for " coca," which is collected here from the plantations of the Yungas of San Antonio and Espiritu Santo, etc., and despatched to the towns of the interior. The tax levied on this article forms a principal item of the budget of the treasury of the republic, and my friend the Bolivian contractor received payment for his road from Arani by the hypothecation of this tax for a certain number of years. Coffee, flour, sugar, and potatoes are also articles of export to other departments, while foreign merchandise finds its way here from Sucre and Santa Cruz, numerous droves or " recuas " of mules and donkeys being met with between Totora and Sucre.

In Totora I sought information with reference to roads leading to the head-waters of the Chimoré, and was introduced to two of the principal men of the place, Don Eugenio Soriano, and Don Saturnino Vela. These gentlemen are owners of " cocales," or plantations of coca, in the hills which form the watersheds of the affluents of the Mamoré, and of those of the Rio Grande. Señor Soriano has made a track from Totora to Arepucho, where his cocales are situated, and is now cutting a further track from Arepucho to the Chimoré. He assured me that a much better road is found by Arepucho than by Espiritu Santo and the Yungas of San Antonio, and gave me the distances thus: Totora to Arepucho, fourteen leagues, and Arepucho to the Chimoré, twelve leagues; total twenty-six. The road from Cochabamba to Coni, *viâ* Espiritu Santo, is forty-four leagues. If the road from Arepucho to Totora be made, the twenty-six leagues can be easily ridden in two or three days at most; and from Totora to Cochabamba, the road being good, can be done in two days, making, say, five days in all, the last day of which can be done in coach from Arani. The Espiritu Santo route cannot be got over with any degree of comfort in less than seven days, and the road is not susceptible of much improvement; whilst the wide crossing of the river San Antonio renders the route almost impracticable for general traffic. It appears, therefore, that future efforts for the opening up of the interior of Bolivia by the Amazon and Madeira route, should be directed to the construction of a road from the Chimoré, *viâ* Arepucho, to Vacas or Totora, this latter place having the advantage of being a good starting-point for a road to Sucre, as well as to Cochabamba and Oruro. These roads may, at some future date, be developed into an internal system of railways for the eastern part of Bolivia, in connection with the Madeira and Mamoré Railway.

The next day's journey was to terminate at Misque, distant about twelve leagues. The arriero and his mules were despatched early, whilst I waited till about nine o'clock, by which time a breakfast was prepared for me by the family that, through the introduction of my Bolivian companion, had given me lodgings for the night.

The height of Totora is about 10,000 feet above sea-level, and the surrounding country is rocky and barren. The road rises slightly on leaving the town, and soon falls on to a large plain, about 500 feet below the Totora hills. It then rises very sharply to 11,500 feet, only to descend, by a very steep and bad " cuesta," into a narrow and tortuous quebrada, up which it runs for about a couple of leagues. This part of the route was said to be infested by robbers, but though I passed up it alone I was unmolested, except by stray cattle, that several times disputed the right of way with me. Certainly a better place for attacking travellers could scarcely be imagined, for the ravine was in many parts not more than twenty yards in width, its steep sides being covered with brushwood, affording capital cover for an ambush.

Road-making in Bolivia is still in its infancy, and in the hilly parts of the interior the tracks are taken up the bottom of the ravines, as, during the dry seasons, a better riding road is found there than could, without considerable work, be had on the sides. This arrangement is all very well when the ravines and rivers are dry, but in the rainy season they become quite impassable, and con- sequently all communication between towns situated as Totora and Misque are, is at an end until dry weather returns. Riding in these ravine roads is also very dangerous in unsettled weather, for a storm may occur on the hills from which the ravine leads, and a flood will then come down upon the unfortunate traveller, with but little warning of its approach.

I overtook the arriero, with his train of cargo-mules, about two o'clock in the afternoon, and the whole day was passed in very rough riding, the "cuestas" and "bajadas" or ascents and descents being frequent and severe. At Misque, where we arrived about 7 p.m., I presented a letter of introduction with which I had been favoured to one of the head men of the town, who I will leave nameless, on account of the shabby manner in which the people of his household treated me. The patron himself was not at home when I arrived, and it seemed that his people had been celebrating his temporary absence with a drinking bout; for when I knocked at the door, I was greeted with shouts of derisive laughter, and roughly told that I had better take up my quarters in the "cabildo," or town gaol. This incivility mattered but little to me, personally, as I had my small tent and plenty of provisions, and could therefore pitch my camp in the plaza of the town with perfect comfort to myself; but I always preferred getting house quarters, if possible, as, the nights being cold, my arriero and servant-boy required shelter also. However, we found an empty room in the town hall, and took possession of it, cooking our supper in the courtyard; and during the night the patron returned, and immediately came to see me, tendering profuse and profound apologies for the way in which his people had treated me. Such an occurrence deserves noting, on account of its being the only instance that ever I heard of upon which a traveller has been turned away with inhospitality from a Bolivian house of any pretensions to respectability, and I am sure the owner, in this case, was very much annoyed at his family's rudeness.

Misque is an old cathedral town, once of considerable importance, as is evidenced by the many pretentious buildings, now empty and falling into decay. It is said that the abandonment of the town during late years has been caused by a curse that has fallen on it, because of the murder, during a revolution, of one of the bishops of Misque, who, after death, was dragged through the town at a horse's tail. The true reason for the desertion of the place is more probably to be found in the prevalence of an aguish fever, caused by bad drainage. The town is situated in a beautiful plain, about 7000 feet above sea-level, and should, therefore, be very healthy. Irrigation has been carried to some extent, several fields and " potreros," or feeding-grounds for cattle, in the immediate neighbourhood of the town being in very fair order. Due provision for the escape of surplus water has not, however, been provided, and the stagnant water, left to dry up by evaporation, is doubtless the cause of the sickness.

The next stage, done on September 4th, was from Misque to Aiquile, about ten leagues. The first half of the day's riding was made up a very wide and almost dry river-bed, the slopes of the hills on either side being dotted with comfortable-looking farmhouses. The road travelled over during this day was much more level than that of the previous days, the greatest altitude passed being about 9000 feet, and we arrived at Aiquile early in the afternoon. The corregidor of the town was a very amiable and pleasant man, who soon procured very comfortable lodgings for me, in the house of an old lady said to be 105 years old. This age was duly attested by the church books, and certainly the appearance of the old lady seemed to give authenticity to the statement. She herself told me that she attributed her great age to the miraculous care of a " Crucified Christ " that she had in a glass case, and under lace curtains, in her principal room ; but the climate of the place seemed to me so delightful, that I should not have been surprised to have heard that people generally lived to great ages there. The town is a thriving place, of about 4000 inhabitants, the streets being broad and well laid out. The trade seems to be entirely in agricultural products, principally carried on with the town of Santa Cruz de la Sierra, to which place a road branches off from Aiquile. Flour, potatoes, coca, and salt are sent to Santa Cruz, in return for sugar and chocolate. Aiquile is 7850 feet above sea-level.

September 5th. We were in the saddle by 8 a.m., and on for Chinguri and Quiroga, another stage of about nine leagues. Both these places are small hamlets of little importance, the only thing worthy of mention being that at Quiroga, about 7000 feet above sea-level, there are several very large and fine " cañaverales," or fields of sugar-cane, small in height and of slender growth, but said to yield good produce. Cultivation was well carried on, considerable work in aqueducts, channels, and other irrigational requirements having been executed. The corregidor of Quiroga was not so amiable as his official brother of Aiquile, and refused to give me any assistance in obtaining a night's lodging. We therefore looked about the town to shift for ourselves as we best could, and entering the courtyard of the largest house in the place, we found that the owner was absent, and therefore we appropriated the " patio," or central courtyard, to our use, and made up our beds under the verandah, which protected us a little from the dew at night.

From Quiroga to Palca forms the next day's journey of about twelve leagues, mostly through a succession of ravines, the bottom lands being cultivated with sugar-cane and maize, or lucerne (" alfa "), wherever irrigation has been found practicable. At about the middle of the stage the traveller enters upon the course of the Rio Grande, flowing between two ranges of hills, on either of which a road might, with considerable ease, be constructed. Bolivian road-makers, as I have already observed, prefer the bed of a river to its banks, and so the road or track is taken up the stream, crossing it about seven times. The river was rising rapidly as we rode up its course, and I therefore looked out anxiously for a bridge, which is much talked of as a wonderful work of art; but, on getting to it, found that, as is apparently customary with bridges in Bolivia, it consisted of abutments only, the roadway being missing entirely; so we had to ford the river again, the water coming well up to our saddles. This bridge had a suspended road-way on chains, to which so great a sag or curve was given, that during a heavy flood the whole top structure was washed away. The site was well chosen at two points of rock jutting out from the main hills on either side, and approaching each other to within about 100 feet, the foundations for the abutments being so good, that, notwithstanding the badness of the masonry, they had for some years resisted the frequent floods. The Rio Grande, therefore, does not offer any very great obstacle to the formation of a good road to Sucre, which will some day be constructed—that is, when the Bolivians begin to think more of road-making, and improving the interior of their country, than of revolutions. In the rainy season, when the river is full, and, by reason of its extremely swift current, quite impass-able to animals, a " balsa," or raft, worked somewhat lower down the river than the site of the broken bridge, forms the only means of communication. The day's ride terminated at Palca, a small farm, or " hacienda," where, the proprietor being absent, we could get no other accommodation than a bare room to sleep in and fodder for our mules.

The last stage commences at Palca, and ends at Sucre. The ride is a short one of about eight leagues, but on account of the many ascents and descents it is advisable to set out early. We left about 6 a.m., and soon reached the " Cuesta de Jaboncillo," so called from the greasy nature of the earth—apparently a steatite, or soapstone—on which the mules find great difficulty in keeping a footing.

This cuesta, short but sharp in slope, is of no great height; but the next, called " Masa Cruz," rises to about 8550 feet above sea-level, and on the Sucre side falls 1350 feet in about a couple of miles. This was perhaps the steepest hill that I ever recollect riding over; for although the ruling gradient would be only about 1 in 9, or say 11 per cent., many parts of the descent were 1 in 4, or 25 per cent., and in these places it was as much as I could do to preserve my seat in the saddle. A traveller in the interior of Bolivia must be careful to purchase a stout and strong crupper—the best being the native-made ones—to be made fast, by at least three thongs or laces, to as many rings or D hooks at the back of the saddle. These do not gall the mules so much as the English make; but many travellers prefer a breeching and breast-strap, so that they are ready for both ascents and descents.

At the foot of Masa Cruz, on a small plot of flat land, formed at the junction of three large and deep ravines, are a few houses and a flour-mill called " El Canto Molino." Here most of the maize and wheat grown in the Cochabamba districts is ground. It seemed strange that corn should have to be brought all the way from Cochabamba to this place to be ground, and the fact offers a striking example of the difficulties caused by the want of good roads; for, just as Mahomet had to go to the mountain when he found that the mountain could not go to him, so the corn of Cochabamba has to be taken to Canto Molino to be turned into flour, for there only is good material for millstones to be found. It would be almost an impossibility to drag grindstones up the ascents be-

tween the Canto Molino and Cochabamba, but the corn
and flour can be easily carried, and affords remunerative employment to a small army of mule and donkey
proprietors. The machinery of the mill is, as may be
supposed, of very old-fashioned and primitive construction, being principally made of hard wood. The
power is obtained from a vertical wheel, driven by
water led down from the neighbouring ravines.

From Canto Molino the road leads up a ravine
of from 200 to 300 yards in width, with hilly
country on either side offering good sidelong ground
for a road; but here again the road is taken up
the bed of the river, which, from being dry for the
greater part of the year, offers a ready-made road
quite good enough for animal traffic. At Huata,
in this ravine, there is a thermal spring, at which
a bathing establishment, much patronized by the
residents of Sucre, has been built. The spring is
led into a receptacle about twenty feet square by
five or six feet deep, the water flowing constantly
through, so that one can enjoy its delightful temperature notwithstanding the smallness of the bath.
I had no means of gauging the temperature, but
should guess that it was about 75° or 80° Fahr.; and
it is necessary to be rather cautious about exposure
after bathing, as the place being about 8000 feet
above sea-level, changes in the temperature are not
infrequent. Beyond Huata there is a very sharp
cuesta, which rises to 10,000 feet elevation, and
shortly after surmounting the crest of this hill, the
capital of Bolivia, Sucre, or Chuquisaca as it is called
in the Quichuan tongue, comes into view. The first
appearance of the town is' both pleasing and im-

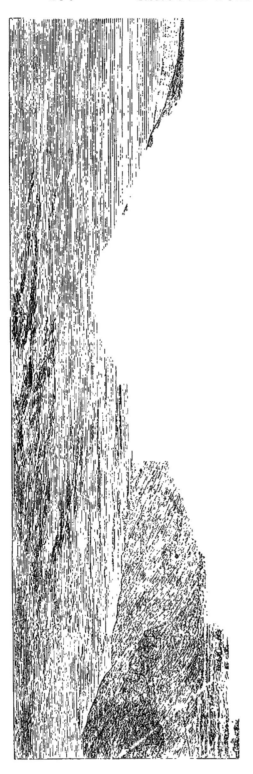

posing, **for** the number of churches, convents, and other large public buildings give an air of importance to the place, which is not maintained upon closer inspection. The country round about is very bare and dull-looking, vegetation being, it may be said, entirely absent from the prospect, as water in the district is very scarce, and only to be met with in the bottom of the numerous ravines, with which the surrounding hills are deeply scored. On the eighth day from Cochabamba I arrived at Sucre, the time usually occupied in travelling between the two places being five to six days; the *détour* that I made, by Totora, occupying two days more than the route by the valley of San Pedro.

## CHAPTER XXV.

THE capital of Bolivia was formerly called "Chuquisaca," which in the Quichuan tongue is said to
mean "River of Gold," but at the establishment of the
independence of the republic, the town received the
name of "Sucre," in honour of Bolivar's celebrated
coadjutor. If General Sucre gained fame by the
nomination, the town certainly lost a pretty name
and received a very commonplace one. Amongst
the Indians and lower orders the prettier title is
preserved, but as amongst the educated classes the
ugly one prevails, I suppose one must, in writing of
the town, follow the lead of the upper ten.

Sucre owes its importance to its being theo-
retically the constitutional seat of the government
of the republic, but as, owing to the frequent revolu-

tions, the government is generally " en campaña," or " on the war path," the other towns, such as La Paz, Oruro, and Cochabamba, have the responsibility of housing the president and his ministers quite as often as the capital. Both Cochabamba and La Paz possess larger populations than the capital, which may be said to have about 25,000 people, who are of very mixed races, ranging from the pure-blooded descendants of the "Sangre Azul" of Old Castile, through the "cholo," or half-breed, down to the Quichuan and Aymará Indians.

There are no manufactures whatever carried on in the town, and but little commerce, the merchants of the district being numerically far below those of Cochabamba, La Paz, or even Santa Cruz de la Sierra. In former years the Indians appear to have been well skilled in the art of inlaying in mother-of-pearl and ivory. Many beautiful specimens of this work, in cabinets, crucifixes, and ornaments, can be seen in Sucre, although they are now becoming very scarce, as travellers have nearly exhausted the stocks, and the art seems to have entirely died out. There are a few well-stocked drapery stores, and a well-managed and completely equipped " Botica Inglese," or English chemist and druggist's establishment, to which is attached an American bar for soda ice-cream drinks and other curiously compounded and consoling beverages, which receive a fair share of the patronage of the young men about town.

It is said that Sucre owes its origin to the proximity of the famous Silver Hill of Potosí, the wealthier miners of that place having chosen it as a preferable place of residence to the cold and bleak slopes of the mineral district of Potosí, from which it is distant about twenty-five leagues. Universities and ecclesiastical establishments were erected, and in the early part of the seventeenth century the town became the seat of an archbishopric and of a supreme court of justice for the Spanish acquisitions in South America, with the titles of "San Arzobispado y Real Audencia de la Plata y Charcas," and jurisdiction from the river Plate up to Alto Peru, formerly the country of the Charcas Indians, a race said to exist prior to the Incas. Most of the universities have been allowed to decline, so that to-day there are but two that have maintained any degree of repute. I did not have an opportunity of becoming acquainted with the routine of academical life in Sucre, but judging by the number of diploma'd men in the country, the acquisition of the title of "Dr." cannot be a very difficult task. In Bolivia, as indeed in most South American countries, one is quite safe in accosting a stranger or chance acquaintance as "Señor Doctor;" and if this be not the right title, then one may try "Mi General," or at least "Mi Coronel."

Churches and conventual establishments abound in the city, but none of them are at all remarkable for their architecture, which is of the plainest possible style, the simplicity being spoiled by a thick coat of plaster. The largest of these edifices, the cathedral dedicated to "Nuestra Señora de la Guadalupe," standing in one corner of the principal square, is a spacious building, the interior of which, on account of its extent, presents an imposing appearance on festival days, when it is filled with a well-dressed congregation. This church must, in very recent times, have been the receptacle of an enormous wealth of jewels and precious metals, poured into its treasury by the successful miners of Potosí. The principal object of value, and of interest to strangers, is the image or picture of " Our Lady of Guadalupe," from whom the church takes its name. The figure is rather more than six feet in height, and is formed in jewels of many kinds, set upon a plate of gold. All the precious stones are of great size and of first-rate quality, but some of the pearls are of especial beauty, advantage having been taken of peculiarities of shape to fashion them into representations of animals or birds, which adorn the virgin's robe. Thus, a pearl about the size of a pigeon's egg, and with a peculiar shape, has, by the addition of a golden head and legs, been made to represent a slender Italian greyhound ; another represents an ox, another a frog, whilst the whole of the figure gleams resplendently with rubies, diamonds, emeralds, and jewels of all kinds. Some authorities set down the value of the image at 2,000,000 dollars, but I think this must be an exaggerated estimate, as probably, had the church been in the possession of such a large amount of convertible treasure, not even the sanctity of the patron saint of Sucre would have saved her from the rapacious hands of some of the adventurers that have occupied the presidential chair. On high festivals the image is carried round the principal squares of the town, under the escort of a procession, including the president and his ministers, the archbishop and his principal clergy, a battalion of infantry, bands of music, and the most important merchants, lawyers, doctors, and gentry of the town. Upon these occasions " Sucre " is *en fête*, fine weather being almost always to be relied upon; the streets are full of people of all ranks and conditions, the gay colourings of the ponchos, shawls, and petticoats of the lower orders affording a lively contrast to the black coats and silk dresses of civilized society.

Besides the rich image of the virgin, the cathedral contains a very valuable collection of vestments and plate, and it is said that a few years ago it possessed twenty-four massive silver candelabra; but President Melgarejo, being pressed for silver to continue the coinage of his bad money (" Moneda de dos Caras"), melted down all these magnificent candlesticks except two, which alone remain to testify of the splendour of the church in former days, and of the ruthless vandalism of a Bolivian in power. The two remaining are about seven feet in height, and appear to be of solid silver. There are also several fine paintings, some of which have been attributed to Velasquez and Murillo; they may be worthy specimens of the masters, but the taste displayed in the exhibition of these pictures in a church is, to say the least, peculiar, as the subjects portrayed are of the most revolting character. One is a representation of the flaying alive of a saint (St. Bartolomeo, I think) : a dreadful picture, with full life-size figures, representing an executioner tearing the skin from the saint's body, while he holds between his teeth the knife which he has been using during his ghastly work. The horridly cool and unconcerned look of the wretch, who goes about his business as steadily as though he were skinning the hide from a dead bullock, is most marvellously painted; whilst the suffering, yet resolute look of the saint, can be more easily imagined than described. Another of these pictures depicts the martyrdom of a saint in a cauldron of boiling oil, another a saint being impaled, and each one of these pictures perpetuates the memory of a dreadful crime that has, at some period of the church's history, either been committed or imagined. The policy of accustoming unreasoning Indians to such scenes seems to be a very unwise one.

The whole of Bolivia may be said to be priest-ridden, but Sucre, perhaps, suffers more than any other place in the republic from the incubus of a numerous and not over scrupulous clergy. Travellers in South America will scarcely need to be told that the Roman Catholic clergy include men of all shades of character; but though I have met many worthy pastors in other countries of the continent, I must unwillingly say, that I cannot recollect having met with any very striking excellence of character amongst the priesthood of Bolivia. Open violation of the vow of celibacy, insobriety, passion for jewellery, fine horses, and other worldly gear, are amongst the most venial of the charges that might be brought against many members of the clergy; so that one is tempted to think that the first reform the country requires is a reform amongst its pastors and teachers.

The streets and squares of the town are broad, and fairly well paved, and the town has altogether a rather imposing appearance, although it is to be regretted that the sanitary arrangements of the municipality should in Sucre, as well as in the other principal towns of Bolivia, be remarkable and conspicuous solely from the utter absence of care or attention to the commonest requirements of our times. The description that I have given of the state of Cochabamba will apply equally to Sucre, and need not, therefore, be repeated. For this reason it is, that small-pox hangs for such long periods of time about these cities, and kills yearly large numbers of the Indian population, who, averse to vaccination in ignorance of its benefits, fall easy victims to this terrible scourge of South American cities. Whilst I was in Sucre this plague was rife, my own servant-boy, the Cruzeño who accompanied me from Exaltacion, falling a victim thereto.

Two sides of the principal square of the town are occupied by the Government House, the Hall of Congress, the Municipal Buildings, and a Barrack. The first, dignified with the name of " Palacio del Gobierno," is a very plainly-built edifice, with interior and fittings of the simplest possible style. Here the president has a suite of apartments, and the several ministers have offices. The " Sala del Congreso," or House of Commons, is arranged after the usual South American fashion, with a " barra," or outer bar, to which the public are admitted without any restriction, except on occasions when the house itself votes a secret sitting. A president of congress, and two secretaries, are elected by ballot from amongst the deputies every month, the president's duties being to preserve order, whilst the secretaries regulate the proceedings and edit the reports of the speeches ; but, as these reports seldom leave the printer's hands until some months have elapsed, they cannot be said to be of any very great value, either to the deputies themselves or to the country. The barra divides the hall into two equal parts, so that when a debate of interest takes place, the public present far outnumbers the deputies, and does not fail to make its presence felt by frequently interrupting the speakers with approving hurrahs for a popular sentiment, or groans, cat-calls, hisses, and other lively expressions of disgust, for one that does not coincide with the mob's whim of the moment. The members of the house generally speak from their seats, but at times the public shout for them to ascend the tribune, as a small pulpit placed at one side of the hall is grandiloquently termed. Two soldiers, armed with rifle and bayonet, standing at the centre of the barra, curb, in some measure, the fury of the mob that at times fills the hall, and protect unpopular deputies from actual violence. During my stay in Sucre, a treaty of boundaries with Chili, which, being very adverse to Bolivia in its terms, was naturally much disliked by a decided majority of all classes, came on for discussion, and at several sittings I fully expected to see a free fight in the Congress Hall. Popular deputies would harangue the crowd at the barra, which would loudly cheer the sentences that sympathized with its patriotic notions, whilst those members who dared to differ from the opinions of the mobocracy were scarcely allowed a hearing. Republican institutions may be acceptable dispensations of Providence to well-settled countries, but

probably a European, visiting the Congress of Bolivia at a stormy sitting, will carry away with him
the belief that the advent of a thoroughgoing
despot would be about the best event that could
happen to the country.  The Bolivian House of
Commons may, however, in one respect, be considered an improvement upon our English one, for
the presence of ladies is not supposed to be a hin-
drance to the proper discharge of the functions of a
deputy.  The ladies of Sucre, instead of having to
hide behind a grating, are accommodated in an open
gallery, occupying a prominent position at one end
of the hall, so that a susceptible deputy may be
animated to oratorical effect by the smiles and appro-
bation of his fair countrywomen.  During the debate
on the Chilian question, several very excellent
speeches were made, and though I was much im-
pressed with the eloquence displayed by many of
the deputies, I could not help especially remarking
the speech of a youthful deputy from Cochabamba,
who, apparently scarcely of age (although he must
have been, or he could not have been elected), spoke
for about three hours, in a style that showed he had
thoroughly mastered his subject ; but doubtless the
presence in the gallery of a young lady to whom he
was paying his addresses, and who was one of the
prettiest girls of the city, gave him courage to offer
his opinions at length to his fellow-deputies, the
majority of whom had, in age at least, a better right
to the title of " patres conscripti."  This question
of settlement of boundaries with Chili occupied
the attention of the Congress for nearly a whole
month, being argued with  much warmth  by the

opponents and supporters of the treaty which the government had made with the Chilian minister, Señor Carlos Walker-Martinez. The final modifications, as agreed to by the Congress, defined the twenty-fourth degree of latitude as the northern Chilian boundary, from the Pacific coast to the highest points of the Andean range, excepting towns already under Bolivian government, such as Antofogasta—not to be confounded with the town of the same name on the coast. This treaty, therefore, reduced the Bolivian coast-line to even less than that afforded by the miserably small slip given to the republic at the time of the partition of the Spanish empire of South America.

A sort of private box is apportioned to the members of the diplomatic body, from which, for some years past, a representative of Great Britain has been missing, Brazil, Peru, Chili, and the Argentine Confederation only, maintaining resident ministers. As long as there was any chance of raising a loan on the London market, the presidents of Bolivia managed to accredit ministers to England, but as soon as it became evident that there was very little prospect of launching further loans, the envoy invariably found that the state of his private finances necessitated his departure from the court of St. James, for the poverty of the treasury of Bolivia is, apparently, so great, that the country is unable to maintain any paid representatives abroad. A misunderstanding seems to have occurred between the last English minister to Bolivia and one of the numerous presidents that have, during the past few years, successively usurped the powers of govern-

ment, the president going so far as to send the
minister his passport; since when, the English
government has declined to accredit any one to the
republic. As this happened some years ago, it
might now be an assistance to a struggling country,
if the recognition of European governments were
afforded by the presence of ministers or consuls.

Politics in Bolivia are best described as purely
personal, for the different political parties seem to
spring up, change, and die out according as some
ambitious leader comes to the front, and soon gives
place to a newer man. During my stay in the
republic I tried to discover whether there was any
difference in the policy of the parties, but, to my
perhaps limited vision, they all seemed embued with
the same creed, namely, either to turn or keep your
adversary out of place and power. One party,
called " Rojos," or " Reds," may perhaps be deemed
" Liberals," whilst another, " Los Oligarcas," may be
supposed to be the " Conservatives "; but it was
difficult to see that either of them had any other
platform than the ruling maxim just mentioned.
The political division was, however, at the time to
which I refer, a threefold one—Quevedistas (Oligarchs), Corralistas (Liberal Oligarchs), and Balli-
vianistas (Rojos, or Radicals). The party once led
by General Melgarejo, a former president, had then
for its chief General Quintin Quevedo, and its supporters were therefore termed Quevedistas. They
were decidedly in a minority, but their activity and
good organization, aided by the unpopular course of
action taken in the disputes with Chili by the party
in power, enabled them to commence a revolution

which very nearly succeeded in placing General Quevedo at the head of the country. However, the old adage of "many a slip, etc.," is very applicable to the fortunes of revolutionists ; and the final result of Quevedo's enterprise was that he had to seek a refuge in Puno, where, I regret to hear, he has since died. There are rumours that he was poisoned, and

GENERAL QUEVEDO.

*(From a photograph taken at Cochabamba.)*

it is quite probable that this means of breaking up the party may have been resorted to, for by Quevedo's death only could it have been entirely defeated, all his followers being greatly attached to him. He was universally looked up to as the future president, and his career ′ seems to have been singularly free from the faults that have, with few exceptions, been recorded of the rulers of Bolivia.

The " Corralistas " were led by Dr. Casimiro Corral, minister of home government and foreign affairs under the presidency of General Morales, and seemed to me to embrace the most talented men of the country. This party was, however, singularly unfortunate, not being popular with the lower orders. Its leader had to expatriate himself to the town of Puno, which, together with Tacna, seems to be the refuge of disappointed Bolivian revolutionists. The government of the day did not, however, come out of the dispute with Dr. Corral with any great *éclat*, as they gained a very bloodless victory over the gallant doctor and some of his adherents, who, to the number of about twenty, were holding a conference in the doctor's house at La Paz on a certain evening in September, 1874. The meeting probably was a political one, but there was no immediate danger of a disturbance of the public peace from the fact that politics were being discussed. However, the government determined that the assembling of a caucus opposed to their own *régime* was a movement that must at once be suppressed *vi et armis*, so they sent a general in command of a company of infantry, with a field-gun, which they loaded with grape shot and laid point blank on Dr. Corral's front door. Then, after a flourish of bugles, the general summoned the doctor and his friends, mostly young men, to surrender, and upon their declining to open the said front door, the cannon was discharged, and a way made for the entrance of the soldiers. Then, whilst part of the troop fired from the street at the

closed windows, the remainder entered, firing upwards through the floor, so that the gallant doctor
and his adherents were exposed to a curious style
of cross-fire. Of course, resistance was out of the
question, and Dr. Corral, with about half a dozen of
his friends, after being well buffeted by the soldiery,
and after witnessing the sack and destruction of the
contents of the house, were marched off to the
military prison, where they remained until they
could raise sufficient funds to pay their jailers for
conniving at their escape. Occurrences such as
these are very frequent in Bolivia, notwithstanding
that it is supposed to enjoy the free liberty of republican institutions.

The third party in Bolivia has been in power for
about three years, and therefore has had a long term
of office, although it has hard work to keep its place.
The terms " Rojos," or " Reds," and " El partido
Ballivian " are somewhat indiscriminately applied to
this section of public opinion, which includes many
independent members, as well as many of the supporters and co-political religionists of the lately
deceased President Don Adolfo Ballivian. At the
time I write of, it was nominally headed by Dr.
Tomas Frias, who was apparently far too old to be
at the head of a turbulent republic, and he was
evidently only a puppet in the hands of his able
minister of " all work," Dr. Mariano Baptista, one of
the cleverest men Bolivia has ever produced. However, Dr. Frias and his " alter ego," Dr. Baptista,
have lately been jockeyed out of the reins of government, and exiled from the country by an unprin-
cipled adventurer, one General Hilarion Daza,

whose advent to power must universally be allowed
to be the greatest misfortune that could possibly
have happened to the republic. He commenced
life, I have been credibly informed, as a "mozo,"
or waiting-boy, in the house of an Englishman in
Sucre. He was then a tailor for a short time,
after which he became fired with military ardour,
and, joining the army, his audacity and unscrupu-
lousness made him so useful to his first patron,
General Melgarejo, that he passed rapidly from the
appointment of "full private" to that of "general
of division." Arrived at this position, he took the
earliest opportunity of deserting his benefactor,
and selling himself and his battalion to General
Morales, after whose death by the hand of his
son-in-law, Daza became generalissimo of the army,
and subsequently minister of war to President
Frias. Being thus practically in command of the
republic, he soon usurped the supreme power, for
notwithstanding that at the commencement of the
last Quevedistic movement he voluntarily took an
oath to support the civil power of the state, exemplified in the person of Dr. Frias, he so manipu-
lated matters that poor old Dr. Frias was driven
into exile, and the quondam "mozo" installed himself at the head of the republic. Of all the adventurous careers recorded in the annals of South
American republics, Daza's, when written on
history's page, will perhaps stand out as the most
glaring instance of successful perfidy and audacity.
The secret of his success is, however, easily discovered, and proves how little suited are republican
institutions to countries which, like Bolivia, contain

such a mixture of races that adventurers are never at a loss to find elements of discord ready to be set in action against the respectable portion of the community. Daza, throughout his career, made it his study to keep one battalion of soldiers, well clothed, fed, and paid; the result being, that whilst the soldiers talked loudly of their "country," they really served their chief, who thus had unlimited power at his command. The finances of Bolivia have generally had to be balanced by means of forced loans or contributions; but whether the treasury had or had not the wherewithal to pay the salaries of the ministers and the employés of the various departments, it had, somehow or other, to find pay for the first battalion; and on the shoulders of this battalion, composed entirely of uneducated Indians, Daza has ridden to the presidential palace. Installed in power, he seems, however, to be endeavouring to conduct himself in somewhat more civilized fashion than when he was a simple general of division, for one of his principal supporters (an Englishman) tells me that he rules his countrymen excellently well, and that, as to his moral character, whereas he was formerly drunk *every evening*, he now only allows himself to be thus overcome on *three nights in the week.* Let us hope, therefore, that he will go on improving in respectability until, if he stays in office long enough, he becomes a model for South American presidents. But to what a pitch of degradation must the country have sunk, when a man of Daza's antecedents and character is elevated to the seat once honoured by occupants such as the great liberator, Simon Bolivar, and his famous coadjutor and friend, General Sucre.

A great deal of the time of the Congress, which, I believe, only sits for two or three months in the year, is always taken up in considering new schemes, which speculators are continually bringing forward with the object of breaking up Bolivia's isolation from the civilized world. Not that I would by this be understood as saying that I consider the republic to be outside the pale of civilization but, hemmed in, as she is, by the Andes and her neighbours, Peru and Chili, on the west, and by the impenetrable swamps and morasses of the yet unexplored Gran Chaco on the east, she may with truth be said to be so secluded as almost to form a small world of her own, and will continue to do so until the magnificent route of the Amazonian watershed is accepted as the natural inlet and outlet of trade. In the Congress of 1874 most of the schemes for which new concessions or renewal of old ones were being sought, were connected with the opening up of the eastern side of Bolivia. On the Pacific side, the only enterprises are connected with the silver mines and nitrate deposits of the desert of Atacama—a district so rich in minerals, that alone it should be sufficient to form the basis of the well-being of its fortunate owners, the Bolivian nation. From La Paz many efforts have been made to conduct the trade of Bolivia, by the lake of Titicaca and Puno, to the Peruvian seaboard, but up to the present time little has been done except the granting of concessions for projected railways, although a couple of steamers have with great trouble been carried up to and launched on the lake.

The applications for concessions on the eastern

side were four in number, all having for their object
the construction of roads across the unknown territory which separates Bolivia from the river Paraguay.
One scheme which met with a good deal of favour
in Sucre, was started by a Señor Antonio Paradiz,
who obtained the renewal of concessions granted so
long ago as 1853, for the construction of a cart-road
from Santa Cruz, *viâ* Chiquitos, to a port on the
Paraguay, to be called Port Vargas, and to be situated about 180 miles below the Brazilian port ot
Curumbá. The projector of the enterprise estimated
that with about £60,000 he could complete his track,
establish a rural colony at the port, and place two
steamers, a schooner, and sundry lighters upon the
river. He secured the right to all duties that might
be levied at the port, for a period of eight years.
But the scheme has doubtless fallen through, for
poor Señor Paradiz lost his life in his patriotic
endeavour to open up a new trade-route for his
country, being killed by savages in 1875, while
ascending the river Paraguay, exploring for a good
situation for his proposed Port Vargas.

The second scheme was propounded by Señor
Miguel Suarez Arana, a Bolivian gentleman of good
family. He proposed to construct two cart-roads.
one from Santa Cruz to an undefined port on the
Paraguay, and the other from a town called Lagunillas in the Cordillera to the same undefined port,
This *concessionnaire* asked for two-thirds of the
duties to be created at the proposed port, for a
period of forty years, together with tolls, premiums,
and other special advantages ; but nothing was done
in the matter by the Congress, and doubtless the
scheme remains on record as a project only.

The next scheme was one brought forward by one Captain Greenleaf Cilley, a retired commander of the United States navy, who had married in Buenos Ayres a lady descended from one Oliden, who received a concession of lands from Bolivia nearly fifty years ago, and whose name is still recorded on all the maps of the republic. These lands are high and well-suited for the cultivation of coffee or cocoa, and Captain Cilley hoped to be able to attract emigration to them, if he could obtain a concession for a railway and funds wherewith to construct it. He therefore asked for a concession to construct a railway from Santa Cruz to the territory of "Otuquis," on the upper waters of the river of the same name, an affluent of the river Paraguay, and in which the Oliden lands are situated. The length of this proposed line would probably be not less than 300 miles, and Captain Cilley, who estimated the cost of construction at £8000 per mile, asked for a guarantee of seven per cent. on the expenditure, and for two leagues of land on either side of the line. But even Bolivia was not reckless enough to promise a guarantee on such an enormous capital, and this scheme has also gone to the region of cloudland.

The fourth and last scheme was "invented and arranged" by Dr. Reyes Cardona, some time minister to the court of St. James, and to the Brazilian court at Rio Janeiro. This enterprising statesman proposed a colossal scheme of railroads, commencing at Bahia Negra on the Paraguay, crossing the deserts of Izozo to Santa Cruz, and thence passing by Sucre on to La Paz. The doctor wrote pamphlet after pamphlet and paper after paper concerning the merits of this vague scheme, but the only settled idea that he seemed to have was to seize the funds belonging to the Madeira and Mamoré Railway. In what part of the grand scheme of internal railways for Bolivia the fund was to be spent did not appear to be of much consequence, so that it was handed over to the doctor, to be dealt with as his much-vaunted " honor, talento, y patrio-tismo " should direct.

These numerous and spasmodic efforts to obtain an outlet for trade in an eastern direction, made by Bolivians themselves, prove satisfactorily that the proper route for the commerce of the country is acknowledged to be one that shall lead to the Atlantic Ocean. Whether this route should be down the Paraguay or the Amazon is, in my opinion, sufficiently well determined in favour of the latter river, whose affluents spring from the richest slopes of the republic, and flow through its most fertile plains. Whatever opposition there is in Bolivia to the opening of an eastward trade route, is kept up by a small minority of interested parties, principally some of the leading merchants of La Paz and Tacna, who see in the success of the eastward route a break-up of the monopoly of trade that they have so long enjoyed, and a consequent probable diminution of their profits. Another influence re-tarding the development of the trade of Bolivia, is the jealousy that exists between the principal towns, and which, instead of finding vent in a healthy com-petition of trade, occupies itself with any sort of project calculated to hinder the legitimate progress of one town or province above its neighbours. The Paceños are, as a rule, very jealous of the growth of Cochabamba, and of the importance that will accrue to that town from the opening of an eastward route; and many of the deputies of the La Paz provinces have systematically voted against enterprises whose realization would improve the condition of the eastern provinces: but in the Congress of 1874 three deputies, Dr. Belisario Salinas of La Paz, and Señores Roman and Merisalde of the Yungas of La Paz, deserve to be mentioned as having emancipated themselves from these narrow ideas, preferring to assist in the general development and welfare of their country, rather than restrain their efforts to the benefit only of their own immediate provinces.

One of the most talented ministers that the republic ever possessed, Don Rafael Bustillo, writing to the Brazilian government in 1863, described in forcible language the position of his country. "Bolivia," he wrote, "occupies a territory entirely central in the vast continent of South America. She has but five degrees of latitude on the Pacific Coast, and even this is disputed, in part, by the Republic of Chili. (This five degrees has been reduced to two and a half by the treaty of 1874, and one almost certain result of the war now being carried on by Bolivia and Peru against Chili, will be that Bolivia will lose all her seaboard; for if Chili prove victorious, she will certainly annex the whole of the desert of Atacama, whilst if Bolivia and Peru succeed in their ill-advised enterprise, Bolivia will probably have to cede the same much-coveted territory

to Peru in payment for her assistance.) Bolivia
is seated upon the masses of silver of the double
range of the Andes. She has a territory fertile
beyond measure, where the treasures of the most
opposite climates are grouped together. With all
this, Bolivia perishes from consumption for want
of methods of communication which may carry to
the markets of the world her valuable productions,
and stimulate her sons to labour and industry."
These words, which forcibly depict the condition and
requirements of the republic, are almost household
words in the country; yet, although they are well
known and thoroughly appreciated, the interests of
the monopolizing merchants of the Pacific seaboard
have hitherto been powerful enough to preserve the
isolation of Bolivia, which they have only allowed to
be communicated with through their narrow toll-
gates of Arica, Tacna, and La Paz. The only certain means of providing efficient modes of transport
for the, at present, useless riches of the country, lie
on its eastern side, for nature has declared that the
route to Europe shall not be a western one; and the
navigation of the Madeira and Amazon Rivers, when
the railway of the rapids is completed, will offer a
more speedy and economic transport than can be
afforded by any scheme having the river Paraguay
for its basis. In regard to time, the Madeira and
Mamoré Railway can with ease despatch its freights
from the port of San Antonio to Europe in twenty-
eight days or possibly less, whilst the Paraguayan
route from Bahia Negra to Europe will occupy at
least forty. In reference to cost, the Madeira and
Mamoré Railway offers to carry a ton of freight from

the centres of Bolivia to the markets of Europe for
£15, whilst the lowest estimate by the Paraguayan
route was that of £26 per ton, proposed in 1858 for
the navigation of the Vermejo.

Another reason for the present deplorable condition of the country may be found in the absolute
non-existence of any financial talent, or even ordinary knowledge of national account-keeping amongst
the ministers and officials in power of late years.
This has been thoroughly exposed in the matter of
the loan raised in London in 1872; and if the short-
comings of the officials of the finance department
are not to be set down to want of knowledge, they
must be charged to want of candour or straight-
forwardness.   In the financial accounts for 1873
the debt appears as 8,500,000 Bolivian dollars, or
£1,700,000, the correct nominal amount of the loan;
and although no notice is taken of the operation of
the sinking fund, which by the end of 1873 had
paid off a first drawing of £34,000, there is in the
estimated outgoings of the treasury a credit taken
for the service of a loan of £2,000,000.

The national receipts at the time the country
gained its independence amounted to 2,500,000 of
hard dollars, and in 1873 were as nearly as possible
of similar amount, being 2,566,034 Bolivian dollars,
or say £513,207, showing clearly the state of stag-
nation in which the country has vegetated during
its fifty years of independence.   In the same year the
minister of finance declared a required expenditure
of 3,660,679 dollars, or say £732,135, thus showing
a deficit of £218,928; and, nevertheless, the minister
did not propose to Congress any plan for equalizing

the national accounts; whilst it is a fact that in the Congress of 1874 not one proposal, either financial or political, except the treaty with Chili, emanated from the ministry. In the ministerial statement of the national finances, or budget, for 1874 one sees at a glance that there is no effort made to equalize income and expenditure, for not much more than £20,000 per annum is got from the Bolivian people by any kind of direct taxation.

Customs' rentals cannot be expected to increase until the completion of the Madeira and Mamoré Railway creates new entries on the eastern side of the republic, for Peru only can benefit by any growth of commerce on the western side, having stipulated with Bolivia that it shall only pay her £81,000 per annum out of the receipts of the port of Arica. It seems certain, therefore, that direct taxation must be resorted to, and as there is no individual poverty visible in the country, there is no reason why the government should not be able to show easily a fair balance-sheet, which should meet the current wants of the nation, and provide honourably for the service of the public debt.

It is not, perhaps, too much to say that the realization of the joint enterprises of the Madeira and Mamoré Railway, and the National Bolivian Navigation Company, will change the entire character, not only of the eastern provinces of Bolivia, but also of the republic itself; whilst, at the same time, the Brazilian provinces of Matto Grosso and the Amazons will be most materially benefited. It may, in the case of Bolivia, seem absurd to say that its mineral wealth can ever appreciably decrease; and,

certainly, such an assertion must, to any one that
has passed over the highly metalliferous districts
of Potosí, Oruro, and the whole central plain of
the country, appear entirely groundless; but the
examples of California and Australia teach us, that
though mineral discoveries are the first cause of the
creation and settlement of new countries, it is the
development of their agricultural and industrial
resources that causes them to take rank amongst
the nations of the world : and this it is that Colonel
Church's enterprises will do for Bolivia, for there
can be no doubt but that their realization will place
Bolivia in the foremost rank of the republics of
South America. No scheme that has for its object
the opening-up of the country on any other sides
than its northern and eastern can effect this result;
for there alone exist immense plains and tracts of
country suitable for any kind of agriculture or
cattle-rearing. On the western side, the barren
and inaccessible heights of the Andes forbid any
attempts at settling, while the southern and eastern
territory of the Gran Chaco is a cheerless swamp,
never capable of affording a home to other than
the irreclaimable savage, or the wild animals of the
fast-decreasing forests of the continent.

Few, perhaps, are the enterprises that can hope
to create and unfold such vast industries as those
found in the districts to be benefited by the opening
of the Amazonian route to the interior of the conti.
nent; for as the traveller descends, in an eastward
journey, from the barren summits of the Andean
Mountains, he will find that the railway will prove
the outlet, not only for the mineral riches of

Bolivia, her wools, hides, and other animal products, the cinchona bark (cascarilla), and other
drugs, dyes, and commercial values of her unexplored forests, but also for the agricultural riches
that already exist in considerable scale on the
descending plateaux of her eastern plains. At altitudes of 12,000 feet, barley and potatoes are grown ;
at 9000 to 6000, corn, potatoes, apples, pears, and all
kinds of fruits ; at 6000 to 2000, coffee, coca, cocoa,
and plantains ; and from 2000 to the plains, cocoa,
plantains, sugar-cane, maize, mandioc, arrowroot,
yams, tobacco, and other tropical products. The
republic, therefore, in addition to the speculative
allurements of mineral wealth, can hold forth substantial inducements to the breeder of stock, or
the tiller of the soil; and there is no doubt that
the character of the people will improve when,
through facilities of communication, remunerative
work is afforded them, for Bolivians, whether of
Indian or Spanish extraction, are very industrious,
differing greatly in this respect from the inhabitants
of many other countries of South America.

Politically considered, the enterprise will be of
vast benefit to Bolivia, for her population will find
employment in the impetus given to commerce, and
will consequently become less turbulent, as revolutions will decrease commensurately with the interest that each one will find in their increasing
prosperity. A bond of unity will also be created
for Bolivia, with her powerful neighbour Brazil,
whereby she will be rendered more secure from the
encroachments of the republics of the Pacific seaboard.

The results, financially considered, will be, that a trade, equal, if not superior, to that now carried on through the Peruvian towns of Tacna and Arica, will be created on the eastern side of the republic; and from the custom's receipts of this trade, Bolivia would have far more than sufficient to keep up the service of, and rapidly pay off, both her internal and external debts. Taking the year 1873 as a guide, we find that the imports through the port of Arica amounted to £1,422,369, and the exports to £860,607. Of these figures, three-fourths of the imports, or £1,066,766, and £842,345 of the exports, fairly belong to Bolivia, making a total of £1,909,121 in value of Bolivian commerce that passes through Peru. The duties arising from this trade may reasonably be averaged at twenty per cent. of the gross value, so that Bolivia annually affords Peru a rental of more than £381,000, out of which she magnanimously grants Bolivia a subsidy of £81,000. That Bolivian commerce is not decreasing is proved by the fact that the exports of Arica for 1874 exceeded those of 1873 by nearly a million hard dollars, or about £200,000. These statistics sufficiently account for the opposition offered by the parties interested in the above trade to the opening-up of the Amazonian trade-route. (See Appendix, p. 400.)

Bolivia is generally supposed to have rather more than 2,750,000 inhabitants; the above figures give, therefore, an average trade of about 14s. per head per annum, and it is not unreasonable to suppose that a similar amount of trade will soon be carried over the Madeira and Mamoré Railway. The loan of 1872 demands an annual service for interest and sinking fund of £136,000, and the gradual payment of the other debts of the country would require about £120,000 more. This total requirement of £256,000 would, in a very few years, be provided by the custom's duties collected on the eastern route, for the amount is not equal to three-fourths of the duties shown to be received by Peru from Bolivian commerce.

Bolivia would still have the Peruvian subsidy, the profits received from sale of the nitrates and guano of the desert of Atacama and islands near the Pacific coast. These sources of revenue, together with the departmental rentals, would more than suffice for the general government expenses and the improvement of her internal means of communication. It is not, therefore, too much to say that the realization of the Madeira and Mamoré Railway may be made the means of materially changing and improving the present deplorable financial and political situation of the republic. It is, however, hopeless to expect that the men in power should have sufficient foresight or courage to enable them to foster such an important and promising scheme of progress for their country. No, the policy of the so-called *statesmen* of Bolivia is the short-sighted one of self-interest, and because the realization of Colonel Church's enterprises would not be attended by immediate pecuniary advantages to themselves, they have of late years placed every possible impediment in his way. Fortunately for the masses of the population, Colonel Church has proved himself to be of sterner and honester metal

than Bolivian statesmen are made of, and has refused bribes innumerable, offered him with the
view of tempting him to abandon his enterprise,
and leave the Bolivian people to the mercies of their
gaolers of the Pacific seaboard; and so the country
will, in spite of its leading men, probably receive
the immense benefit of communication with Europe
by the Amazon River within a reasonable time. I
can only hope that Colonel Church may be spared
to a long life, during which he may reap the due
reward of his steadfastness of purpose and integrity
of motives, by seeing the development of the country, which will then hail him as its best and truest
friend since the days of the great liberator Simon
Bolivar, who may be said to have given it independence or birth, while Colonel Church will
have given it lungs, through which to breath the
invigorating stimulus of intercourse with the civilization of Europe.

The labours of a Bolivian Congress generally
last about sixty days, and for the rest of the year
the president and his ministers reign supreme.
The closing of the house is celebrated by a procession of the ministers, who, led by the president,
and escorted by a body-guard of soldiers, go from
the Casa del Gobierno to the Sala del Congreso,
where they are received by the members, standing
and uncovered. By the way, Bolivian deputies,
though representatives of a land of liberty, are
not allowed, as our members are, to wear their
hats in the House, but have to leave them in the
lobby. The president, arrayed in a gorgeous
uniform of dark blue, embroidered heavily with

gold lace, begirt with a tricoloured scarf round his waist, with a tricoloured plume in his cocked hat, gives the spectator a curious notion of re_ publican simplicity. On every state occasion the president is immediately preceded by the national flag, which is, perhaps, the prettiest flag to be found (barring, of course, our own Union-Jack). It is composed of three colours, yellow, red, and green, arranged in three wide parallel bars; and I have heard it said, that the three colours were adopted to typify the green earth, and the rising and the setting sun, the founders of the republic wishing their Indian population to believe that their country included the whole of the world.

At the ceremony of closing Congress in November, 1874, Dr. Tomas Frias, the reigning president, who was, I believe, upwards of eighty years of age, carried himself right royally, and read his speech to the deputies with quite as much *hauteur* as a crowned monarch might be expected to employ. He was answered by the President of the Congress, who congratulated the members upon the termination of their labours, which, as far as I could discover, had consisted mainly of squabbling amongst themselves and vilifying the government. The result of their labours soon proved to be disastrous in the extreme, for the country was again in revolution within less than a fortnight after the closing of the session. If the members could have agreed together upon a ministry to replace the then existing one, peace would have been preserved; but though the majority worked well together in abusing all who were then in office under Dr. Frias,

U

they could not at all agree as to their successors. Under these circumstances the government encouraged the Congress in wasting time in fruitless recriminations and discussions until the closing day came, when, as the deputies were anxious to return

PRESIDENT FRIAS.

(*From a photograph taken at Cochabamba*).

to their respective districts before the rainy season should set in and render the roads impassable, they easily succeeded in hurrying a short bill through the house, giving them powers to raise a revenue equal to that of the previous budget. The government were thus masters of the field, but were not left in peaceable possession very long, for as Daza's battalion, which was then in Sucre, was the only one that had received any pay for many months, the other battalions, termed the second and third, then stationed near Cochabamba, took the opportunity of the return of General Quevedo from Congress to revolt and declare him president of the republic, *vice* Frias, to be deposed in due course. It is quite possible that Quevedo thought the second and third battalions were not strong enough to fight " Daza's Own; " but, anyhow, he refused to head the proposed revolution, and endeavoured to induce the revolted troops to remain quietly in their barracks, promising to represent their claims to the government at Sucre. But Daza, seeing an opportunity of ridding himself of one of his probable rivals for the presidency, managed to get the government to decree that Quevedo had incited the soldiery to rebel. He then made a declaration of steadfast attachment to Frias, and marched to Cochabamba to put down a revolution which would never have existed but for his violence. This was his programme, but his real object was to get Quevedo into his power, succeeding in which, he most probably would have had him shot without any trial; indeed, it was currently reported that he had said publicly that he would do so. This threat coming to Quevedo's knowledge, made him pause while on his return to Sucre to lay the complaints of the soldiery before the government, and obliged him to take measures to secure his own personal safety. His partisans, in various parts of the republic, then very unwisely rose in his favour, and attempted to take possession of Oruro and Cochabamba; but, as they were very badly armed, totally undisciplined, and almost entirely without leaders, they were soon beaten and dispersed. There was a good deal of desultory fighting, and a number of the revolutionists, under a Dr. Miguel Aguirre, entrenched themselves in Cochabamba, where they were attacked by President Frias and General Daza. Daza's star was, however, in the ascendant, and though the besiegers were driven to great straits for ammunition, so much so that if the Quevedistas had attacked vigorously they must have been victorious, after about a week's fighting the revolutionists withdrew, and left the city in the hands of Daza, who shortly after followed up his victory so rapidly, that near La Paz, at the battle of Chacomo, the revolutionary party were utterly defeated, their leader, Quevedo having to fly to Puno in Peru, the usual sanctuary of losers in the political struggles of Bolivia. This crushing defeat of the revolutionists, who included partisans both of Quevedo and Corral, ought to have had the effect of firmly establishing the civil power of the state, exemplified in the person of the venerable President Frias ; but Daza, who had probably fermented the rebellion even while he combated it, would not be satisfied with a settlement that did not fully realize his ambition. Revolution therefore again raised its hydra-head; and Daza, making terms with a Dr. Oblitas of Cochabamba, one of the most unscrupulous partisans of Quevedo, soon drove poor Dr. Frias from the country, and reaching the summit of a Bolivian's aspirations, installed himself in the coveted presidential palace. Here we will leave him, hoping that the reports which have reached England of his changed demeanour now that he has obtained the supreme power, have some truth in them, and that his country, as I fear it will, may not progress, land-crab fashion, backwards to the miserable state of tyranny and oppression under which it groaned and suffered in the times of Belzu and Melgarejo.

# CHAPTER XXVI.

The Prado of Sucre—Belzu's Rotunda—The President's evening constitutional—Personal politics—Quevedo's birthday banquet—Dancing
with the general—Ball at the Chilian Embassy—Baile caramba!—
Environs of Sucre—La Paz not visited on account of revolution in
progress—Routes to ocean and home—Santa Cruz, Curumbá, and the
Paraguay—Oran and the Vermejo—Tarija and Cinti—Cinti wines
and spirits—Cobïja and Desert of Atacama—Silver mines of Caracoles, etc.—Encroachments by Chili—Official report on the Desert of
Atacama, published by the Government of Chili—Description of the
road to Tacna and Arica commenced—Preparations for journey—
Servants and their pay—"Postas"—Buying and selling mules—A
few requisites for a land journey.

BEFORE leaving Sucre notice should be taken of the
public gardens here, called the " Prado," although in
other towns the gardens are generally termed
"alamédas." The prado occupies a very fine site
on the outskirts of the city, and might, with a slight
amount of judicious expenditure, be made an exceedingly beautiful recreation-ground. The site slopes
gently downwards from the city to a ravine, and an
attempt at hanging gardens has been introduced, but
the idea has not been fully developed, the poverty or
apathy of the municipality having allowed the whole
affair to remain in an unfinished state. Notwithstanding this, I must allow that some little care has
been bestowed in the way of beds of flowers, gravel
walks, and seats, etc., so that the prado of Sucre has

not such a melancholy look as the alaméda of Cochabamba, which was entirely deserted and neglected by
the authorities of that town. During my stay in
Sucre, I, at the request of a friend, designed a plan
for completing the prado ; and presented the drawings
to the municipality, who acknowledged my labours
by a courteous letter of thanks. The designs were
framed and placed upon the walls of the council
chamber, but I soon found that there was not public
spirit enough in the august body of councillors to
carry out the work, although the cost would have
been trifling, considering the improvements that
would have been effected. I have no doubt that my
plans are still hanging on the wall, a memorial of
labour thrown away ; but as I was only *en route*
through the city, I had no intention of making
profit out of the execution of the work, and
probably as there was no scope for making a job out
of it, the apathy of the councillors is easily accounted
for.

At the bottom of the prado is a rotunda, erected
by General Belzu, to commemorate his escape from
the bullet of an assassin, who attacked him at that
spot whilst he was enjoying his evening stroll. By
the way, this evening stroll, or one may almost call
it "parade," of the president, seems to be an established institution in Sucre, for every evening the
venerable Doctor Frias, followed by two aide-de-
camps, was accustomed to take his daily constitutional. General Quevedo, who was looked upon as
the probable future president, was also in the habit
of taking exercise about the same time, but as he was
only a candidate for the presidency he was not able

to have a military escort, although he never lacked a goodly following of the younger members of his party; and on Sunday evenings and fiesta days, it was quite amusing to see the parade of the different political sets. On these occasions a visitor had frequent opportunities of observing that the rancour and ill-feeling that existed between the several parties was evidently not caused by differences of political feeling, but rather by personal hatred; for any chance that occurred of offering a slight insult one to the other, such as occupying the centre of the path, or the best seat, was eagerly made use of, and on several occasions I quite expected to see the pocket revolvers drawn and made free use of; certainly, if fierce looks could have wounded opponents, they were freely given and returned. I have mentioned before that politics in Bolivia are purely personal, and in the case of the Quevedistas I can quite understand why they were so, for a more amiable and pleasant man than General Quevedo it has rarely been my lot to meet. I remember well the anniversary of his birthday that occurred on the 31st of October, 1874. His friends then gave him a supper at his lodgings in Sucre, and it was very pleasant to see the zeal with which every one present joined in doing him honour by toasting him in champagne while it lasted, and afterwards in bitter beer. After the banquet a number of speeches followed, some of which were exceedingly eloquent, though, perhaps, a trifle too bombastic in style. This part of the ceremony over, the company could not separate without further testifying its enthusiasm by an impromptu ball; but, as it was a bachelor's party, this part of the entertainment promised to become rather slow, until the general got on his feet to acknowledge the good feeling of his entertainers by dancing a " baile suelta," or Spanish dance, with each one in succession. At home we should, perhaps, fancy it rather a queer proceeding on the part of one of our leading statesmen, if after their whitebait dinner, or other friendly gathering, they were to perform a Highland fling or hornpipe with each of their political supporters, but in Bolivia it is quite *en règle* ; and as in Rome one must do as the Romans do, I joined with great gusto in the ceremony, and had the honour of specially trotting out the general in a grand *pas de deux à l'Anglais.* As the company present were all of one political colour, the utmost good humour prevailed, and notwithstanding the absurdity of the affair, I think we all enjoyed the evening thoroughly.

Talking of dancing reminds me of a very different affair that took place whilst I was in Sucre, when the Chilian minister gave a splendid ball at his residence to celebrate the treaty of boundaries that by skilful diplomacy he had obtained from the Bolivian Congress. The house tenanted by the minister was the property of the Melgarejo family, and, as is usual in the best buildings throughout not only Bolivia, but most Spanish South American countries, was built in the form of a square enclosing a handsome " patio," or court, which was roofed in with awnings for the occasion ; while the side walls being decorated with flags and a profusion of lamps, the effect of the whole was very charming when " the lights shone o'er fair women," for the *élite* of

Sucre were present, the fair Chuquisaqueñas coming out very strong both in numbers and in quality. The rest of the quotation as to the "brave men," is perhaps best omitted, although the Bolivian race bears a high reputation for courage amongst South American people; indeed, there is a story current, that after a battle in Peru in which the Bolivians succeeded in capturing the entire Peruvian army, the Bolivian commander had the Peruvians formed up in line, when, placing his own band of music in the front, he ordered the unfortunate prisoners to dance to the tune, exclaiming "Baile caramba!" and the story goes that the Peruvians obeyed the strange order rather than be shot down by their conquerors. I could never obtain exact information as to the date or place of this occurrence, but every Bolivian firmly believes it to have happened, so much so that the words "Baile, etc.!" accompanied with an offensive expression, are universally used in depreciation of the Peruvians; but a traveller's idea of Bolivian bravery would, I think, be that it is rather of a Falstaffian order, "much cry and little wool."

To return however to our particular "baile," altogether about 500 people were present, and the evening was a great success, although at one time it ran great risk of coming to an untimely end, owing to the imprudence of the chief of the embassy, who, possibly elated by his diplomatic victory, aided, perhaps, by the exhilarating effects of Clicquot and Mumm, so far lost his balance as to inform one of his fair partners, a lady of one of the best families of the town, that she was an angel, but that she had married a brute of a husband. This pleasant remark was unfortunately overheard by the happy " brute," who very pluckily at once reclaimed his bride, and having placed her under the protection of her mother, he sought the Chilian, and challenged him to immediate mortal combat out in the street. Mutual friends intervened to prevent the further progress of a dispute that looked ugly enough, and dancing being kept up with vigour matters quieted down. The next day the Chilian apologized, and although the gossips of Sucre kept the squabble alive as long as possible, nothing more came of it.

Beyond the public buildings and conventual establishments to which I have already referred, Sucre offers nothing of interest to a traveller, who, unless he has business to transact or friends to visit, is likely to make his stay in the town as brief as possible, for although the climate of Sucre is almost as good as that of Cochabamba, its environs do not offer any special attractions for short excursions. The only places near that are worthy of notice, are Huata, which has already been described, and where the thermal spring repays the visitor's trouble with a grateful and welcome bath. On the road to Potosí, a ride of about a couple of hours brings one to a village called Nutschucc, where the wealthier inhabitants of Sucre have built their " quintas," or country residences. The road goes out on the south side of the town, and, as usual, is taken up a ravine, which at the time I rode up it had a good deal of water, in places reaching to the horse's girths.

But this being on my way to the Pacific, and my business in Bolivia being completed with the close of the Congress, I may continue the description of my journey, first premising that at Sucre a homeward-bound traveller will probably determine which route he will take towards ocean and home. My business engagements rendering it of the greatest urgency that I should arrive in England with as little delay as possible, I chose the shortest land journey *viâ* Potosí, Oruro, and Tacna to Arica on the Pacific coast. I greatly regretted having to leave Bolivia without visiting La Paz (which is the first city of the republic in regard to commerce and population, although politically second to Sucre), but owing to the revolution having made its head-quarters there, it was impossible to find " muleteros " that would expose their animals to the risk of being taken either for the service of the revolution or of the government, so that I was forced to give up the idea of visiting La Paz, and must therefore refer intending travellers to other writers for a description of that city.

In deciding upon the route, the first consideration will be whether the traveller wishes to reach the Pacific or Atlantic Oceans. Should he desire to avoid either the land transit over the Panamá railway, or the bad weather so prevalent in the Straits of Magellan, his course will be directed to the Atlantic. As I have before stated, the best route to this ocean is down the Madeira and Amazon Rivers, but if our traveller has arrived in Bolivia by ascending those rivers, he will be anxious to see new worlds, and will steer his course either for the Paraguay or the Vermejo.

Should the former river be chosen, the traveller

must, from Sucre, make his way to Santa Cruz de la Sierra, from which town there is a track running through the villages of the Cordillera to Curumbá, a Brazilian town on the western bank of the Paraguay. From this place there are occasional steamers trading up and down the river, by which Asuncion can be reached, and from thence to Buenos Ayres there is a regular service. This route involves a land journey of about 850 miles, being about 300 from Sucre to Santa Cruz and 550 from thence to Curumbá. A straight line from Sucre to Curumbá would be under 500 miles, but there is no known road running direct between the two places; and in 1875 a Bolivian Commission, sent for the purpose of opening up a track, returned without success, having been unable to attempt to cross the lagoons and swamps of Izozo. The road *viâ* Santa Cruz is a well-known one, and in fairly dry weather presents no obstacles that a good mule cannot overcome, the principal difficulties being those presented by a journey through sparsely inhabited districts almost entirely destitute of resources for a traveller, who must therefore depend upon his own animals and what he can carry with him in provisions, bedding, and other requisites. Arrived at Curumbá the rest of the journey to Buenos Ayres would probably be a very pleasant one, navigating down the magnificent river known above Corrientes as the Paraguay and below as the Paraná and Rio de la Plata.

If the Vermejo route be attempted, a land journey of about 400 miles to Oran, *viâ* Potosí, Cinti, and Tarija, must be undertaken, and from

Oran, I have been informed, canoes can be obtained for Corrientes, a distance by river of about 900 miles. The land journey is a rough one, as it passes over a very mountainous country, but probably a traveller would find more resources *en route* than by the Santa Cruz and Curumbá line. Both Cinti and Tarija are places of considerable trade, and the former is specially noted for its wines and spirits, which find their way, not only all over Bolivia, but into the neighbouring republics of Peru and Chili. The Cinti wines are very excellent in character, and compare very favourably with ordinary wines of Portugal or Spain, whilst the "aguadiente de ubas," or "strong waters of the grape," of Cinti is far preferable to the greater part of such spirits as gin or common whiskey and brandy, and is quite equal to the best white rum of the West Indies or the best "Pisco" of Peru. In Sucre and Cochabamba this spirit is called "cingani," and costs ten reales, or 4s. 2d. per bottle, whilst the Cinti wine of fairly good quality costs half that price for the same quantity.

There is a route to the port of Cobija, the only Bolivian seaport on the Pacific coast, but the entire journey from Porco to Cobija, being through a perfectly deserted country of most mountainous and barren character, should not be undertaken unless the traveller has special reasons for visiting the desert of Atacama with its silver mines and "salitreros," or nitrate deposits.

The department of Atacama has been a constant cause of envy to Chilian adventurers, and consequently, for many years past, frequent disputes as to the boundary line have occurred; but these have now been settled for a time by the treaty made in 1874, to which I have already referred, and by which the astute Chilian minister Don Carlos Walker y Martinez succeeded in transferring about sixty miles of coast-line from Bolivia to Chili. This was a most serious loss to Bolivia, already almost land-locked, but doubtless the Chilians will not be content until they have gained all the Pacific sea-board available, and have united their territory to that of Peru at the river Loa, thus entirely isolating Bolivia from free communication with the Pacific. The unfortunate internal dissensions of the Bolivians assist the Chilians greatly in their efforts to absorb the whole of this rich mineral district of Atacama, but as the Chilians are a far more enterprising people than the Bolivians, one can scarcely regret that such a rich territory should become the property of a people capable of developing its resources. For information upon this part of Bolivia an inquirer should procure a work entitled " Ten Years in South America," written by Benjamin S. Dingman, an American engineer, and published by Messrs. Trübner and Co. The following remarks on the desert of Atacama are therein found, and as I had no opportunity of visiting the district I may perhaps be excused for making the following quotation, as being the best testimony available to me of the richness of this part of Bolivia. The volume devoted to Bolivia opens with an account of " the Caracoles silver mines which were discovered in 1870 in the desert of Atacama, by Don José Diaz Gana, whose innumerable explorations have been the means of

opening an extensive horizon to the capital and
industry of Bolivia and Chili.  It appears that Diaz
Gana, not being satisfied with the result of his
explorations on the borders of the desert, sent a
part of his company to the interior to explore some
mountains where he had reason to believe some rich
veins of ore would be found.  His envoys, Saavedra,
Mendez, Porras, and Reyes, arrived at the table-
land which serves as the base of those beautiful grey
mountains.  Reyes, climbing up the easy slope,
picked up loose pieces of silver where now are the
Merceditas and Deseada mines, and continued
picking them up in different directions, not knowing
their value, but thinking possibly they might be of
service.  Later on he joined his companions, who
had also found loose pieces of ore, and had made
marks in the lead with their knives.  Two of them
immediately started to the coast to inform their
patron.  They had been to Diaz Gana what Sancho
Mundo was to Columbus.  The discovery was made,
and that dry and solitary desert a short time after
was the centre of an active population.  Diaz Gana
baptized that emporium of riches ' Caracoles,' for the
fossils characterizing the lias were abundant, and as
a matter-of-fact man he fixed upon this notable
geological formation to give a name to his discovery.
The young Chilian Francisco Bascunan Alvarez is
another of those untiring explorers who have helped
to convert the desert into a field of industry and
labour.  After long and laborious explorations in
Copiapo, Bolivia, and Catamarca in 1857, he returned
to the desert in 1870 and discovered in Caracoles
the group called Isla on account of its topographical

position. The mines are from 10,000 to 15,000 feet above the level of the sea, and among the richest may be noted the Deseada, Merceditas, Flor del Desierto, Esperanza, San José and Esmeralda. Then there are the Federico Errasurig, Sud America, Salvadora, and a host of others, some of great promise, others worth little or nothing. The experiments made by men of science resulted in the encouragement of all kinds of enterprises, and Caracoles soon became an immense field of speculators disposing of large capitals. The merchants of Chili, both native and foreign, were the founders of these companies, the stock of which was sold at fabulous premiums. In Caracoles fortunes were made in a day, and not insignificant ones either, but of millions. But in this, as well as in other pursuits of life, all cannot have the same luck, and thousands went there only to bury their fortunes and their bones also in their vain search for the hidden treasures."

After the celebration of the treaty whereby the boundary line between Bolivia and Chili was fixed at the 24th parallel of latitude, the government of the latter republic lost little time in commencing to utilize the treasures of the desert which would probably remain undeveloped as long as they were in Bolivian hands. A commission of exploration was sent under the auspices of the government, and the results obtained are given to the world in a pamphlet whose objects are therein thus set forth : 'The Chilian government, desirous of rendering aid to private enterprise, has sent thither two commissioners, one for the purpose of discovering the natural sources of wealth existing in this desert and now hidden from view, and the other to study the means of affording ready access for those who may be engaged in the work of bringing its produce within reach of the markets of the world." The pamphlet is entitled " Nitrate and Guano Deposits in the desert of Atacama; an account of the measures taken by the government of Chili to facilitate the development thereof," and was published by the Chilian Consulate in London.

With these few remarks upon the routes from Bolivia to the ocean, I will take up the description of the road *viâ* Potosí and Oruro to Tacna and Arica. In preparing for this journey a traveller should engage a servant who knows the road well; and there are plenty of handy fellows always on the look out for such service. I was to be accompanied to England by the son of an old English resident in Bolivia, a young lad who was being sent to England to complete his education, so that we required two servant boys, as we had, what with baggage and saddle mules, too many animals for one boy to look after properly. My companion's father sent with us as his son's factotum, a very handy Argentine gaucho who was most useful on the road, as he thoroughly understood the management of the mules and their pack apparatus, which, if not kept in good order, is sure to give the travellers endless trouble. I selected one " Juan de la Cruz Peña," a man from the province of Valle Grande, who had made the journey several times, and turned out a very fair servant, although he was not nearly so handy with the animals as the Argentine " Marco." A fair sum to pay one of these men for the journey from Sucre to Tacna is forty-five pesos, about £7, and he will want his food, or a payment of two reales (9*d.*) per day in lieu thereof. A mule must be provided for him, and he will generally find his own saddle, bridle, and sleeping-blankets.

Occasionally arrieros, who are going down to Tacna with minerals from Potosí or Oruro, and returning to Sucre with European goods, will undertake the carriage of a traveller's baggage on some of their spare animals ; but it is scarcely safe to trust any of these gentry, as they are quite likely to leave your baggage anywhere on the road wherever their animals may break down ; and as they always require pay before they start, it is not a very safe proceeding to trust one's belongings to them.

"The Posta" is an institution that I have only met with in Bolivia, and if it were properly worked, it would be a great assistance to travellers in a country where there are scarcely any roads ; but the government in this, as in every other branch of the public service, seems to look only to the one end of making as much as possible out of it. As soon as a revolution is over, the ministers who have installed themselves in Government House, call for tenders for farming the " postas " between the principal towns of the republic. The successful contractor having paid to the government the purchase price of the contract, is supposed to supply a sufficient number of mules for the post-houses on the route he has contracted for. These postas are generally about four to six leagues apart, and a few Indian huts are found in their neighbourhood. The contractor sells to these Indians the right of carrying the travellers and their baggage ; and screws as much as he can out of them for the transfer of the monopoly of the work between each station. The tolls are fixed by the government, and the corregidor of any town will furnish the traveller with a " guia," or list of the postas and the tolls to be paid per mile between each of them. The rates vary slightly, according to the situation of the posta, but are generally from two to two and a half reales per mule per league, which would be about 3*d.* to 3½*d.* per mile ; and this price includes the services of an Indian in charge of the animals. Of course, the Indians, who have to pay heavily for the privilege of working the posta, provide wretched animals, whilst the government contractor, who rarely, if ever, visits the route, but lives either at La Paz or Sucre, never troubles himself as to whether the post-houses are kept in good condition, and supplied with sufficient and proper animals.

Between Potosí and Oruro there are very fair post-houses, in which, in times of peace, baggage mules can be depended upon from post to post ; and if one can be sure that everything connected with the posta is in good working order, and that there is no probability of a revolution coming on, this becomes a very good plan of getting over the road quickly and economically ; but you must take your own saddle animal, for it is simply impossible to ride the rough posta mules.

About buying mules for a journey in Bolivia many opinions prevail ; for some people think it best to buy low-priced animals, so that the loss in

selling upon arrival at one's destination may not be
great; but I think that loss is better avoided by
purchasing good animals, which, although costly,
are more likely to find a buyer at a good price.
There is, however, great difficulty in selling animals
in Tacna, for after such a long journey it is almost
impossible to avoid their arriving in poor condition;
and then the arrieros of Tacna, knowing that the
traveller is obliged to leave for Arica and the ocean
steamer, conspire together and refuse to give anything at all like a proper price for the animals,
alleging their condition as rendering them valueless. Good mules are, however, certain to pass
through the trials of the road better than low-priced
and weedy animals; they therefore are likely to
find a buyer, as there are generally travellers for
Bolivia looking out for a good mount for their
journey. For ours we had to provide eight animals,
namely, four good saddle mules, three for baggage,
and one spare one that could take its turn either
under saddle or pack, as required. This last we
found a very useful assistant, as, when a sore back
or lameness occurred, we thus had means of freeing
the injured animal from its burden until recovery.
The saddle mules cost from 150 Bolivianos, or pesos
fuertes (4s. 2d. each), up to 400, the highest price
being for a very fine " macho," or he-mule, belonging
to the father of my young *compagnon de voyage*, Don
Alfredo. This macho, a beautifully marked grey,
standing perhaps fourteen hands in height and pro-
portionately well built, would always command a
high price, as, on account of his great strength, he
was capable of becoming a "pianera," or carrier of

dianos over the Andes. This task appears to be the highest test of strength for a mule; but I have been told that an animal seldom makes more than three journeys under the burden, as the third essay of the herculean feat appears to break down the poor beast's constitution entirely. The profits to an arriero on the transport of a piano from Tacna to Bolivia are so great that he could almost afford to slaughter his mule at the termination of a successful journey, and thus spare the poor brute a repetition of the dreadful ordeal; for the weight of a piano is fully equal to two ordinary mule burdens. Our baggage mules were bought in Oruro, costing from 80 to 120 Bolivianos each, and whilst all the saddle mules arrived in Tacna in fair condition, we found notwithstanding our having a spare animal, and all the care that we could exercise, the trials of the road were so great, that the four cheaper-priced animals finished their journey in such a bad state that we found ourselves only able to realize but a small portion of their cost. The saddle mules could, however, have been easily and well sold had we not been under engagement to send them back to Bolivia with the servants; and, after the double journey, those that had to be sold realized very nearly their cost price. Certainly my experience is, that it is cheaper in the long run to buy first-class animals only.

For a journey over the Andes, a traveller must provide himself with a good poncho as well as a good overcoat, for the early mornings and the nights are sometimes very sharp and cold. A waterproof sheet, that will come well over the shoulders and fall over the pommel of the saddle, is also not at all to be despised, as nothing is more objectionable than to get one's knees thoroughly soaked in some of the heavy rain storms that are frequently encountered at all seasons of the year. It is a good plan to carry a cot that will fold up into a small compass and lay between the two packs of a baggage mule; a mattress and blankets are also necessary; whilst it is as well to have a mosquito bar with one, as, in case of being obliged to pass a night in the open, it will be found very useful in keeping off the heavy dew.

For eatables, a sheep can be purchased on many parts of the route for about a dollar; so that, with mutton or a fowl, a good chupe can be made at the postas, if one's servant has any idea of cooking it. A few tins of green peas or carrots help one to do without the dreadful " chuño," which is the only vegetable obtainable; and, above all, some Liebig's extract of meat should be carried, as it is a most welcome addition to the cuisine. A little coffee, tea, and sugar should also be taken, and then one is independent of the keepers of the "pulperias" attached to the postas. At these shops bad bottled ale can be bought at prices varying from four to eight reales (1s. 8d. to 2s. 2d.) the small bottle; but it is well to avoid this as much as possible, and carry with one some of the best Cinti cingani, which is a safe and wholesome beverage when used moderately. I have found it excellent when taken with a dash of Angostura bitters, a bottle of which forms a very acceptable addition to one's baggage. The following are some of the retail prices in Bolivia of things useful for the journey.　Tea, three pesos, say 9s. 4d. per pound; coffee six reales, 2s. 3d. per pound; brandy (Martel's) two pesos and a half (7s. 10d.) per bottle; tinned meats, such as paté de foie gras, etc., three pesos (9s. 4d.) each; tins of sardines, four pesos (12s. 6d.) per dozen.

Before starting, a traveller should be very careful to see that all the pack saddles of his mules are complete and in good working order, otherwise he will suffer endless annoyances on the road.　An " aparejo," or pack-saddle, with " reatas " (hide ropes), " cinchas " (belly-bands), " sogas," (head-ropes), " caronas," skins for placing under the saddle to preserve the mules' backs from injury, and every necessary, costs from fifteen pesos to twenty, say £2 6s. 8d. to £3 1s. 8d.　A good " tapa-carga," or cover for the baggage, costs about nine pesos, or, say £1 10s.　The best made in Oruro are an entire hide, roughly dressed, with the hair on, cut square and bound with white leather curiously pinked out into quaint patterns.　A small handy set of shoeing tools, a few shoes, and a supply of nails should be carried; and attention to these minor details of a journey will save much trouble, as, when all appliances are in good order, the stages of the road pass by pleasantly enough, and the travellers arrive at the posta which marks the end of the day's work in good temper, inclined to do good justice to whatever is forthcoming for the nightly repast, after which the thoroughly earned rest is heartily enjoyed both by masters, men, and animals,

# CHAPTER XXVII.

MY homeward journey from Bolivia was commenced
on the 22nd of December, 1874, when Don Alfredo
and I left Sucre, accompanied by Alfredo's father
and three other English friends, who formed the
entire British community, and who very kindly
escorted us for a few miles on our way, so that
we might be fairly started with a hearty English
farewell and good wishes for a successful journey.
About four o'clock in the afternoon we rode out, in
number eight horsemen, making quite a commotion
as we clattered through the roughly paved streets of
the town.

That evening we only intended to ride as far as

the village of Nutshucc, where we had been invited
to pass the night at the house of Doctor Calvo,
formerly minister of justice and public education.
Nutshucc, distant about three leagues from Sucre, is
a place of resort of the principal residents of the
capital, who have built themselves country residences,
termed " quintas," or farmhouses, but which are
generally much more pretentious than farmhouses in
our own country.  A smaller village, called Yotala,
which lays between Sucre and Nutschucc, is a small
and slovenly-looking place, in which chicha making
and drinking appear to be the principal occupations
carried on.  Between Yotala and Nutshucc there are
some well-built quintas on either side of the road,
several of which have substantially-built retaining
walls round the grounds, to protect them from the
scour of the floods, which even at the time we rode
up the ravine, in many places reached up to the
girths of our animals.  One of the finest of these
quintas belonged to Señor Arturo Arana, a successful
miner, who had made a large fortune out of the silver
mines of Huanchaca.  In contrast to this really fine
house was a little den in course of erection by
Don Tomas Frias, the then president of the republic,
who was having a most curious little box, about
sixteen feet square and three stories high, built as
his place of refuge when seeking relaxation from the
cares of state.  The fact that the president was
building himself a country residence was so much
talked of in every town of the republic, that I had
expected to see quite a palatial edifice, or at least a
building as imposing as many of the quintas of the
rich mine-owners of Bolivia, or some of the mansions

built by the Melgarejo family during the presidency
of the general of that name; but if all Doctor Frias's
requirements were on as limited a scale as his
country house in the Cachimayo valley, the country
could not have suffered much from him personally,
Yet, although he was a man of most modest and un-
ambitious desires, his minister of war, Daza, made
up in show and extravagance for his leader's
economy.

At Nutschucc the ford of the river Cachimayo,
which must be crossed by travellers to or from
Potosí, is very frequently impassable  On the Sucre
side stands the handsomest villa residence in Bolivia,
the property of Don Gregorio Pacheco, who, I
believe, has also made his fortune in silver mining,
which seems to be the only occupation in Bolivia
that leads to affluence.  The house is well built, of
stone, with a stucco front, having a spacious corridor
supported on well-proportioned pillars; the whole
arrangement being very comfortable, and the owner
is proud of it accordingly.  On our arrival we found
that the Cachimayo was coming down in flood, we had
therefore to leave our animals at Señor Pacheco's,
and cross the river, about eighty yards in width, in
a basket bridge, the property and invention of Señor
Pacheco, and therefore universally considered to be a
most marvellous and clever enterprise.  The river is
spanned by a stout rope hawser, about three inches
in diameter, supported on either bank by a tripod of
poles, well guyed down on every side.  Under the
tripods are placed drums, turned alternately by
manual labour, as it is required to cause the basket
to cross over from side to side.  The basket is slung

from roughly-cut wooden pulley wheels, which work
on the hawser, but as the whole affair is of the
roughest workmanship and materials, the motion is
so jolty and erratic that the occupant of the basket
is generally sea-sick before getting half-way over the
stream, while the chances are that the hauling ropes
break down during the passage, when the *voyageur*
is left in mid-air and mid-stream until he can be
rescued from the unpleasant position by an acrobatic
performance of an Indian, who has to go out on the
hawser with a new hauling rope.

Nutschucc is considered a very charming place by
the Chuquisaquenos, who think it the height of
luxury to be the owner of a quinta in the narrow
ravine of the Cachimayo; but although it is pretty
by contrast to the dreary plain in which Sucre
stands, I did not think it at all equal to some of the
environs of Cochabamba. The hills on either side of
the Cachimayo ravine are of a shaly rock, which
crumbles down in regular slopes with a uniformly
dull and heavy look, that quite take away any idea
of the picturesqueness which the valley might have,
were the rocks of a more solid character. My
experience of the place was not altogether pleasant,
for on my first visit there I was taken with a severe
attack of ague-fever, probably the last lingerings of
the usual ill effects of a stay amongst the rapids of
the Madeira River, and which the damp climate of
Nutschucc brought out. This illness came upon me
whilst visiting the Calvo family, and I was greatly
indebted to the extreme kindness with which I was
cared for during the three days upon which I was
too weak to attempt the return journey to Sucre;

but kindness and hospitality are, I must say, the rule in Bolivia, for in all my travels through the country I only remember one house, already mentioned, where I was treated with anything but the greatest courtesy and friendship. This good account of Bolivians, refers, however, only to those of Spanish descent, for the Indians, both Quichuans and Aymarás, as a rule, especially in the small villages and at the post-houses, are brutish and rude in the extreme, and even the offer of ready money payment will not, in some places, procure for a traveller fodder for his animals, or a few simple necessaries for himself.

However, to continue the journey, our animals, which had remained the night at Señor Pacheco's, were the following morning, the floods having abated, ridden across the ford; and at early dawn, having been fortified with a cup of coffee, we started on our way, intending to make Quebrada Honda our resting-place at night, as this forms the first stage between Sucre and Potosí. Leaving Nutschucc, which I make to be about 8000 feet above sea-level, the road lays up a very narrow quebrada, or ravine, at the head of which a steep ascent, or cuesta, called El Cruzero, has to be ascended to a height of nearly 9000 feet above sea-level, from whence the track rapidly falls again, until, after passing a small village called Calara, the river Pilcomayo is reached. The altitude has then fallen to about 7000 feet, and the river, which flows through a valley about a mile in width, in flood-time is impassable; but we were able to ford it easily, carefully avoiding some very treacherous-looking quicksands that were dotted about the river bed. A short distance above where we crossed, the valley narrows considerably, and there is high ground on either side of the stream. The track would conduct one to the ruins of a bridge which has been built over the Pilcomayo, but the road bed of the structure was in such a rotten condition, that the arrieros do well to trust themselves to the chances of the ford rather than risk falling through from the bridge into the river. On either side of the ravine are patches of cultivated land, watered by "azequias," or irrigation channels, led from the necessary distance up the stream.

Leaving the Pilcomayo, the road again ascends a cuesta, at top of which are the stations of Terrado and Pampa-tambo, at an elevation of 9850 feet above sea-level. These are not good places to stop at, being small farms and not regular "postas," so we kept on our road, which crosses cuesta after cuesta, until we arrived at a deep and wide ravine, called Quebrada Honda, where we intended to stay the night, at a post-house in the bottom, having travelled about twelve leagues during the day. The general elevation of the country has somewhat increased, the summits of the hills on either side of the ravine being about 12,000, whilst the post-house in the bottom is about 11,200 feet above sea-level. At this place we had great difficulty in getting the public room opened for us, and were refused forage for our animals and food for ourselves, under the plea that the owner of the house was from home; but by a slight display of firmness, and a few hints as to the great importance to the government of the business upon which we were travelling, we got the Indians in charge to produce the keys, and open the room appropriated to the use of travellers. For barley in the straw, which is the fodder generally given to mules in this part of the country, we had to pay four pesos per quintal, or about 13*s.* for a bundle supposed to weigh 100 lbs. Our-servant boys managed to get themselves some chupe, made from dried mutton and chuño, whilst Alfredo and I supped off some cold provisions which the kindness of our friends in Sucre had provided for us. The temperature at night was low enough to make the use of blankets desirable, and as the post-house was new and clean, we passed a good night, and rose betimes, intending to get to Potosí before nightfall if possible.

Starting soon after six o'clock on the following morning, we made good and rapid progress. Ascending the cuesta on the Potosí side, there is nothing noteworthy on the road until, at about a league and a half from Quebrada Honda, some small lakes are seen in a plain surrounded by high hills. These drainage pools of water are a common feature amongst the Andean ranges, and are many of them situated at very high altitudes, those we passed to-day being at about 11,750 feet above sea-level. They are very shallow, and cattle were walking across them at pleasure, whilst several couple of ducks and some teal were on the margin of the water, together with numberless " gabiotas," or tern, which rose up screaming at being disturbed from their work of searching for worms in the wet sandy mud over which the track passes. About mid-day we arrived at Bartolo, a small and miserable village, at which the traveller should arrange to stay as short a time as possible, for the dust and dirt of the place are intolerable. We refreshed ourselves with our cold provisions, and a bottle of ale from our travelling larder, whilst our " mozos," (servant-boys) indulged in copious draughts of chicha mascada, which horrible beverage is the only drink purchasable at Bartolo. Riding hard all the afternoon, we arrived at Potosí about half-past six, just as night was closing in, having done fourteen leagues and a half in the day's journey. We were so fatigued that I did not care that evening to present a letter of introduction that my German friends in Sucre had given me to their correspondent in Potosí, so we made straight for the best tambo in the town, called the " Tambo Artéche." This tambo is a very large building, forming a square, with yards for the animals at the rear. The square has galleries on every side, and reminded one of some of the old-fashioned inns of home. We got a very good room off one of the galleries, and after partaking of some poached eggs and chupe, procured from a " fonda " near by, were very glad to see our cots put up, and to have the prospect of a good night's rest. This tambo was one of the best that I recollect in my travels through Bolivia, but the only accommodation afforded consisted of an empty room for ourselves, and the use of a yard, or " corral," for our animals. For the former we were charged six reales, say 2s. 3d. per day, and this sum was the sole demand made upon us for the use of the hotel, as we only had to pay for the barley that our animals consumed, and nothing at all for their safe custody, so that if the entertainment offered a traveller at a Bolivian tambo be small, the charges are moderate in proportion. Barley was the same price as at Quebrada Honda.

The next day was Christmas Day (1874), and we rose up to so cold, clear, and bright an atmosphere, that I might well have fancied that we were in Old England, especially as snow had fallen during the night, and lay thick on the courtyard. Soon after rising I experienced an unpleasant sensation in the throat, which caused a feeling of faintness, and was said to be the effect of the sickness called "soroche," that attacks all new comers to Potosí. It is not, however, a specialty of the place, but the effect of the high altitude, and is not felt so severely by travellers passing from the interior of Bolivia to the Pacific, as, in consequence of the more gradual nature of the ascent, probably their lungs have time to adapt themselves to the rarified condition of the atmosphere. Persons arriving from the Pacific are much more exposed to the bad influences of this sickness, and several fatal cases are recorded of almost sudden death amongst new comers direct from westward. The first symptoms are giddiness and vomiting, and sufferers are advised to lie down at once, or at all events cease any kind of exertion. The scent of ammonia and garlic are said to be good remedies; whilst the use of spirits is advocated by some, but by others considered to be sure to bring fatal consequences with it. My own personal experience was that a moderate quantity of spirits, taken at the first feeling of faintness, arrested its progress; but the balance of opinion is so entirely against the use of alcohol by sufferers from soroche, that I would be loath to place my single evidence in the scale. The Indians aver that their favourite stimulant, coca, is a complete preservative, and some recommend the addition of a mouthful of snow or ice to the " chew."

The soroche did not, however, prevent our feeling the want of a good breakfast, so we left our tambo and proceeded to the Fonda Coca, a very decent and clean little restaurant near by, where we had a very nice mutton chupe, with eggs poached in it; some so-called beef-steaks, which were hard

EL CERRO DE POTOSÍ.

and greasy; a very good bottle of Cinti wine, and some coffee. The charge for this breakfast for two was eleven reales and a half, or about 4s. 10d., a sum which was certainly not unreasonable. We then strolled out to see the city, which is built at an elevation of about 13,500 feet above sea-level, at the foot of the magnificent Cerro de Potosí, an immense white-capped cone, whose summit is probably more than 2000 feet above the city, the most interesting in Bolivia, having at one time a population of probably over 200,000, but now only being able to boast of about a tenth of that number. The famous Cerro, which might well be termed the "Silver Hill of Potosí," has in times of recent date yielded immense stores of treasure, and was doubtless the principal source of Spain's former great wealth. Whilst the mines were workable without machinery the profits derived from them must have been enormous, but even the seemingly fabulous riches of this hill of silver will not tempt speculators to attempt the impossible, and try to drag powerful pumping engines over the Andes from the Pacific to Potosí. Consequently the output of mineral has so decreased that the population has emigrated or died off, and the greater part of the city is in ruins, which standing desolate and forlorn on the barren hill-side, only serve as a monument of the departed activity of the place. The city has also suffered more from revolutions than any other in the republic, having been a continual bone of contention between opposing factions, many of the houses bearing marks of the severity of the struggles of which they have been the silent but suffering witnesses. Some few interesting remains of former prosperity may still be seen, the twisted columns of the façade of the church of the "Matriz" are marvels of architectural effect, and the reservoirs for the storage of the water supplying the power for the stamping-mills constructed during the time of the Spaniards, show that though the Spanish government was a despotic one, it designed and carried out works that its republican successors

seem quite unable to match, for I do not recollect
to have seen anywhere in Bolivia a single public
institution that has been erected since the War of
Independence, saving some paltry-looking " cuartels,"
or barracks, of which there are two or three to
every town ; whilst churches, convents, colleges, and
other buildings, dating back before the war, are
seen in every city of importance.

The streets of Potosí are very narrow, the houses
very old-fashioned, much smoke-begrimed, and
blackened with the accumulated dust and dirt of
years; for although water is laid on from the
reservoirs for the supply of the town, its use seems
to be avoided as much as possible. This fear of
water may be the result of the constant coldness
of the climate and the piercing winds which
are seldom absent from the bleak heights of the
Andes. The Indians all have a dreadfully un-
washed look about them, and their places of public
resort, such as the " recoba," or market-place,
are perfect pig-sties. The principal object of
interest in Potosí is the mint, where is to be
seen the only steam-engine at work in Bolivia.
The machinery was made by a Philadelphian firm
of engineers, and, being under the superintendence
of Americans, is kept in very fair working order,
the coins struck being very good impressions, though,
as the feeding is done by hand, many of them
come out in incomplete shape. This machine was
set up by General Melgarejo, who is said to have
pressed on its erection as rapidly as possible, in
order, probably, that he might lose no time in
flooding the country with his abominable base

coinage. He certainly would not have taken so much pains and trouble with any other enterprise; for it is said that the beams for the stamps were dragged by oxen all the way from the forests of Tucuman, and considering the numerous hills and ravines that have to be crossed between Tucuman and Potosí, one may say that Melgarejo is to be credited with a considerable achievement, even though the object he may have had in view was a rascally one. The coinage that has been struck recently, consisting of Bolivianos, or dollars, of 4s. 2d. value, half Bolivianos, reales, and medio reales, is of first-rate quality, and is so much sought after by the Indian population that it has been found extremely difficult to keep pace with the demand, the Indians of Bolivia having the propensity, in common with all other uncivilized peoples, of burying their earnings, and they are cunning enough not to bury the bad Melgarejos, but only the good new money. The Quichuan Indians apparently do not care much for ornaments, such as bangles or armlets; the women wear a kind of spoon-headed pin, made of silver or baser metal, according to the wealth of the wearer. These pins, or skewers as they might more properly be termed, seem to do the double duty of pinning up a shawl or head-gear, and of being used as spoons in the consumption of chupe and chicha. The women are also fond of amassing as many different coins as possible, and attaching them to a knitted bag, which they use as a kind of market purse. These " murchilas," as they are termed, are often covered with silver moneys of all sizes and nationalities, and some very rare old Spanish coins

may thus be met with by amateurs who will pay
the owner a good price in current money.

Among other curiosities worth looking for are
the "mechas," and "yescas," or tinder-cases and
steel-strikers, for which the town is noted. Some
of these yescas are true works of art, the engraving
being executed in good style; whilst many of them
are inlaid in gold on hard steel in a wonderful
manner. The "mechas," or tinder-cases, are also
very nicely designed and executed, in silver or
gold, and together with the steel-strikers form a
good memorial of the cleverness of the art-workers
of Potosí.

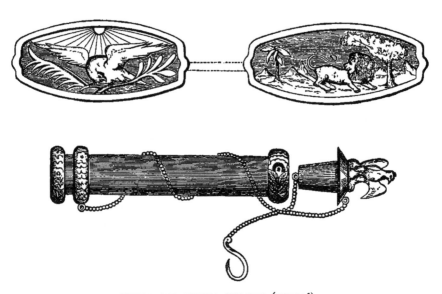

YESCA AND MECHA HOLDER (POTOSÍ).

There does not seem much *immediate* future
for the mining interests of Potosí, although it is an
undoubted fact that the Cerro still contains in-
exhaustible supplies of silver ore, but none of the
old levels and shafts can be worked, nor can new

ones be sunk advantageously, without heavy pumping machinery, which it is practically impossible to carry up from the coast. But, at some future day, when railways shall have opened up the interior of Bolivia, these mines will again become valuable; but even then, the mines of Oruro and Huanchaca, and others located in the central plains of the republic, are much more advantageously situated for purposes of export than the deposits of Potosí. A great drawback to successful mining in these regions is found in the total absence of fuel for smelting purposes, as the forests that once existed in the lower ravines of the metalliferous districts have been entirely exhausted, and no discovery of coal has yet been made, or is, perhaps, likely to be made, within a reasonable distance for transport.

We remained a couple of days only in Potosí, perfecting our arrangements for the next stage of our journey, namely to Oruro, a distance of about 200 miles. Three of the baggage mules that we brought from Sucre had been hired only, at the rate of fifteen pesos each, and we had to decide whether our onward march should be continued with hired animals, or whether we would chance finding the posta in good working order. For hired pack mules to Tacna, the end of our journey, we were asked sixty pesos each, with the condition that we should find forage on the road; thus, probably the three animals we required would have cost us altogether about 250 pesos for the trip, whilst, travelling posta, the same number of animals ought not to cost more than about half that sum: we therefore decided to risk it, especially as we were assured in

Potosí that the posta to Oruro was in excellent
working order.   I was very glad to get away from
the town, for the climate did not seem to suit me,
as I had a return of my Nutschucc experiences of
ague; and on the 27th of December, a Sunday
morning, having arranged that the posta mules
should be at the tambo by 6 a.m., we should have
started early had we not been delayed by the
absence of one of our mozos, who had been indulging too freely over-night.   It seemed that we were
fated to suffer delays and difficulties, for soon after
starting I was again attacked with a fit of ague and
vomiting, which came on so severely that on
reaching a small village called Calamarca, scarcely
a league out of Potosí, I found myself quite unable
to proceed, and had to dismount at a small and
horridly dirty chicheria, where I was allowed to lie
down in a corner on some mats and rugs.   After
taking warm water to aid the vomiting, and going
through the regular stages of cold shivers and
burning heat, I managed to get half an hour's sleep,
and rose up sufficiently recovered to be able to
mount my mule again.   In consequence of this
delay we made but a very poor day's work, and only
got as far as Tarapaya, distant about five leagues
from Potosí.   On our road we met the posta
Indians returning with their mules, and they informed us that they had left our baggage in charge
of the " maestro," or keeper of the posta at Tarapaya, and they told us that we should be sure of
getting animals there for the next stage to Yocalla.
We were much pleased with the celerity with which
the muleteers of the first stage out had done their

part, and thought that it augured well for our onward progress ; but, alas, on arriving at the post-house we found our baggage placed in an empty room with open doors, and not a living soul about the place. The village was about half a mile away from the post-house, so Alfredo went on with the mozos, to buy barley for our saddle mules, some supper for ourselves, and engage baggage mules for the next day's work. The speed shown by the Indian muleteers from Potosí was now explained, for they feared that had we arrived at Tarapaya before they had left, and found no animals ready to take us on, we should have forced them to wait till the following day, and carry our baggage the next stage to Yocalla and they would thus have had double duty to do, so they hasted to return that they might pass us on the road and shirk their work by telling us the flattering tale that other animals were in readiness for us. As travellers have to pay for the first stage out of a town before starting, and at double the rate of the other stages, they are exposed to such tricks as the one played upon us ; and as we had paid the maestro at Potosí, we let the fellows pass us, thinking all was right. However, I congratulated myself that our baggage was safe, and had a nap until Alfredo returned with the eatables and fodder, but with the doleful intelligence that no mules could be got without sending on to Yocalla, four leagues ahead. I am afraid that we made some rather hard remarks upon our friends at Potosí, who had so strongly advised us to travel posta, for had we agreed to pay the price asked by the arriero who offered us animals for Tacna, we should have been independent of the tricks of the Indian post-boys; however, we had our supper, and turned in, hoping that our troubles would be confined to the first day only.

The next day we started Marco, the gaucho, on to Yocalla, to return as quickly as possible with baggage mules, and waited as patiently as we could. I felt much better than yesterday, and this being an off-day for the shakes, I took a good dose of quinine, and hoped that, as we were getting to a somewhat lower level, the attacks of ague, or soroche, would cease. The post-house of Tarapaya is about 11,200 feet above sea-level, and the small village, about half a mile distant, seems to be entirely deserted, only one or two Indians being visible, and they were very much disinclined to sell us any provisions; indeed, we had to threaten to shoot a fowl for ourselves, before we could induce the owner to sell it to us for a very fair price of two reales and a half, or about 1s. It was not till nearly two o'clock in the afternoon that Marco returned with baggage mules, and we then made haste to saddle up and get on the road. Alfredo and I started on ahead of the boys; but, as I was not over strong, we could not ride at any but a walking pace; it was therefore quite dark before we arrived at Yocalla, near which we crossed the best masonry bridge in Bolivia—a single arch of about thirty feet span, and of masonry excellently well put together. The Indians of Yocalla say the devil built it in a single night; if so, his satanic majesty must be a very good mason. I wondered whether the explanation of this tale might not be that the bridge was one of the last works carried out under the Spanish government's *régime*, and that possibly the builder might have been a free-mason, in which case the priests would most probably have told the Indians that it was built by *a* devil.

The mozos and the baggage mules did not arrive at Yocalla until nearly ten at night, as they had encountered a very difficult task in driving the posta mules, which were very wild ; at least, this was the explanation that the boys gave us of their delay ; but, as we left Tarapaya before they did, I am rather inclined to think that they had a good long visit to a chicheria on the road. Until they arrived with the beds, we passed a bad time, for the mud berths in the post-house were not the softest couches, even when we had spread out all our rugs and saddle-cloths ; and we were very glad to see them arrive safely with their cargoes, for we had got quite downhearted with surmising all manner of accidents that might have happened. This tedious waiting and uneasiness brought back my old enemy, the ague, so that I passed a bad night, and on the following morning could scarcely summon up courage enough to mount my mule and take to the road again. About eight o'clock, however, we managed to get off, after a cup of tea, and started for the next posta, called Leñas, about seven leagues distant.

Our road here lay principally over two long and steep cuestas, the one nearest to Yocalla rising to nearly 14,000 feet above sea-level, at which height there is a small lake or pool with a few ducks. On either side of the road the mountain tops, which were covered with snow, rose probably 1000 or 1500 feet higher than the summit of the pass. The next ascent, which is nearer to Leñas, rises about 5000 feet higher than the elevation assigned to the Yocalla cuesta, and on passing over it we met with a slight hailstorm. We arrived at the Leñas posta about three o'clock in the afternoon, having travelled slowly on account of my weakness, and we thought it prudent to be content with our day's work of seven leagues. So we decided to rest for the remainder of the day, that our saddle mules might also refresh themselves thoroughly and be ready for a good day's work to-morrow. Leñas is a single house, situated in a small plain surrounded entirely by rugged rocky eminences, amongst which Alfredo and the two mozos had great sport hunting "biscachas," a lively little animal that makes its home in the holes of the rocks, and is so much like them in colour, a dark bluish grey, that a very sharp look-out is wanted to distinguish them. In shape they appear to be a cross between a squirrel and a rabbit, having the tail and ears of the former, and head and body of the latter, to which, when cooked, they assimilate greatly in flavour.

Barley was very scarce here, the Indians asking as much as six pesos two reales, or £1 sterling, per quintal of 100 lbs.; but, by a few threats of complaint to the corregidor of the district, although we had not the slightest idea who he might be or where to find him, we got the price reduced to five pesos, about 16s. To a quintal of barley in the straw, we added an arroba (25 lbs. weight) of the grain, costing twelve reales, about 5s., so that the mules, five in number, both feasted and rested well. The keep of the animals is the most costly part of the expenses of a journey in Bolivia, so that there is no doubt but that posting is the best way to travel, provided that one can be sure before starting that the posta arrangements are complete and in good working order throughout the route, and that the traveller has provided himself with a good saddle mule.

Shortly after arriving at Leñas, I set to work to write up my diary; and, looking for my aneroid barometer, I found, to my sorrow, that I had lost it on the road. I recollected that when the hailstorm commenced, as we were ascending the last cuesta, I put my heavy poncho on, and when the storm was over the sun came out so strongly that, being unable to bear the heat and weight of the said poncho, I had to take it off again, and so must have lifted the aneroid, which hung in its leather case by a small strap round my neck, over my head at the same time, without noticing its fall. This might easily have happened at any time, as it was a very small one, scarcely as large as a good-sized watch, and I would certainly recommend the use of the larger sizes, although they are much heavier and more cumbersome. No doubt it was careless in the extreme to drop an aneroid without noticing its fall; but when one is suffering from fever, perhaps shaking with cold and scarcely knowing how to sit on the mule, a small watch-sized article may easily drop unnoticed. The loss was most annoying to me, as one of the chief pleasures of the road was at an end, namely, the noting down of the differences of elevation of the different ravines and cuestas. In order to make every effort to recover my loss, I sent an Indian on foot and my mozo Juan on a mule, with orders to return as far as Yocalla, if necessary, as possibly the postilions who took back the mules belonging to that place, might have found it, and have taken it along with them. Juan returned about ten at night, saying he had found the postilions in a hut about half way to Yocalla, resting for the night, but that he could not get any tidings from them of the missing aneroid, although he searched their packs and pockets; so probably some of the llama men that passed us on the road had found it, and it was lost to me altogether.

We left Leñas on the following morning about eight o'clock, being furnished with very good posting mules, that were to carry our baggage to the next posta, Lagunillas, distant seven leagues. The road crossed the " cabeçeras," or head-waters, of the Pilcomayo several times, the broadest stream being about half-way between Leñas and Lagunillas, and flowing through a valley that would be very pretty scenery were there any trees or other vegetation than the brown tufted grass, which is all the sign of life to be seen at these great elevations, except the " vicuñas," which we met for the first time hereabouts. These animals are about the size of a small fallow deer, which, when seen at a distance, they very much resemble. They seem to confine their wanderings to the central plateau of the Andes, for they are not found eastward of Potosí, or westward of the pass of Tacora. Probably they keep to these limits because they form the zone in which fewest villages or towns are found; they cannot be influenced by elevation or climate, for similar circumstances may be found in many other parts of the country. They go in droves of different sizes, sometimes not more than four or five being together, whilst at times droves containing as many scores are met with. Their fur is of a light dun colour on the back of the animal, the breast and neck being almost white. The skins are not much valued at home, although they make beautiful rugs for carriage use, or in place of quilts as bed coverings, for which purposes they are very suitable for elderly people, as, while they are warm and soft, they are exceedingly light. A good rug takes, I was told, about twenty skins; but it is a bad plan to buy the made-up rugs in Bolivia, as the makers there charge a very heavy price for putting the skins together, whilst their work is of such very ordinary character that the skins have to be resewn and relined after arriving in England. For some rugs that I bought in Tacna I paid about £7 each; but the bargain was a very bad one, for although the price was not above that usually asked in Bolivia, I found, on getting them home to London, that at the principal furriers of the West End much better vicuña rugs, well sewn and preserved, could be bought for about one fourth of the price that I paid in Tacna. If the skins were more valuable, so as to make it worth while killing vicuñas for the sake of the furs, some excellent sport might be had in the Andes, for they are nobody's property, and as free to all comers as are the ducks in the lagoons. They are, however, so tame, that there would not be much glory in stalking them, for many times on the road I could have knocked them over with a bullet from my revolver;

and I passed several that had evidently been wounded
by passing travellers, and left to drag out their life
in pain and misery.   Wherever practicable, we shot
the poor beasts, and left their carcases for the condors,
eagles, and vultures that are continually soaring
over the mule tracks of the Andes on the look-out
for their horrid banquet.   Often, when riding over
the Andes, a huge dark shadow comes suddenly
over the path, and the traveller, looking upwards,
sees the magnificent condor floating in the bright
sunlight and rising to his resting-place amongst the
snow-clad peaks.   These birds are seldom to be seen
at rest, but occasionally they may be observed feasting
on some poor mule that has fallen exhausted by the
way-side.   The eagles may then be noticed flying
round in circles, watching for their turn, which
comes next, whilst the vultures are dotted over the
plain, waiting contentedly until the more lordly birds
have satisfied themselves, when they will fall to and
not leave the carcase until nothing but the skeleton
remains.

We arrived at Lagunillas about one o'clock,
having done the seven leagues in the five hours,
and we found good mules ready for the next stage,
which would take us to Tolapalca, about four leagues
distant.   Lagunillas is a small "aldea," or village, of
perhaps a dozen small houses and a church, built like
the houses, of sun-dried adobes, or mud-bricks, and
roofed with rushes.   The place is named from two
lagoons close by, where we saw many ducks and
large flocks of tern, or "gabiotas," some of the ducks
being regular "pato royales," like the black and
white ones of the Mamoré River.   I tried a shot at

them from my revolver, but the range was too great, although they seemed so tame that I was almost sure of them. As the Indians have no guns, the ducks very rarely get disturbed; this probably accounts for their tameness. After resting a couple of hours, during which the saddle mules enjoyed a feed of barley and had a roll in the dust of the corral, we took to the road again, and, leaving the hilly country, got on to an elevated pampa land, over which we made pretty rapid travelling, getting to Tolapalca about half-past five, before night closed in. During the afternoon ride, rain threatened to come down heavily, but confined itself to the neighbouring hills. The post-house of Tolapalca is a very desolate place, and must be at a great elevation, possibly 14,000 feet; here I began to miss my poor lost aneroid. The rooms are deplorably small and abominably dirty; but, at these elevations it is impossible to sleep out-of-doors, as the nights are not only very cold, but the storms of wind, rain, and snow are very frequent, so there is nothing to be done but to put up with the dirt and discomfort of the postas. Travelling on the Andes is very different to a journey in India, where, if the bungalow be not to one's liking, the absence of dew at night allows one to sleep either in the verandah or out in the open. In most parts of South America, a man who slept out of doors whilst any sort of a roof was within a reasonable distance would be looked upon as little less than a madman. At Tolapalca, we got some fresh but lean mutton, and made a very fair chupe for supper, after which we hoped for a good night's rest; but alas, my hopes were vain, for, no

sooner had I blown out the candle than I was
attacked by an army of Bolivian Norfolk-Howards,
called here " chinches " or " vinchutas." As I was
hours before, thoroughly wearied out, I at last got
a little broken sleep. The night was very cold, so
that I was obliged to keep under my blankets along
with the bugs, and bear it out as best I could. The
strange thing was, that when I struck a light, not
a single brute could I discover; yet immediately I
put the light out and courted sleep, my horrid per-
secutors re-commenced the torment. How I envied
my young Bolivian friend and the two mozos, who
all snored away with most dismal regularity, whilst
I was tossing about on my cot and venting smothered
" blessings " (?) on the invaders of my rest.

The next day was the last of the year 1874, and,
rising early, we settled our account at the Tolapalca
posta for barley, at five pesos the quintal, and for
posting mules on to the next stage at Vilcapujio. I
endeavoured to have a deduction made from our bill
for the entertainment I had afforded to the vinchutas
during the night, but could not get our Indian hosts
to see the matter in the same light as I did. Soon
after starting, rain, changing into a heavy snow-
storm, began to fall, and kept us company all the
way to the next posta, a distance of four leagues,
which we accomplished in about two hours and a
half. Vilcapujio was the site of a battle in the War
of Independence, and is a fine open pampa, affording
plenty of room for a fight, with hills on either side
for good positions. The post-house is very large,
and somewhat cleaner than that at Tolapalca. Here
we got some very fair mutton and potatoes, so that

arriving early we were able to make a better breakfast than was possible on days when we could not
reach the end of a stage until the afternoon, when,
perhaps, another piece of the road would have to be
got over before nightfall. If an English traveller in
these parts has been fortunate enough to secure a
mozo, that has a little idea of cooking, his plan is
to show the mozo at starting what kind of a broth,
or chupe, he likes, and then, when materials are
available at the different post-houses, he stands some
chance of getting a broth that is both eatable and
nourishing ; but the chupes prepared for travellers
by the Indians of the postas are simply abominable.
Their colour is an earthy red, and they taste of
nothing but fire, grease, and garlic, the first from the
great quantity of " aji," or chillies, put in, the second
from the dirty state of the cooking-pots, and the last
is inseparable from all Bolivian cookery.

On leaving Vilcapujio about mid-day, I was
much amused by seeing three Indian women rush
out of the adjoining huts, each one bearing a few
burning embers in a broken piece of an earthen pot.
These embers they placed in the mule track, and
then, kneeling and crossing themselves, they retired
to their huts, leaving the burning ashes in the path-
way. My mozo's account of this pantomine was that
the women prayed that the mules might travel as
rapidly as the smoke of their fires did, but as the
smoke does not return to the place from whence it
started the explanation does not appear to be a very
good one. My idea was that the women might be
the wives of the postilions, and as the smoke never
returned, so these wives, like many fashionable ones

of Europe, prayed that the husbands might vanish as
the smoke did ; but as there were three wives to two
postilions this theory would not work, so I had to
leave the problem unsolved.

Large droves of llamas and alpacas were scattered
about over the pampa of Vilcapujio, and I observed
that these animals mixed but little together, the one
or two stray ones in each large drove looking like
visitors, out of place. After leaving the pampa the
road becomes more uneven, and crosses the river
Ancacata several times. Ancacata is about four
leagues from Vilcapujio, but the posta way-bills, or
" guias," give the distance as six leagues. We
arrived late in the afternoon, having travelled very
slowly, on account of the strong wind, which blew so
piercingly cold over the pampa that, at times, we
were fain to stop the mules and turn our backs to it.
The village of Ancacata is pitched in a narrow
valley, through which the river of the same name
runs, the hills on either side, although barren and
stony, having rather an imposing look from being
covered with tufts of short dry grass, of a bright
yellow colour, giving quite a golden tinge to them
in the fading sunset.

The houses are all in a tumble-down and ruinous
state, the posta being in the same condition, with
scarcely plaster enough on its walls for the travelling
snobs of Bolivia, both natives and foreigners, to
scrawl their valued names and sentiments. One of
these defacers of public property advises passers-by
that on a certain day he passed through Ancacata
with his " amiable spouse," as he defines his wife :
happy man ! or else given to falsehood-telling to

keep his better half in a state of amiability. So common is the habit of writing one's name in public places, that even the mountain roads of the Andes can show many examples of the abominable practice. Notwithstanding the ruinous state of the post-house, we passed a very good night, as we were, I am happy to record, not troubled with unpleasant companions as we had been at Tolapalca. We congratulated ourselves greatly on this, as the next day we had a very long ride before us, having to get over three stages before nightfall, so as to sleep the following night at Poopo.

The next morning was the first in the new year of 1875, and we rose at half-past four, leaving Ancacata at six o'clock sharp. The morning was fine and clear, but very cold, the tops of the hills being all covered with snow. The road runs down the river for about a couple of leagues, and then gets out on the pampa lands of Aullagas, bordering on the lake of Poopo. The country hereabouts is dotted over with cottages and huts of a much superior character to those of the villages lately passed through, and the Indians seem more well-to-do than those living on the hills.

In this part of the country a traveller going west first comes across those very remarkable and interesting relics of antiquity called "chulpas." They are dotted all over the central plain of Bolivia, and a few are also found on the lower parts of the slopes of the mountains on either side. Whether the chulpa has been a house or a tomb, and who were its builders, are questions that, as far as I know, remain entirely unanswered. As for its builders, the only information to be obtained regarding them from the present inhabitants of Bolivia, whether Indians or Bolivians of Spanish extraction, is that the chulpa was a " casa de los Gentiles," or literally translated, a " house of the Gentiles," and that the Gentiles were the inhabitants of the country before the introduction of the Christian religion by the missionaries who followed in the wake of the Spanish conquerors of the Incas. The explanation does not seem to be a feasible one, as the Incas settled in Peru more than in Bolivia, and have left in the former country many monuments in stonework of their skill as handicraftsmen, while the chulpa is a rough erection of " adobes," or sun-dried mud bricks, and is the only relic of former ages that Bolivia has to boast of. The makers of the chulpa, must, therefore, probably be looked for in a race that existed prior to the Incas.

The chulpas are of various heights, ranging from ten to twenty and occasionally thirty feet high, the difference arising probably from the more rapid decay of the shorter ones. In shape they are at the ground line generally about fifteen feet wide by six feet broad, outside measurements, and as the walls are twelve to fifteen inches in thickness, the inside forms a long and very narrow parallelogram. The doors all have a lintel of stone, and are in every case turned to the east, doubtless in connection with the rising sun, as even when the chulpas are found in groups (although they are generally placed singly or in pairs) I observed they were always pitched so that the eastward view for each one of them was quite uninterrupted. Towards the top the walls gradually approach each other, but as I could not find one that was quite closed in, it is impossible to be certain whether the top was flat, or formed by bringing all the walls together in a point. A remarkable thing about these chulpas is the excellent quality of the adobes of which they are constructed. These are evidently only sun-dried mud or common earth, and have very little straw or fibrous matter in

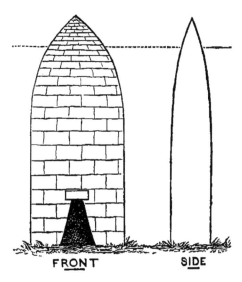

FRONT      SIDE

A CHULPA.

them, yet they must have lasted for many centuries, and will, as they are protected as far as possible, both by the authorities and by the traditions of the Indian inhabitants of the district, probably last for centuries yet to come, and this, notwithstanding the fierce storms that sweep over the desolate plains of the altaplanicia of Bolivia, and the extreme alter-nations of heat and cold which occur in almost each successive day and night. So wonderful is the tenacity of the material of which these adobes are

composed, that I question whether kiln-dried bricks
would have any chance of equalling their durability.
By some people these chulpas are set down as tombs,
but I have not heard of any bones having been
discovered in them, although gold and silver ornaments, as well as pottery have frequently been
found.   One of our mozos told us that there was a
tradition that the builders of these chulpas, whoever
they were, at the approach of death caused themselves to be walled up in them without food, in the
belief that after death they would be transported to
new life, in a land which they called by the name of
" Buenos Ayres," but as this tale was told me by our
Argentino Marco, perhaps it was an invention of his
own, and only served to show the ready wit of a
gaucho.

Arriving at the posta of Catariri about 11 a.m.,
we halted for breakfast, and, changing our baggage
mules, which got over the ground admirably although
they were not promising animals to look at, we took
the road again without much loss of time.   From
Catariri to Pazna, the next post, the road lies
principally over the pampa of Aullagas, which is
capital arable land, planted largely with barley and
potatoes.   Nearing Pazna, we approached more
nearly to the lake of Aullagas, or, as it is called in
most maps, the lake of Poopo, and saw a most
beautiful mirage.   Some distance in the lake are two
small and hilly islands, and these appeared to be
lifted high into the air, whilst on the western side of
the lake a snow-covered mountain was raised quite
into the clouds.

At Pazna we stayed only just long enough to

change our baggage mules, and got a couple of very young mules given us that gave much trouble at first start, as they wished, apparently, to travel any road but the one we wanted them to take. However, when once we got them on the right road they made very good progress, so that we finished our day's run by six o'clock, having done sixteen leagues, say fifty miles, in about twelve hours, including our two stoppages, which occupied two out of the twelve; not bad work! Poopo is a miserable-looking place, built in a ravine, up which the houses are built on either side, the middle forming the "high street." Nearly the whole village seemed to be in ruins, and, as it was New Year's Day, all the inhabitants, at least the few to be seen about, were more or less intoxicated. I have already mentioned the prevalence of drunkenness in Bolivia, but certainly this vile habit seems to be even more general in the mining towns that in the purely agricultural ones. These latter also have better-built houses, and are altogether more cheerful looking than the former. Perhaps these differences may be somewhat accounted for by the dismal prospects that the working miners of Bolivia have before them, for although the mineral extracted is almost uniformly of great richness, the cost of carrying the article to a market is so great that little profit is left to the actual miner. There seems to be but small hope of better times for the mining industry until good roads are made and a route for exportation completed in an eastward direction. At Poopo there are a few mines in which tin, or " estaño," seems to be the principal mineral found. The altitude of Poopo above sea-level is given by

Hugo Reck at 378 metres, equal to 12,431 feet.
The posta was in as ruinous a condition as the other
houses, and a small church seemed to be the only
building that had a complete roof to it.  No provisions were obtainable, so we had to content ourselves with a tin of *rognons sauté* from our travelling
stores, and had it not been for this resource we
should have remained supperless after our long day's
ride.

The next morning we left Poopo early, with very
good posta mules and travelled well, the whole of
the road to the next station, called Machacamarca,
distant about six leagues, being over pampa land.
At Machacamarca we breakfasted and were preparing
to start, when a party, consisting of three Bolivians
and two ladies, rode up from Oruro.  The boss of the
party stared hard at me, and then claimed acquaintance as having met me in Sucre.   I did not recollect
him, so he told me his name, and that he was a
proprietor of tin mines at Poopo.   He confirmed the
rumours that we had heard along the road for the
past two or three days, of a revolution in La Paz, in
favour of General Quintin Quevedo, and told me that
he had received a letter from the general, telling him
that he was *en route* for La Paz, to put himself at the
head of the movement.  This news caused me to give
up all idea of visiting La Paz, as the roads between
Oruro and that city were in the possession of General
Daza and his officers, who, I feared, would not
scruple to take my mules from me, and leave me
without means of travelling.  The only plan I could
adopt, was to push on for Oruro with all speed, in
hope of being able to arrange for a continuance of

my journey to Tacna before Daza or any of his men arrived there. We therefore made all possible haste, but were much delayed by encountering a very heavy storm of wind, hail, and rain, which drove over the pampa with great violence. Before the storm, the mirage on the pampa was the finest I have ever seen. The hill at the foot of which Oruro lies appeared to be separated from us by a lake, and I said to Alfredo that we should have to go round it. The droves of llamas and their attendants seemed to be walking in the lake, but as we approached the water seemed to disappear gradually, at about the distance of a quarter of a mile only from us. I have never seen such a distinct and clear effect on any other occasion, and could not but conjecture that the coming storm had something to do with it.

We arrived at Oruro about 4 p.m., having travelled thirteen leagues during the day, and put up at the house of the Peruvian consul (Señor Urquidi) to whom my young travelling-companion was recommended. The consul received us very kindly, giving us a capital room in his house, and a good corral for our animals, so that our mules were comparatively safe for the present.

# CHAPTER XXVIII.

Oruro—Mineral districts and mining operations—" Barilla "—Freighting
ore by llamas—Future of mining in Oruro—Attempted revolution in
Oruro—Night attack on the Quartel—Start from Oruro for Tacna—
The river Desaguadero—The ferry called La Barca—Llollia—Escape
of the mules during night—Indian cooking arrangements—Dress and
appearance of Indian men and women—El Cruzero—" Quinoa "—
Heavy storms—Electrified state of the atmosphere—Peculiar strata
observed near El Cruzero—Curahuara de Carangas—Its church, people,
and parish priest—Travelling jewellers—Mining prospects of the
district.

ORURO, situated 12,530 feet above sea-level, is a
dreary-looking town, containing about 8000 inhabitants. The plain on which it stands is entirely
destitute of any kind of vegetation, and the hilly
district not far from the town is especially famous
for its mines of tin, copper, and silver. So numerous
are the veins of ore that it may almost be said that a
blind man striking with a pick at the hill-side would
be sure to find mineral of some kind or other, and
the " Cornish divining rod " would be of but little
use here, as it would be attracted in so many
directions at the same time that its miraculous
powers would probably be quite useless. The richest
veins are, however, those only that pay for working
at present, on account of the great distance that has
to be traversed between Oruro and any seaport.
Most of the mercantile houses engaged in Bolivian

trade have agencies in the town, and there are several Englishmen and Americans engaged in mining, with as good results as can be expected in the absence of other means of transport for the ore than llamas and donkeys.

I visited several of the mines, but a description of any one will give an idea of the work carried on at them. One of the English miners, a Mr. Penny, who had been resident in Bolivia for more than twenty-five years, invited me to his property of San José Chica, a flourishing mine about a mile from Oruro. The two working shafts, connected by galleries and with numerous headings were worked by the old Spaniards, but some difficulty is now met with from the influx of water, which cannot be kept under with the limited pumping-power available, until steam machinery can be imported into the district. Apart from this drawback, the mine appeared to be in fair working order, the lode yielding silver and tin ore of various values, percentages of from six to sixty per cent. being named. The mineral, as it came up to the top of the shafts, seemed to me to require only a little picking over, in order to free it from the rocky stuff adhering to the ore; but the practice is to select the best-looking lumps only, the remainder, which would doubtless pay well if passed through proper crushing-machinery and then reduced by smelting, being run away to spoil as valueless. The Indians soon get very expert in the work of picking out the best ore, and the selected mass is broken up by hand into small chips, washed in order to get rid of as much of the earthy impurities as possible, and packed into small bags of 50 lbs. each.

Many of the ores, when thus dressed, yield sixty to seventy per cent. of tin, and the mineral is known in the English markets as " barilla," being shipped per steamer from Arica in the same condition as it is sent from the mine, the small bags stowing capitally between larger cargo. The freight paid for carriage of this ore from Oruro to Tacna by llamas, the cheapest mode of transport that exists at present on that route, is from two to three pesos per quintal, say from £7 5*s.* to £10 15*s.* per ton of 2240 lbs., the distance being said to be from eighty to a hundred leagues. This would give an average rate of about 8*d.* per ton per mile, and as each ton carried requires twenty-two llamas, it follows that each llama earns about one-third of a penny per mile for his owner. It is a very curious sight to see the llamas loaded up for their journey, and upon one occasion I saw over 500 being prepared for the road. Having been driven together as closely as possible, a rope is passed around the crowded animals, being so placed as to hang on the necks of the outer ones, thus forming a perfect ring fence. They are then let out one at a time, a piece of hairy llama hide, or sheep-skin with wool on, is placed on their necks, and a couple of bags tied on, pack fashion. The llama is then left to its own devices until the whole " recua," or drove, have been laden with their burdens, when they are driven on the road, being led sometimes by one of the finest of the drove, or by a tall black alpaca, or sometimes by an old hill pony ; but, what-ever the leader may be, he always has a bell tied round his neck, the ceaseless clangour from which seems to keep the drove together, warning them not to delay too long by the road-side nibbling any stray grass that they can find, and which appears to be all the forage they get. At the close of the day, as soon as night falls, the llamas are again driven closely together, their burdens taken off and stacked up in the form of a rough shed, under which the arriero shelters himself for the night. The burdens being removed, the animals are free to roam around and forage for themselves, having to trust to chance whether there be any water and grass near. At break of day they are all gathered together again, and the journey is resumed, it being perfectly wonderful to see what little trouble the men have to get their droves together each morning.

The cost of freighting the ore by llamas to the seaport is not excessive, but the time occupied on the journey is very great, the principal house in Oruro assuring me that it often took twelve months before they could obtain a return from their investments in " barilla." When the Amazonian route is opened up by the completion of the Railway of the Madeira Rapids, a road from Totora to the port on the Chimoré River will be made, the existing road between Oruro and Cochabamba will be improved, and the whole of the mineral products of the central Andean valley of Bolivia will find its way to European markets over the shortest, easiest, and most natural route, even before the finances of the country shall have sufficiently improved to enable an interior system of railways to be commenced. There is no great difference in distance between Oruro and Tacna, and Oruro and the port on the Chimoré, but a journey with animals by the latter route offers far less risk, as pasturage is everywhere plentiful, and there is no danger of the animals dying from the effects of the soroche, so fatal on the pass of Tacora, the highest point of the Andes, passed on the roads from Oruro to the Pacific coast. If ever the happy day that shall see the opening of the Madeira and Mamoré Railway dawns for Bolivia, then few speculations appear to me to be more promising than that of mining near Oruro. The want of fuel for smelting purposes will not, when good roads are made, be felt so much at Oruro as at Potosí, for Oruro is within a reasonable distance of the eastern slopes of the Andes, which are well wooded.

As I expected, the revolution had entirely broken up the posta service between Oruro and Tacna, as well as that upon the La Paz road, so I had to suffer a week's detention at Oruro, whilst looking out to purchase baggage mules. Animals of every kind were very scarce, but I was fortunate enough to secure a couple, though at very high prices; and our host, finding that we could not purchase any others, lent my companion Alfredo a baggage mule, and so we were at length provided for our journey on to Tacna.

During our stay in Oruro, the townspeople were much excited as to which side to take in the revolution. The prefect raised a small band of recruits and took them out to join General Daza, who was supposed to be encamped about a day's march on the La Paz road. In his absence some conspirators of Quevedistic tendencies formed secret bands, and endeavoured to get up a " pronunciamento" for their favourite, General Quintine Quevedo. The night of January the 8th was chosen by the Quevedists for an attack upon the " quartel," or barracks, which were held for the government by a " comandante" and about a hundred men. We had all turned in early, but about two o'clock in the morning our host called us up, saying that the revolution had commenced in the town. Alfredo and I dressed as quickly as possible, so that we might be prepared for any eventualities. At first the firing was rather rapid, but after about half an hour's smart fusilade, it dropped off to single shots, as though one party were gradually retiring to the outskirts of the town. The shouting ceased by three o'clock, and all being quiet, we turned in again till daylight, when we found that a party of Quevedistas, supposed to be about five and twenty in number, having attacked the quartel, had been repulsed. Two of the defenders of the quartel were killed, and the comandante-general, who appeared to have conducted himself with great bravely, was hit twice in the arm and also in the side, the latter wound being a very dangerous one. The whole proceeding seemed to have been a very senseless one on the part of the Quevedistas, unless, as is very probable, they had a secret understanding with the soldiers in the quartel; if they had, the bravery of the comandante must have cowed his men, so that they feared to assist the attacking party, who were able to retreat without loss. The following morning the authorities were very active, and three or four men were taken into custody on suspicion, but it did not appear to be known for certain who were the leaders of the attack. Rumour said that the plan was, if the quartel had been taken, that requisitions or robberies would have been committed upon the principal mercantile houses, especially upon those that were thought to be favourable to the present government. As our host was agent for Messrs. Campbell & Co. of Tacna, who were thought to be "Gobiernistas," all the mules in his corral, our own amongst the number, had been marked out for requisition,; and, I fancy, not even my own well-known Quevedistic proclivities would have saved them. A forced contribution of 10,000 pesos was also to have been raised from the firm, whilst the other mercantile houses were put on the list for sums varying from a couple to five thousand pesos. However, fortunately for us, the combination did not succeed, and as we had everything in readiness for our onward journey we hoped to get away safely on the following morning. Late the same evening an arriero came in from Tacna with a recua of about fifty mules, and as the animals and their trappings were in good condition they formed quite an imposing sight. From this arriero I was able to hire a couple of "aparejos" in good order, to replace two of mine, which were not complete. He charged me eight pesos for the hire of each one, and this turned out to be a cheaper method of equipping one's self than purchasing new aparejos and selling them at the end of the journey.

The following night passed quietly without any more attempts at revolution. Patrols were kept up in the streets, and although the Quevedistas threatened another row, none took place. The next day, January 9th, at 5 a.m., I called our mozos, and we began to arrange our baggage for a start. As our new mules were saddle animals, and consequently unaccustomed to cargo work, we had a good deal of trouble to get ready; but by about eight o'clock we managed to make a start, intending to travel that day as far as La Barca, a distance of twelve leagues. However, before we were out of Oruro we had more trouble with the animals, as they apparently wished to go every road but the right one.. One mule, a fine grey animal that would have made a perfect match for my young companion's "macho," with which it would have made a fine pair for a coach, was particularly lively, and nearly succeeded in jumping to the top of an almost perpendicular bank, over four feet in height, and this with over a couple of hundred-weight on his pack-saddle. So we went on with many troubles, until getting on the road outside the town the animals behaved themselves better.

The road out of Oruro first crosses the junction of two ranges of hills, in both of which are several mines, the right-hand range behind the town being worked by an apparently very well managed mining enterprise, said to belong to the house of Blondell & Co. The road then is over pampa land, and nothing but pampa of the dullest and flattest kind conceivable. Here a macho, that we were allowing to run loose, took it into its head to bolt back for Oruro, and Alfredo and I had to scamper after him for about a league, until we headed him, and turned

him back on the right road. We arrived at the
river Desaguadero about four in the afternoon,
and to the ferry called La Barca about six
o'clock. Here we found a troop of donkeys crossing,
but made them wait whilst we were ferried over,
much to the disgust of their owners, but the Indians
hereabout are quite insolent enough, and it is
necessary to put them in their proper place now
and then.

The Desaguadero is a riverine canal, which
unites the lake of Titicaca with that of Poopo, or
Choro. The canal has to be crossed on a pontoon
or raft, kept in its course by a hide rope stretched
from bank to bank, a distance of about 300 yards.
The tolls collected are one reale, say $4\frac{3}{4}d.$, per mule,
half a reale for a donkey, and five llamas are passed
for one reale. The pontoon is made of three large
barrels lashed together in a row, and having three
pointed caissoons on the front. A twisted hide
rope, fully three inches and a half in diameter, and
most wonderfully made, is stretched across the river,
being anchored to heavy stones on either side. The
pointed caissoons are placed up stream, and the
proper direction being given to the rudder, the
current lent some slight assistance to the two men
who worked the launch across the river by hand-
work. The launch might have a better flooring,
and the landing-stages might with little expense
be greatly improved; but still, on the whole, the
ferry is very serviceable to travellers, and, as the
traffic is considerable, it must be a fortune to the
old lady who is the proprietor, and who resides at
the house on the western side of the river. The

Desaguadero is the outlet for the surplus waters of lake Titicaca, the largest fresh-water lake of the South American continent, and has a course of about 200 miles in length before emptying itself into the lake of Poopo. At La Barca it is about fifty or sixty yards wide, and has but a slight current, is very muddy, and is said to be about twenty-four feet in depth at the crossing, but did not seem to me to be so deep. Without consider able dredging it would not be available for steamers, as it is very narrow and changes its course con tinually, leaving shallow places and "playas" (sandbanks) at every turn. The level of lake Titicaca is given in Keith Johnston's maps as 12,846 feet above sea-level, whilst the lake of Poopo is probably about 12,400 feet. This gives an incline of about two feet per mile between the two lakes, a fall which is probably pretty evenly distributed over the entire course of the river.

Having crossed the river, we entered the house belonging to the proprietress of the ferry, and engaged a large room where my companion and I could have our cots at one end, whilst our mozos slept on hides laid on the floor at the other. We here made ourselves pretty comfortable, and having bought some mutton, had a good chupe made for supper, after which we turned in for a good night's rest in hope of making good progress on the morrow. At La Barca prices were moderate, barley for the mules being two pesos the quintal, whilst the total charge for the mutton for our supper and the use of the room for the night was only a peso, so that, if there be no great accommodation for travellers at the Desaguadero Hotel and ferry, at least one cannot complain of the charges. Sunday, January the 10th, was to see us to the nearest village, called Llollia, pronounced " Yocclia," an Indian settlement, about twelve leagues from La Barca. We rose at five, but it was nearly eight o'clock before we got the mules all saddled and cargoes up. The road all day lay entirely over pampas which, in most places, were very muddy and covered with the rain which had fallen during the preceding night, and which lay in many places three and four inches in depth. This made the travelling very heavy work ; but, notwith-standing, we did the twelve leagues by four o'clock in the afternoon. The tops of the ranges of hills in sight were covered with snow, and during the greater part of the day a very cold wind blew, with heavy driving rain, but fortunately at our backs. Llollia is a small Indian aldea, or collection of ranchos, built of mud, plastered with a little lime on the inside, and with very small, coffin-shaped doors, which gave one a good idea of what living in a " chulpa " must have been like. The Indians here are Aymarás, and are very cunning,—one fellow came out to meet us long before we neared the village, and tried his best to make us believe that a room he offered us was the only one to be had. On arrival we went to see his hut, and found it was more than three parts full of barley, so we looked round amongst the other ranchos, and soon got offers right and left, securing a tolerably-sized room for ourselves and a corral for the mules.

The next day was a wretched lost one. On waking at 5 a.m., I took my accustomed dose of quinine, and, dressing leisurely, went out to the corral, expecting to find the boys saddling the mules; but neither mules nor mozos were visible, and the unpleasant fact forced itself on my unwilling belief that the mules had bolted during the night, and that the mule-boys were after them on foot. This was confirmed, in mixed Aymará and Spanish, by the old woman of the house to which the corral was attached. About seven o'clock, Marco returned with five of them, the other four having apparently taken the direction of La Barca. Juan had gone after these on foot; so, having dispatched Marco on one of the animals, all Alfredo and I could do was to wait patiently, take care of the four left in our charge, and nurse our discontents as well as we could. We had bought a small sheep for a couple of pesos on arriving at Llollia last night, so we made ourselves a breakfast of roast mutton, which we toasted in one of the ground fireplaces of the country, and waited the day out. These fireplaces are worthy of note. A hole is dug in the ground about eighteen inches in depth and two feet in diameter, and over this a framework of clay is made, with holes of different sizes, to receive the various cooking-pots. Roasting must be done on spits passed through the holes; so the meat comes out very much smoked, unless great care is taken to have only embers in the bottom of the oven. For rough cooking, the affair answers its purpose well, and one would be inclined to think that a good idea for camp ovens might be taken from it, if a curved sheet of cast or wrought iron were used instead of the clay frame, as good clay would in many places be difficult, perhaps impossible, to obtain, and would take too long to manufacture. The plan of digging a hole in the ground for a camp oven is, of course, not a new one;

Section through oven.

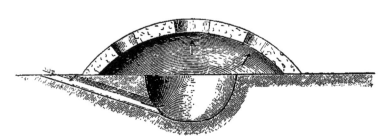

Section through Oven and Air Intake.

QUICHUAN OVEN (LLOLLIA).

but it would seem that the curved top would be much simpler and lighter for transport than the camp ovens that are in general use.

The Indians of Llollia and the district are of the Aymará race, and are strong and well built generally. In their own way they are certainly industrious, for it is very unusual to meet either a man or a woman who is not spinning, whether indoors or out of doors, seated or walking. They are all owners of large flocks of sheep, whilst many of them also have droves of llamas and alpacas, the last of which are said to yield large profits from the sale of the famous alpaca wool. Both men and women wear nothing but dark blue homespun clothing, with stockings of the natural

QUICHUAN WOMAN OF LLOLLIA.

colour of the wool. The men wear their hair long, twisted round the top of their heads in small and narrow plaits, which have very much the semblance of plaited horse-tails. They are scarcely ever seen without the universal poncho over their shoulders. The women wear a countless number of woollen petticoats, which are puckered up round about their waists in a most elaborate manner, and, reaching

about half-way down the calf of the leg, display a
pair of ankles and feet which, to all appearance,
might be made of bronze or copper. A square of
woollen cloth, or shawl, is worn tied round the neck,
secured in front by a couple of spoon-shaped skewers ;
whilst, generally at their backs, a baby is seen stowed
away in the folds of the shawl—for babies are almost
as numerous in the hovels on the tops of the Andes
as they are in some of the back slums or courts of
St. Giles. Their head-dresses are also peculiar,
being something mediæval in shape and look. A
frame of straw is made up in form of a lozenge, with
a hole in the centre to fit the head, and this is
covered with dark blue or red cloth ; a curtain
hanging down on all sides about six inches deep,
making a capital sort of sunshade. One would not
think that the women required any protection from
the sun's rays, for their faces are like their hands
and ankles, of a deep brown colour, from the accumulated dust of years ; whilst a red glow, that the cold
winds give them, aids the semblance of their skins to
well-seasoned mahogany. Washing of any sort is
unknown on the higher Andes, where the strong
cold winds makes even a traveller feel inclined to
follow the universal custom, and let well alone.

Towards the close of the day, much to our joy,
the animals turned up, the boys having had to return
all the way to La Barca, where the four mules had
been captured and placed in the corral. It was
fortunate for us that they did not attempt to swim
across the river Desaguadero, as it was evident that
they had made up their minds to return to Oruro.
Perhaps they thought they would be ferried over

although they arrived without riders, for our boys were told that at daybreak they were all found waiting on the shore close by the ferry-boat. Thus all we lost was an entire day—bad enough, but to have lost the animals would have been much worse; so we consoled ourselves and prepared to continue the journey early to-morrow, making as long a day of it as we could. At first I thought that some of the Indians had done us the trick of letting out the mules, so as to get paid for fetching them back, or as vengeance for our not having bought barley of them; but I convinced myself that the mules got over the mud walls of the corral, they being very low.

On the following day, January 12th, our work was from Llollia to El Cruzero, fourteen leagues, and although we roused up at five o'clock, it took a couple of hours to get the cargoes up and ready for the start. Notwithstanding a heavy hail-storm and rain yesterday evening and during the night, the road was not bad for travelling, as the pampas were more elevated and sandier than those nearer Oruro. Hereabouts there are many ranchos scattered over the pampa, and good crops of barley, potatoes, and quinoa were growing. This "quinoa" is a small grain about the size of millet or rape seed, and is eaten by the Aymará Indians in the same way as gram or rice is eaten by the Indians of Hindostan. When boiled or soaked it throws out a gelatinous substance that causes it to form a mass, in which state it is used by the Indians as their principal article of food. By Bolivians of higher grade, it is only used to thicken the chupe, or soup, and in that way is very agreeable. There were also many flocks of sheep, llamas, and alpacas, as well as many vicuñas, which in these parts are very tame.

From Capillitas, a station about seven leagues from Llollia onwards, the country is much rougher, and the road takes up a very picturesque quebrada, the strata of some of the rocks standing up perpendicular. Here one of the mules that had a very light burden, consisting of bedding only, managed to kick off her cargo, and set to work with teeth and hoofs to tear up as much as she could of it, succeeding in ruining a bag and sundry other articles before we could rescue them from her.

Towards four in the afternoon came on the usual storm of hail, rain, and wind, accompanied by vivid flashes of lightning, some of which were most unpleasantly near us. To know what a hail-storm really means, one must cross the Andes, for some of these afternoon storms were the heaviest I have ever met with either at sea or land. In fact, so large were the hailstones in many instances, that I congratulated myself on being the lucky possessor of two hats, one of which, a large-brimmed thick vicuña felt, I could put on over a soft wide-awake, and then, tying a large scarf over all, so as to cover up my ears and the back of my neck, I could ride out any storm. I recollect many occasions on which the stones came down with such force, being driven by the high wind, that we were fain to turn our backs to the fury of the squall, otherwise I really think the mules would have been stunned had we forced them to receive the hail on their faces.

During the evening the air seemed to be most

highly charged with electricity, and after nightfall the flashes of lightning were intensely vivid, the contrast causing the night to look blacker than usual. Whilst riding slowly along I was for some time puzzled by noticing two luminous points moving backwards and forwards right in front of me, and seemingly accompanying me with great regularity. Reaching out my hand towards these lights, I was astonished to find that they were on the two points of my mules' ears, which, as they wagged to and fro in mule fashion, gleamed like the points of damp lucifer matches. Upon directing my companions' and the mozos' attention to the other animals, we found a similar condition to exist with each one, although it was more distinct in some cases than in others. Every one has heard that sparks can be produced from a cat's back, when the fur is rubbed the wrong way, but I never heard that mules or other animals had the same power of evolving electricity; but probably the wet state of the hair on their ears, and the highly charged condition of the atmosphere, accounted for the phenomenon.

We did not get to El Cruzero, which consists of a few wretched hovels and a small church at the side of a brook, until nearly nine at night, some of us being drenched to the skin, and every one complaining bitterly of the cold. Here we had considerable difficulty in inducing the Indians to open their doors to us and provide us with a shelter for the night. We knocked for some time, at the door of the only hovel in which we could see a glimmer of light through the cracks of the door, and were at length gruffly told to go on our way to the next village, three and a half leagues distant. This we did not approve of, and so we tried the stratagem of shouting to the Indians, that we were part of General Quevedo's advance-guard, and that if we were not admitted in a friendly manner we should return on the morrow with the general, who would visit them with heavy punishment. The name of Quevedo seemed to be a power to conjure by, for after the Indians had jabbered together excitedly, the door opened and a couple appeared, who with a lantern, and many apologies for delay, showed us to an adjoining hovel, which was about large enough to swing a cat round in, as the saying goes. However, we got our baggage inside, and arranged to sleep on top of it, as there was no room for setting up our cots. We tried to light a fire in the doorway, to warm our benumbed bodies and cook a supper, but the smoke filled the hovel, so that we were obliged to put out the fire and content ourselves with biscuits, sardines, and a night-cap of cingani. There was no good corral available, so we had to put the mules in the yard of the church close by, the mozos sleeping in the gateway to take care they did not escape during the night. This was thought to be great sacrilege by the Indians, but necessity knows no law, and Quevedo's name had again to help us through the difficulty.

On the following day we determined to give the mules a short journey only, as far as Curahuara de Carangas, the village to which the Indians had on the preceding night recommended us to go. Fortunately the day was fine, so, having dried our ponchos and rugs as well as we could, and making an early breakfast, we settled up for the barley supplied us, and gave the Indians a couple of dollars for sweeping up the litter made by the animals in the church-yard, thus quite reconciling them to the sacrilege they charged us with last night.

The road from Cruzero onwards is good riding, being mostly sandy, over an undulating pampa. On the way I noticed a very peculiar formation of strata. A plain was completely walled in on either side by upheavals of, in some places, rock, in others earth; the dip on either side corresponding exactly, and being pitched at about an angle of 60° with the horizon.

These inclined walls varied in height in different places, in some having been worn away to the surface of the plain, in others rising, to perhaps fifty feet in height, but their almost parallel lines could be seen along the plain as far as the eye could each. The thickness of these inverted strata might have been about twenty feet, whilst the width of the land between them was probably about half a mile. The effect on the landscape was very striking, and it is exceedingly difficult to set up any theory that may give a reasonable suggestion as to the forces of nature which caused this immense rift in what was once a level portion of the earth's crust.

We arrived at Curahuara de Carangas about mid-day, and put up at one of the principal houses. The pueblo is small, forming one square, or " plaza " only, with a church on one of the sides. This church is said to be upwards of 200 years old, and is a very primitive building of adobe bricks and rush-covered roof, with a tower separated from the main building,

as is frequently the case with old churches throughout South America. The town is not at quite
such a high elevation as Potosí, being only about
12,900 feet above sea-level; but, as it is built on a
slope rising from a vast plain, the climate is frightfully bleak.

The population is probably not more than 800
or 1000 souls, all told, but nevertheless the cura, or
parish priest, seems to make a fine living out of them;
at least, so we thought when we found him bargain-
ing with a couple of travelling jewellers, who arrived
on the same day as ourselves. The cura, who was a
stout hearty man of some fifty years of age, was,
though a priest, the head of a family, consisting
of a buxom Quichuana and half a dozen sons and
daughters. When we called he had just suited his
morganatic wife and daughters with rings all round,
and was debating whether he had sufficient cash or
chefalonia and plata piña with which to purchase a
very large diamond ring, which the "joyeros," or
jewellers, were tempting him to purchase as an
episcopal jewel. The diamond was of rather a
yellowish colour, about the size of a small sugar
almond. The price asked was 6000 pesos, but
doubtless the sellers would willingly have taken
about fifteen hundred; but the priest could not raise
a sufficient amount just at the moment, as his faithful
flock were not in very good spirits, owing to the
slackness in mining operations and the rumours of
revolution.

These travelling jewellers are frequently met
with in Bolivia, and, as they carry a very considerable stock of their wares, they never travel

alone, but always in couples at least. They generally have one or two large diamonds on sale, and sometimes make a very good bargain with a rich priest or a successful miner. In payment they are open to take any other valuables, for they are keen hands at a bargain, being generally of the Israelitish persuasion; and a quantity of "chefalonia," or old silver plate, such as candlesticks, cups or basons, or a few pounds' weight of "plata piña" (pure silver in the moulds, as turned out from the smelting works at the mines), are always as acceptable to them as hard dollars. These joyeros come from either Lima or Valparaiso, and it is said that whenever they sell a *gros lot*, such as a valuable diamond, they always leave the town and neighbourhood as quickly as possible, for fear the purchaser should repent of his bargain; and it is the best policy, whenever a traveller is asked an opinion of a large diamond or other jewel, to give a favourable one, for so many false jewels have been sold in Bolivia that the susceptible feelings of the owner of a rare and precious stone may be easily offended.

About nine leagues from the town there are mines of silver, and the inhabitants expect that the district will some day be equal to the famous Caracoles mines of the coast; but their sanguine hopes are not, in my opinion, ever likely to be realized, as their situation is far away from any possible railway route, even supposing the projected line between Tacna and La Paz should be carried out. The difficulties of transport, fuel, and forage will therefore be always so great as to preclude the idea of successful mining. Provisions of every kind were very dear, and fresh meat seldom to be had, nor even fowls nor eggs. Barley for the mules cost six pesos the quintal in the straw, but was to cost yet more further on the road to Tacna.

## CHAPTER XXIX.

THE following day, January 14th, we called up the mozos about two o'clock in the morning, and by about five we had had our coffee, mules were saddled, packs all up, and a start made. The morning was fine and clear as usual, for the storms come on generally in the afternoon. The road out of the village is northward, and soon gets into a rather wide quebrada with a river, which we crossed and recrossed several times. A small plain, with good grass, plenty of water, a few ranchos, and the largest herd of alpacas that we had yet seen, is called Pichagas. A little distance from this, a short but sharp cuesta—in the ascent of which one of our pack mules fell just on the edge of the precipice—takes up from the ravine to a rocky plateau, which I guessed to be about 800 feet higher than the plain of Curahuara. Arriving at the top of the cuesta, zigzagged out of the side of the ravine, a rocky plateau extends as far as the eye can reach. From thence the ravine looks like a great rent in the earth, the sides being so straight and evenly matched that it is evident some stupendous force of nature must have burst the solid rocks asunder, for the enormous rift cannot have been caused by the action of the small stream that runs in the bottom of the ravine, or " cañon," as it would be called in the northern continent.

On the plateau, the rock is over hard, flat, rocky ground, until it approaches the foot of the noble peak of Sahama. This mountain is always snow-covered at its summit, which Hugo Reck gives as 6546 metres, or 21,470 feet above sea-level. Sahama is but sluggishly active, as nothing but a small amount of smoke has ever been observed to ascend from it. Its outline is exceedingly regular and graceful in form, and as it rises nearly 8000 feet above the plateau from which it springs, it affords a sight that for impressive grandeur is scarcely to be equalled elsewhere in nature. The almost equally beautiful peaks called Las Tetillas are also visible more to the northward, from this plain, and, together with Sahama, form a prospect which alone would repay a lover of mountain scenery for his journey across the Andes.

Hereabouts were many vicuñas, so tame that they allowed one to approach well within pistol-shot. These animals remind one of the deer in many of the parks and forests of our own country, their fawn-coloured backs and white bellies, long necks and slender legs completely carrying out the illusion. In the afternoon we had the usual storm of hail, thunder, and lightning, during which we arrived at Chocos, a solitary house and pulperiâ, well-provided with every necessary except fresh meat. Fortunately we had provided ourselves with this on the road, for, seeing a good flock of sheep, Marco caught one with his lasso, gaucho fashion. This seems to be the proper thing for travellers to do *en voyaye* over the Andes, to help themselves when in want of fresh meat, for the owners of sheep or poultry, for instance, will never sell them willingly except in the market towns; but no sooner had we caught our mutton, than a woman, before invisible, appeared mysteriously from goodness knows where, probably from behind some large boulder, of which there were a vast number scattered over the plain. She did not appear much put out at our summary proceedings, and what little anger she did show was doubtless put on just for appearance' sake, being easily pacified by the present of a couple of melgarejos, with short beards, which **are** the fashion in this part of the country. The sheep raised at such high altitudes are very small, smaller even than Welsh mutton; but the meat is sweet and makes a capital chupe, and a whole sheep for about 3*s.* cannot be dear whatever its size. Our prize was easily carried by Marco across the pommel of his saddle, and, arriving at Chocos, was soon killed, skinned, cut up, and cooked into a good supper for all hands, including our friends the joyeros, who joined us again, and shared our meal, which consisted of the inevitable chupe, a fry of chops, some bottled beer, and an excellent cup of chocolate; the total expense, with the charge for the room and the use of the corral for the animals, being just 10s. between us all. Barley was, however, very dear, being seven pesos, or about 22s., the quintal, and seems to be getting dearer and dearer every stage, until at last we almost expect to have to feed our mules with the money itself. During the night a hail-storm raged with great fury, but being under a good strong roof we did not mind it. Our mules must, however, have suffered greatly in their open corral, and it is astonishing how fresh they always turn out in the morning whatever may have been the weather during the night; indeed, it seems that, so long as they get plenty of fodder, rain, hail, snow, or frost have very little effect upon them.

Our next stage should have been from Chocos to Cosepilla, a run of twelve leagues; but on arriving at Sepulturas we heard that there was no barley to be had at Cosepilla, so we decided to remain the night at Sepulturas. The road travelled during the day had nothing particularly worthy of mention, nearly the whole of the distance being over pampa land, with only one cuesta of consequence which might easily have been avoided. During the day we passed several recuas of mules and donkeys, these having for some days past been very few in number. We also saw an ostrich ("avestruz"), the only one that we saw during the journey to Tacna. It was of dark grey colour and of fair size, and was within easy rifle-shot, but lolloped rapidly away. Further south the ostriches are more plentiful, but there appear to be very few on the Bolivian Andes, whilst the "guanaco," so numerous in Chili, Argentine, and Patagonia, does not seem to come so far north. Vicuña were in great numbers : in one herd, scarcely 200 yards away from the track, I counted twenty-six ; others of ten and twelve were very frequent.

We arrived at Sepulturas about one o'clock in the afternoon, and gave the mules a good long rest, intending to make a long journey of about sixteen leagues (nearly fifty miles) on the morrow. The posada here is pretty fair, though not so good as the one at Chocos. A regular tariff of prices for chupes, etc., is posted up, but bears the comforting announcement that the good things offered to the traveller will be " proporcionado con el mayor gusto cuando posible," or "supplied with the greatest pleasure when possible ; " the two last saving words being doubtless intended to cover a multitude of deficiencies, and to lead up to the old posada answer of " No hay, señor."

Next morning we rose soon after midnight, but my mozo was suffering from a slight attack of ague, so we were delayed until nearly five o'clock before we could get on the road. The air was fine and frosty, and freshened us up famously. Before leaving this place we note why it bears the unpleasant and very suggestive name of Sepulturas, or " the Tombs." For some reason, at present unexplained, it seems to be peculiarly fatal to animals, and has become a perfect charnel-field. The number of dead mules and donkeys, together with the whitened bones of former corpses, scattered over the plain was something extraordinary, giving such a melancholy look to the place that it seems strange indeed that travellers should make it a halting-place ; and how any one could be found to live there, and keep up the posada, was one of those things that pass an ordinary person's comprehension. Probably this excessive mortality is caused by the " soroche," or " mountain sickness," which is doubtless strongest in its effects at this point of the journey over the Andes. Some people blame the water of the locality more than the altitude, but I did not hear that the human travellers passing through or the inhabitants of the posada suffered equally with animals, as would have been the case if the drinking water had been poisonous. However, be the cause what it may, I should advise any wanderer over the route from Oruro to Tacna, or *vice versâ*, to arrange if possible not to break his journey at Sepulturas, the mere sight of the place being enough to give him very melancholy recollections, and had it not been for the report we heard of the lack of fodder for the animals at Cosepillas, we should have ridden on there instead of passing the night in the " Tombs."

Fortunately for us, none of our animals showed signs of sickness before leaving, but we had not been long on the road when one of the baggage mules was attacked with belly pains, and stood still, groaning and shaking violently. I was in great fear for her, as she was the weakest of the batch ; but our gaucho Marco was equal to the occasion, and had the packs off her in a moment, whilst he covered her loins with a rug, and fomented her belly with urine—a treatment that recovered her quickly and completely.

Four leagues from Sepulturas is Cosepilla, a large and well-built tambo, to which we ought to have come last night, as, notwithstanding what was told us at Sepulturas, there was barley to be had, but at ten pesos per quintal. From this place a very high peak, which we were told was named El Cerro del Volcan, was a very beautiful sight, being entirely snow-covered, and of almost equal beauty with the volcano of Sajama. There were no signs of eruption, which is said to take place only in the dry season. The road all day was good, though very stony, with only a couple of cuestas, one of which, called "Las Siete Vueltas," or "The Seven Turns," is a noticeable feature of the journey. The pampas are traversed by numerous small streams that bring down beautiful clear iced water from the snow-covered peaks, some of which display on their steep sides, where the snow cannot lie, a variety of colours that give a most peculiar appearance to the landscape.

The best description that I can give of this, is that the hills look as though they had been draped with immense striped blankets; the bands of colour, which are disposed vertically, consisting of bright red, yellow, and slatey blue. The vertical position of these stripes does not answer to the inclination of the strata, which is probably similar to the peculiar rocky formation noticed near El Cruzero, the different coloured earths lying one upon the other. Some convulsion of nature, or the wearing away of time, has cut through the strata in an angular direction; and at the point where each one of the strata comes to the surface, the detritus or broken earth has fallen, straight down the hill-side, thus giving the appearance to which I have alluded.

We arrived at Tacora, our next halting-place, about five o'clock, having travelled for twelve hours without any stoppages, and having crossed the frontier and entered on Peruvian territory. Here there is a very fair tambo with the usual supply of un-eatables. No barley to be had for the animals,

PASS OF TACORA.

but dried " alfa " was obtainable at eight and a half pesos the quintal, equal to about £29 per ton—a stiffish price for " dried lucerne."

The following day, Sunday, January 17th, we left the post-house of Tacora about 7.30 a.m., the morning being frosty and cold, as is usual on these elevated table-lands. The first league travelled was over a pampa, terminated by a cuesta particularly dreaded for the soroche ; and certainly the number of carcases and skeletons of mules and donkeys on either side of the path was truly appalling. I felt something unusual myself, and notwithstanding that it is said to be dangerous to take liquor when suffering from this sickness, I took a little brandy and bitters, and, attacking the contents of my saddle-bags, ate my breakfast of hard-boiled eggs and biscuits, soon feeling considerably better. The mules also showed, by lagging behind, some symptoms of this dreaded soroche; but our mozos took some cloves of garlic from their "alforjas," and, bruising them, rubbed them into the animal's nostrils. To the one most affected they squirted "aguadiente" into his ears, with which treatment the animals appeared to revive; but we got on slowly, the boys telling us that it would not do to urge the mules beyond a walking pace.

Passing the cuesta and arriving again on flat lands, we crossed a river called El Rio de Azufre, the water of which has a most unpleasant taste and smell, the latter reminding one of the odour exhaled by rotting seaweed. The banks of this stream were encrusted with a yellow deposit, whilst the bed also was covered with a bright yellow slime. This stream is the last that runs eastward, and soon after crossing it the track comes to the highest point over which the road to Tacna passes. Before descending, one notices to the northward, deeply indented on the side of the peak of Tacora, the aqueduct which conveys the water of the river Maury, an affluent of the Desaguadero, to the town of Tacna. This pass, which is called Chulancani, is surmounted by a huge cairn, or "apacheta," composed principally of the bones of the mules and donkeys that have fallen victims to the soroche. To this heap every passing arriero adds either a stone or a whitened bone, picked up from the way-side, and devoutedly crossing himself, prays to the Holy Virgin or to his patron saint for a safe passage to his home. Close by the cairn, which stands probably at an elevation of rather more than 15,000 feet above sea-level, grows a rough and gnarled tree of the kind called " kenña " in the district, and forming a remarkable feature of the route.

After crossing the summit of the pass the descent to the Pacific coast is commenced, and the steep nature of the western slope of the Andes becomes conspicuous at once. Indeed the whole aspect of the country changes, for there are no more pampas or table-lands in sight, and no grass or other signs of vegetation. Owing to the almost total absence of rainfall, nothing green or growing is to be seen on the western slopes of the Andes, except in the bottom of the ravines, where, by skill and hard labour, some industrious " ranchero " has been able to effect a little irrigation. Owing to the broken and ravined character of the hill-side but a short view is to be obtained, from which one would almost be inclined to fancy that the mountains had split asunder; the part towards the Pacific having, as it sank down, broken up into inextricable confusion, whilst the bulk, remaining unshaken towards the interior of the continent, preserved its original formation of valley, plain, and hill.

But notwithstanding the rough nature of the

descent to the Pacific, engineers bold enough to
project a railway down it have been found, and we
observed several bench marks indicating the course
of the once-intended line from Tacna to La Paz.
The obstacles to be overcome between Tacna and
the summit pass, will, in my opinion, render this

LA PORTADA.

undertaking most difficult, if not impossible ; but
once the Cuesta of Tacora is passed, and the
pampas entered on, the line would be comparatively
easy, although, if the La Paz road is like the Oruro
one, there would be some difficult cuestas to descend
before gaining the lower plateau of the Desaguadero.

About five leagues from the Tacora post-house
the track follows a very steep and stony descent to

the Portada, where there is a mining establishment belonging to Messrs. Blondell of Oruro and Tacna. The mines were not being worked, but one could not but notice the neat look of the buildings, which were mostly roofed with corrugated zinc, as also were the " pulperias " adjoining, of which there are four very good-looking concerns with well-stored shops and good rooms for travellers ; but I wondered how so many of them could find a living for their proprietors. Alfa at eight pesos the quintal was to be had, but no " cebada," and on this side of the Andes, alfa, or " lucerne," dried or fresh, with an occasional feed of American oats, seems to be the principal fodder for the animals.

Entering another ravine, called Angostura, which forms the direct descent to Tacna, and is a very stony and bad road, descending probably one foot in every yard or thereabouts, we passed several pulperias or ranchos where the numerous arrieros stop. One of these, sometimes recommended to travellers, and called El Ingenio, must be avoided, as it is in ruins. We had arranged to close the day's journey at Palca, where we arrived about 4 p.m., and found very fair lodgings, chupes and coffee, whilst alfa, now descending in price, was to be had at six pesos the quintal. At this posada we met a French Abbé who was going to Bolivia with intent to earn a livelihood as a professor of French, either in La Paz or Sucre, and as I could converse with him a little in his own language, we passed a pleasant evening, and he continued his solitary journey about two in the morning. He had only one mozo with him, and as he could barely make himself understood in

Spanish, he must have had rather a bad time on the road. He seemed to have no idea of the hard_ ships before him, but as I was very near the con_ clusion of my journey, and he was just commencing his, I was glad to be able to fit him up with sundry

ANGOSTURA.

rugs, and a waterproof sheet, of which he would stand in great need during the afternoon storms off the higher Andes.

Leaving Palca at half-past seven, we rode down the quebrada at a slow pace, on account of the very rough and stony nature of the ground and the tired state of some of the mules, which were evidently beginning to feel the effects of the long journey. The bottom of the ravine, from Palca down to the plains of Tacna, is generally well cultivated, pro- ducing alfa and maize ("maïs") in good quantity, by dint of much irrigation from the small stream which flows down the ravine, aided by the water brought over the summit from the river Maury. About three leagues distant from Palca, we got on to the finished part of the new road, which was then in course of construction from Tacna towards Bolivia. Some hundreds of men were at work, and their rough encampments on either side of the ravine gave it quite a busy look. The road was being very well made, and was, I understood, being worked as nearly as possible to the lines laid down by the railway engineers; so that if at any time the railway scheme becomes financially practicable, the road will be partly available for the railway cuttings and embankments. But even if the more ambitious enterprise should never be attempted, the new road will be a great improvement on the old track, and proves that Peru is straining every nerve to keep her monopoly of Bolivian trade.

About two in the afternoon we rode out of the hills, and entered on the plains on which the town of Tacna and its environs stand. Passing through Pachia, the principal suburb, the gardens of which are all wonderfully cultivated considering the fearfully dry nature of the soil and the distance from which water has to be brought, we arrived at the city about 4 p.m., very dusty and tired, and put up at the hotel " Bola de Oro," or " Golden Ball," a very fair establishment, and decidedly the best that I had met with in all my journey from the Atlantic to the Pacific, for even the town of Pará, Brazil's principal city on the Amazon, cannot boast so good an hotel as the Bola de Oro of Tacna.

From the material of which the houses are composed, the town and its environs have a strange and somewhat dull and heavy appearance, notwithstanding that the houses are mostly built as lightly as possible, in order the better to withstand the frequently occurring earthquakes. The walls are generally lath, plastered over with mud, or adobes, one brick in thickness; and the roofs are also of mud, tempered so well that even the intense heat of the sun does not cause it to crack. These roofs are made in a very peculiar shape, and generally the houses have quite the appearance of toy houses; but at night, when the windows are opened and the interiors well lit up, they look very cheerful and lively. The streets are broad and kept very clean, with gaslights in the principal ones. The plazas are neat, though small, and there is a prettily arranged garden with an elegant cast-iron fountain in the principal square, where the " society " of Tacna meet in the cool of the evening to enjoy a promenade, enlivened by the strains of a military band.

The commerce of Tacna is undoubtedly of very important character; but one sees at a glance that the only *raison d'être* of the city is its being situated on the one exit practicable at present for Bolivia to the Pacific coast. There are no Peruvian towns in communication with Tacna. The long lines of donkeys and mules seen continually entering or leaving the town, are all either destined for, or coming from, the neighbouring republic of Bolivia, and the few merchants with whom I conversed seemed to have the idea that the realization of the

Madeira and Mamoré Railway would materially affect
their trade.

After having rested a night in a bed that was a
real luxury after our long ride and rough quarters, and
having had a look round the town, we arranged that
we would leave for Arica in time to catch the first
steamer for Callao, leaving on the 23rd of the month.
We then presented our letters of introduction, one
that I had to a German merchant being very serviceable, for, like all Germans .with whom it has been
my good fortune to meet abroad, this gentleman was
exceedingly kind and disposed to serve one in any
way possible.   The streets of Tacna are well supplied
with shops and stores of every kind.   Drapers,
hatters, shoemakers, and others all make a great
display of their wares, which, like most of their
*confrères* in our European towns, they are always
selling at a great sacrifice.   The latest French
fashions soon make their appearance in Tacna, and
" La Bella Boliviana," the " Bon Marché," and other
establishments, have always a good display of the
most tempting materials of dress, which they sell at
reasonable prices, considering the long route they
have had to be brought over, either by Panamá or
the Straits of Magellan.

As there is nothing in the neighbourhood of
Tacna worthy a visit, the four days I had to wait
would have hung very heavily on my hands had it
not been for the occupation I found in trying to sell
my mules, which, having landed me safely as far as
they could take me, were now of no further service.
But buyers, thinking that I must sell at any price
on account of my leaving for Europe, thought it, as

usual, one of their many opportunities for making a good bargain out of travellers from the interior, and would not offer anything like reasonable prices. Thus, for five mules, costing nearly 1100 pesos, of which four were in excellent condition considering the long journey and hard work they had gone through, the best offer I could get was 600 pesos, or little more than half the cost; and I was advised by my merchant friends of the place that this offer was not a very low one, and probably only made because of the very excellent character of two machos, these being so strong and sound as to be valuable as "pianeras," or pianoforte carriers. I offered to sell the lot for 1000 pesos, and to give in with the bargain my travelling cot, a revolver, a couple of excellent "tapa cargas," and all the "aparejos," or pack saddles and gear. These sundries would all be very useful to intending travellers, and were well worth at least another 100 pesos. However, I could not find a buyer at my price, and therefore determined to sell the mule that was in worst condition, and send the others back to Bolivia for sale there, as our two mozos had to return, and would require at least three animals for their journey. Sometimes it happens that travellers bringing servants down from Bolivia are lucky enough to meet others returning, who will engage the mozos, and thus save the first hirer further expense; but the revolution going on had stopped all business between Tacna and the interior. The result of the course adopted was, that instead of losing about 500 or 600 pesos (nearly £100), I only lost about 100, or £15, which was the cost of fodder for the animals and rations to the mozos on their return journey to Sucre. True, I ran the risk of losing the animals altogether in the revolution that was then going on ; but fortune favoured me, and they got back to Sucre safely, as I had calculated that they would ; for I knew the boys would naturally be very averse to being pressed into the service of either the government or the revolutionists, and would give both parties a wide berth should they come across either of them on their way back. There is no doubt that the best and only way to avoid loss in realizing the cost of the animals necessary for crossing the Andes, is to buy the best class of mules, and, if the journey ends at Tacna, send them back to Bolivia, where they are always worth their cost ; and one can generally manage to draw the value of the mules returning, from one of the mercantile houses of Tacna, less a small commission for selling the mules in Bolivia.

We left Tacna, on the morning of the 23rd, by the ten o'clock train, arriving at Arica about mid-day, the distance being about forty miles, and the fare three pesos for first class, and four reales for each package of luggage. The line runs over a sandy plain like that on which Tacna is situated. At times a small cutting had been made ; but there were none more than some six to eight feet deep, and very few banks, and only two or three bridges. The rail used is a flat-footed one, of perhaps sixty-five pounds per yard, and the road is very well maintained, being well ballasted and boxed up. Nearing Arica the road runs close along by the sea, and we saw several remains of the effects of the great hurricane wave of

1869. The hull of a steamer of perhaps 600 or 800 tons, was quite a quarter of a mile inshore, where it had been deposited by the retiring wave; and there was a great deal of damaged and now valueless machinery scattered along the line of railway and sea-coast.

The Peruvian coast offers very little facility to shipping, and most of its ports, except Callao, are scarcely more than open roadsteads. Arica has been built at a small bay which has a few rocky islands to defend it from the south winds. The town, never very large, is now much reduced in size, the greater part of the inhabitants living in huts built up of tarpaulins, boards, etc., placed well up the side of the hill, apparently to be out of the way of another earthquake wave. The custom-house has been re-built with brick walls and zinc roof; a small church also has zinc roofing—an article which enters largely into the composition of all the houses, and gives the place a very temporary and make-shift look. There is a neat pier, erected on six-inch wrought-iron piles, which enables passengers to embark clear of the surf. The steamship *Lima* being in port, we took tickets at the mail-agent's office, paying 353 soles each for passage to Southampton, and thirty soles each fare over the Panamá Railway, and at once went on board, leaving Arica about five in the afternoon. The *Lima* is a very long and narrow screw boat, with state cabins on deck, and she rolled considerably from having her main decks crowded with bullocks, and her upper deck littered up with merchandize of all sorts. Indeed, her upper deck was in the utmost confusion, caused by a peculiar practice which exists on nearly all the Pacific Steam Navigation Company's boats. This is, that dealers in all kinds of provisions are allowed to take passages principally between Valparaiso and Callao, and exhibit their wares on the deck, so that the ship is completely cumbered with their goods, and the crew have little chance of managing the ship properly. The practice may remunerate the company, as each dealer pays according to the space of the deck that he occupies, but passengers are greatly inconvenienced and endangered thereby.

The next day, Sunday, we passed Islay, Mollendo, the shipping port for the railway to Arequipa and Puno, and Quilpa, stopping only to land and receive passengers. On Monday we spent the greater part of the day at Lomas, shipping sugar, rum, and bullocks. This place consists of about half a dozen huts only, and the coast is as arid and wretched-looking as the whole line of the Pacific coast really is. It is said, however, that there is good cultivable land, with haciendas for sugar and pôtreros, or grazing grounds for cattle, a few leagues inland. The Tuesday was passed principally at Pisco, a dull and miserable-looking place, worthy of note only for its capital aguadiente, or white rum, said to be made from grapes, but probably made from sugar-cane. It is, however, a very pure spirit, and an opportunity of tasting it genuine should not be neglected. A great many Chinese are settled at Pisco, and there is a railway to the town of Yca, about fifty miles southward. During the run up from Arica, every morning had been foggy, necessitating a very slow rate of speed, and a continual sounding of the foghorn, and on Wednesday morning, the 27th, we anchored in Callao Bay, about seven o'clock in the morning.

Callao Bay is a remarkably fine piece of water, of large extent, and so well defended from all winds, that the water is always like a mill-pond. It has, however, like all the other ports of the Pacific coast, suffered from earthquake waves, though in a far less degree than many others. Much shipping, two monitors, and other Peruvian men-of-war were in harbour, also two other men-of-war, one English and one American, and the whole scene betokened the near presence of a large city. We dressed hastily to go on shore to the office of the Pacific Steam Navigation Company, in order to secure a good berth on the steamer which we had to change to for Panamá, the *Lima*, etc., being on the berth between Callao and Valparaiso, while the *Oroya* and others run the Callao and Panamá trip. Finding the office did not open until ten o'clock, we remained on shore to breakfast at a very good restaurant in the Hotel de Comercio, near the " Plaza Principal." This necessary duty duly performed to our high satisfaction, both as regards quality and price, we chose our berths at the office, and returned to the *Lima* to shift our baggage to the *Oroya*, a fine paddle steamer, whose captain, a worthy old American, who had been at sea for more than fifty years, kept her in better order than, perhaps, any other mail steamer that floats. Everything in the shape of paint, brass, and plain wood, was most delightfully clean and well scoured, whilst the cabins were a real treat to see. Certainly the contrast from the confused decks of the

*Lima* to the order and neatness of the *Oroya* was very striking. Returning on shore again, we passed the floating dock, in which was the steamship *Payta*, also of the Pacific Steam Navigation Company's fleet, and which had a short while previously been run on a rock at the port of Santa, near Truxillo. The government foundries, with several private establishments of a similar nature, also attract attention; and, indeed, the whole aspect of the bay showed that a large amount of work was going on. Callao itself is like most other Peruvian towns, not at all striking, the houses having the same toylike and temporary look that one notices on arriving at Tacna.

There being nothing to detain us in Callao, and the *Oroya* not leaving until the following day, we determined to pay Lima a visit, and taking tickets at four reales each, a twenty minutes' ride brought us to the capital of Peru. It is situated at the foot of the hills which, all along the Peruvian coast, run sometimes close to the sea, and at others recede somewhat inland, leaving a sandy plain from their slopes seawards. On one of these plains Lima is built. Entering the city, the European-like look of the shops is the first thing that claims attention; and were it not for the flat roofs, and the unfinished look of the houses, the tops of which are not even graced with a cornice, one might easily imagine one's self to be in a large European town. We put up at the Hotel Maury, the *table d'hôte* dinner at which did not come up to that given at the Golden Ball of Tacna.

Of churches there are many, the principal ones being, the famous Cathedral in the Plaza, with its two towers, where the Brothers Gutierrez were hung by the townspeople after their brutal murder of President Balta ; and the church of Panamá, with a wonderful façade of images, curved pillars, etc. The Plaza de Armas, is pretty though small. Here the military bands play every evening ; and as chairs can be hired, the time passes away pleasantly. Over a river that flows through Lima is a very old bridge, solidly and well built, and bearing an inscription with the date of 1608, " regnante Felipo III." The alaméda close by is very little cared for, and appeared to be falling into ruins, the society of Lima apparently caring more for a stroll along the well-paved Calle de Comercio, than for public gardens. In the evening an alarm of fire brought out three com-panies of " bombarderos," a sort of volunteer fire brigade. They looked very gallant and gay in their well-appointed uniforms, which did not appear to have seen much service. The hat they wore was of curious shape, made of black shining material, and in form a cross between a very large solah topee and a coalheaver's bonnet ; it did not seem so suitable as the helmet our own firemen wear, but the corps being a volunteer one, probably something must be sacrificed to effect. I noticed some of them return to their rooms in the hotel after the alarm had subsided. They were evidently men of good position in society, and went to their work with kid gloves on ; but possibly, as the alarm was a false one, they did not require to take them off. I should think that a bad fire in Lima would be a most serious matter, for the houses are of a flimsy nature, and have a great deal of wood in their composition.

The next day, the 28th of January, we left Lima at 8 a.m., and had an hour or so in Callao to get a few newspapers and books for use on the voyage to Panamá. The *Oroya* started about mid-day, but once outside the harbour we got into a thick fog, which is said to hang about these coasts at this time of the year. This fog accompanied us all the day, and the early part of the next, when we passed H.M.S. *Repulse*, flying Admiral Cochrane's flag, and on the 30th we arrived at Payta at mid-day. This is a small town in the usual Peruvian tumble-down style, and not worth landing to see. We had to take in some sugar as cargo, and were detained till evening. The next three days passed without anything worthy of note, save, perhaps, that though the weather was fine, the ocean was anything but " Pacific," the breezes being strong from the north and west.

On the 3rd of February, the seventh day out from Callao, we arrived off Panamá about mid-day. The approach is exceedingly pretty, as the steamer passes several islands clothed with bush to the water's edge, and forming a pleasant contrast to the arid coasts of Peru. On one of these islands, Taboga, the Pacific Steam Navigation Company have a station and pier, and there is a good-sized village with fields of maize and plantains, looking fresh and green. The ocean steamers stop at an island about a mile and a half from the town, and from thence a smaller steamer conveys passengers, mails, and specie up to Panamá. From this island the town looks pretty, but on arriving one sees that it is old and somewhat dirty. The wharves are large, but have been patched up and enlarged from time to time.

Two severe fires, that occurred in the city within eighteen months, had destroyed many large houses; the central hotel and adjoining buildings in the plaza being in ruins. The insurance companies, Imperial and Sun, of London, lost large sums of money; the agent in Panamá, a Monsieur de Roux, telling me he had sent in claims for more than a million dollars, and now the companies wisely decline any further risks. The cathedral is a plain old-fashioned edifice, the towers of which are spotted with pearl-oyster shells, probably to put one in mind of the pest of small-pox, which is at times very bad in the town, although on the whole it seems to have a very fair climate, and not to deserve the bad reputation that is universally attributed to it. The Grand Central Hotel, at which we stayed, is well managed, and the prices charged are reasonable. Before leaving Panamá we paid a visit to the prison, where the criminals are kept in large rooms, having barred windows opening to the ground, through which the prisoners are allowed to converse freely with all comers. They may also divert themselves with the manufacture of small curiosities, the best being engraved cocoa-nuts and gourds, on which they carve very pretty designs, and for which they ask about a dollar apiece.

The royal mail steamer *Tasmanian* being announced to leave Aspinwall at 5 p.m. on the 5th, we decided to go there by the early morning train, leaving Panamá at 7 a.m. in order to have a few hours to look round the town of Aspinwall, or Colon,

as it is called in the country. The transit by railway
across the Isthmus of Panamá is so well known by
travellers that very little description is now needed.
The notorious incivility of the employés and the
discomfort of the carriages, coupled with the ex-
orbitant tariff of £6 for about fifty miles distance,
render this part of the journey so unpleasant in
every way that no one would use this railway were
there any other means available of passing the
Isthmus ; but as the Panamá Railway Company
have at present a monopoly of the inter-oceanic
traffic, they probably think that civility and reasonable treatment of passengers is quite an unnecessary
item of management, their trade not being likely
to be driven away until they have had a lifetime
of their profits.

The country on the Pacific side of the hills that
run through the Isthmus, and on the upper parts of
the Chagres River which flows into the Atlantic, is
pretty enough, there being several small villages
through which the line passes, at each of which the
clearings made in the bush show the usual luxuriant
tropical growth of maize, plantains, and other
products ; but the flat country nearer Aspinwall is
one vast swamp. The completion of the line
through this is one of the most notable feats of
engineering, and the passage over it recalls vividly
to the mind the dismal story of the numerous deaths
that occurred during the construction, the number
being so great that it is said, the laying of each
sleeper cost a life. Aspinwall is also built amongst
the swamps, and were it not that the miasma rising
round the town is blown inland by the fresh sea

breezes, it would certainly be a most unhealthy place.

The city is small and uninteresting, and the less one stays in it the better. We found the *Tasmanian* in the agonies of coaling, and who shall describe the grim state of dust and dirt that afflicts mail steamers when this unfortunately necessary operation is being carried on. Although all doors and windows between the saloons and the hold are carefully closed, the dust permeates everywhere; whilst the noises, foul odours, and still fouler language, that rise from the crowd of negroes following one another in quick succession up and down the planks leading from the vessel to the shore, are so unbearable, that to remain on deck is absolutely impossible; a stroll even along the hot and uninteresting streets of Aspinwall therefore becomes preferable to going on board before the hour of departure. The longest day has, however, its ending, and what with buying a few shells and other simple curiosities in the market-place, inspecting the statue of Columbus, and breakfasting at one of the very second-rate restaurants, we managed to pass away the time until the coaling of the *Tasmanian* was completed, and the bell rang to warn passengers to go on board.

The voyage home from Aspinwall commenced on the evening of the 5th; on the 10th we were at Jamaica, on the 14th at St. Thomas', and on the 1st of March I landed at Plymouth, well pleased to be home again in Old England after so long and varied a journey by river, land, and sea.

# APPENDIX.

## TABLE OF APPROXIMATE HEIGHTS.

| Name of place. | Height above sea-level. Feet. | Productions. |
|---|---|---|
| San Antonio, lowest rapid | 250 | Sugar, maize, yams, plantains, mandioca, tobacco, cocoa. |
| Guajará Mirim, upper rapid | 510 | |
| Exaltacion | 710 | |
| Trinidad | 800 | |
| Coni | 950 | Ditto, and coffee and coca. |
| Santa Cruz | 1,615 | |
| Cristal Maio | 1,920 | |
| El Chaco | 3,250 | |
| Cuesta del Lina Tambo | 6,150 | Barley and potatoes. |
| Inca Corral | 7,715 | |
| Los Jocotales | 8,000 | |
| Cuesta de Malága | 12,550 | |
| Cochi-janchi | 10,950 | |
| Cochabamba | 8,450 | Ditto, and wheat and fruits. |
| Pass near Totora | 11,500 | Barley and potatoes. |
| Totora | 10,000 | |
| Misque | 7,000 | Wheat, barley, etc., also fruits. |
| Aiquile | 7,850 | |
| Chinguri | 6,850 | Sugar, maize, etc. |
| Quiroga | 7,000 | |
| Rio Grande | 5,925 | |
| Palca | 6,800 | |
| Jaboncillo, top of cuesta | 8,615 | Barley and potatoes. |
| Masa Cruz, ditto | 8,550 | |
| Canto Molino | 7,200 | |
| Huata, foot of cuesta | 8,200 | |
| „ top of cuesta | 10.100 | |
| Sucre | 9,200 | |

| Name of place. | Height above sea-level. Feet. | Productions. |
|---|---|---|
| Nutschucc . . . . | 8,000 | Maize, fruits, etc. |
| Rio Pilcomayo . . . | 7,000 | |
| Pampa Tambo . . . | 9,850 | |
| Quebrada Honda, top . | 12,000 | |
| ,, ,, bottom . | 11,200 | |
| Potosí . . . . | 13,500 | |
| Cerro de Potosi, summit | 15,500 | |
| Tarapaya . . . | 11.200 | Barley and potatoes, up to about 12,500 feet. |
| Yocalla . . . . | 11,450 | |
| Cuesta de Leñas, top . | 14,400 | |
| Pampa de Aullagas . | 12,400 | |
| Poopo . . . . | 12,430 | |
| Oruro . . . . | 12,530 | |
| Curahuara de Carangas . | 12,890 | |
| Sajáma, summit . . | 21,470 | |

EXPORTS FROM THE PORT OF ARICA DURING THE YEARS 1872—4, THE BULK OF THE ARTICLES BEING THE PRODUCE OF THE REPUBLIC OF BOLIVIA.

| *Minerals and precious metals.* | | Soft dollars. | Soft dollars. |
|---|---|---|---|
| Barilla copper . . . | 178,748 cwts. of 100 lbs. @ | 18 | 3,217,464 |
| ,, tin . . . | 29,923 ,, ,, ,, | 16 | 478,768 |
| Copper, in bars . . | 1,078 ,, ,, ,, | 38 | 40,964 |
| Tin, in bars . . | 29,255 ,, ,, ,, | 30 | 877,650 |
| Silver, pure . . | 424,600 marks of 7·4 oz. ,, | 12½ | 5,307.500 |
| ,, old plate . . | 2,083 ,, ,, ,, | 10 | 20,830 |
| ,, money . . | 5,265 cases . . ,, | 90 | 473,850 |
| ,, hard dollars . | . . . . ,, | . | 1,414,880 |
| ,, soft dollars . | . . . . ,, | | 265,149 |
| Gold, dust and grain . | 11,945 oz. . . ,, | 20 | 238,900 |
| Ditto, coin . . | 6,010 ,, . . ,, | 20 | 120,200 |
| *General Merchandise.* | | | |
| Chocolate, manufactured . | 67 cwts. of 100 lbs. ,, | 65 | 4,355 |
| Cocoa, in nibs . . | 50 ,, ,, ,, | 36 | 1,800 |
| Coca . . . . | 531 ,, ,, ,, | 60 | 31,860 |
| Cochineal . . . | 750 lbs. . . ,, | ⅜ | 562 |
| Coffee . . . | 943 cwts. of 100 lbs. ,, | 38 | 35,834 |
| Cotton . . . | 1,856 ,, ,, ,, | 36 | 66,816 |
| Elixir of coca . . | 9 dozen . . ,, | 15 | 135 |
| Guaraná . . . | 40 cwts. of 100 lbs. ,, | 15 | 600 |
| Maté . . . | 153 ,, ,, ,, | 50 | 7,650 |
| Olives . . . | 77 ,, ,, ,, | 18 | 1,386 |
| Peruvian bark . . | 28,835 ,, ,, ,, | 80 | 2,306,800 |
| Ratania root . . | 20 ,, ,, ,, | 60 | 1,200 |

Carried forward . . 14,915,153

|  |  | Soft dollars. | S ft dollars. |
|---|---|---|---|
| Brought forward . | | | 14,915,153 |
| Spirits, Italia . . . | 139 dozen . . . ,, | 18 | 2,502 |
| Tobacco . . . | 226 cwts of 100 lbs. ,, | 40 | 9,040 |
| Hides, ox . | 15,136 . . , | 5 | 75,680 |
| Skins, Chinchilla . . | 7,179 dozen . ., | 25 | 179,475 |
| ,, Biscacha . | 16 ,, . . ,, | 10 | 160 |
| ,, Vicuña . . | 4,586 . . . ,, | 1 | 4,586 |
| ,, Goat . . | 2,532 . . . ,, | ¾ | 1,899 |
| ,, Sheep . . | 150 dozen . ,, | 10 | 1,500 |
| Wool, Alpaca . . | 17,807 cwts. of 100 lbs ,, | 61 | 1,086,227 |
| ., Vicuña . . | 21 ,, ,, ., | 80 | 1,680 |
| ,, Guanaco . . | 1½ ,. ,, , | 70 | 105 |
| ,, Sheep . . . | 1,153 ,, ,, ,, | 29 | 33,437 |

$16,311,444

At 6½ per £ = £2,509,453

Average value of twelve months' export    ...  £836,484


TABLE SHOWING THE TEMPERATURE, RAIN-FALL, AND DEPTH OF
FLOOD-WATER BELOW THE FALLS OF SAN ANTONIO ON THE
MADEIRA RIVER, FROM OBSERVATIONS TAKEN BY THE AUTHOR
IN 1873.

| Month. | Average Temperature. | | Rainfall in inches. | Flood-water in feet. |
|---|---|---|---|---|
| | Lowest. | Highest. | | |
| January . . | 75° | 83° | 15·85 | 34 |
| February . | 73° | 82° | 10·97 | 42 |
| March . . | 74° | 82° | 14·59 | 46 |
| April . . | 73° | 83° | 11·01 | 42 |
| May . . | 73° | 83° | 5·96 | 35 |
| June . . | 70° | 85° | 2·56 | 27 |
| July . . | 71° | 87° | 0·32 | 21 |
| August . . | 71° | 88° | 1·07 | 15 |
| September . | 72° | 88° | 5·70 | 7 |
| October . . | 73° | 88° | 1·94 | 9 |
| November . | 73° | 84° | 11·32 | 9 |
| December . | 74° | 86° | 10·03 | 27 |

ESTIMATE OF TIME AND EXPENSE OF A JOURNEY FROM LIVERPOOL TO PARÁ, THENCE ACROSS THE CONTINENT, AND RETURN TO ENGLAND.

| Stages. | Days. | Conveyance. | Approximate Expense. | |
|---|---|---|---|---|
| Liverpool to Pará . . | 12 | Steamer, Red Cross Line or Booth's | Passage . . £25 | |
| | | | Personals 5 | |
| Pará to San Antonio . | 13 | Steamer Amazon Steam Ship Company, Limited | Passage . . 15 | |
| | | | Personals . 5 | |
| San Antonio to Exaltacion | 50 | Canoe . . | Pay of 14 hands say 2 months | 85 |
| | | | Keep of same . 85 | |
| | | | Personals . 30 | |
| Exaltacion to Trinidad . | 10 | „ . . | . Say ⅛ of above 40 | |
| Trinidad to Coni . . | 18 | „ | „ ⅖ „ 80 | |
| Coni to Cochabamba . | 7 | Mule . | Hire of 4 mules and 1 arriero | 12 |
| | | | Personals 3 | |
| Cochabamba to Sucre . | 7 | „ . | . Loss on purchase and sale of 4 mules say | 50 |
| Sucre to Potosí . | 2 | „ . | . | |
| Potosí to Oruro . . | 7 | „ . | . | |
| Oruro to Tacna . . | 9 | „ . | . Personals . 50 | |
| Tacna to Arica . . . | 1 | Railway . | Say . . 1 | |
| Arica to Panamá . | 10 | Steamer . | soles Royal Mail 353 | |
| Panamá to Aspinwall . | 1 | Railway . . | Railway 30 | |
| | | | say — 80 | |
| Aspinwall to Southampton | 23 | Steamer . . | Personals, say 50 | |
| Total days | 170 | | Total . £616 | |

NOTE.—The foregoing is a very liberal estimate, particularly in the items of pay and keep of crew from San Antonio to Coni, but it is well to be liberal to the Indians both in pay and keep, as a traveller thereby ensures the health and contentment of his men. Also the item of loss on sale of mules is the outside amount that could be spent, but by good management it should be saved altogether. The cost of my journey from San Antonio to Southampton was as nearly as possible £400; adding £50, from Liverpool to San Antonio, would ma e the round trip to cost £450, and I believe it can be made for this amount. k

LONDON: PRINTED BY WILLIAM CLOWES AND SONS, STAMFORD STREET AND CHARING CROSS

*A Catalogue of American and Foreign Books Published or Imported by* MESSRS. SAMPSON LOW & CO. *can be had on application.*

Crown Buildings, 188, *Fleet Street*, **London,**
*April,* 1879.

# 𝔄 𝔏𝔦𝔰𝔱 𝔬𝔣 𝔅𝔬𝔬𝔨𝔰

PUBLISHED BY

## SAMPSON LOW, MARSTON, SEARLE, & RIVINGTON.

———◆———

### ALPHABETICAL LIST.

*A* CLASSIFIED *Educational Catalogue of Works* published in Great Britain. Demy 8vo, cloth extra. Second Edition, revised and corrected to Christmas, 1877, 5s.

*Abney (Captain W. de W., R.E., F.R.S.) Thebes, and its Five* Greater Temples. Forty large Permanent Photographs, with descriptive letter-press. Super-royal 4to, cloth extra, 63s.

*About Some Fellows.* By an ETON BOY, Author of "A Day of my Life." Cloth limp, square 16mo, 2s. 6d.

*Adventures of Captain Mago.* A Phœnician's Explorations 1000 years B.C. By LEON CAHUN. Numerous Illustrations. Crown 8vo, cloth extra, gilt, 7s. 6d.

*Adventures of a Young Naturalist.* By LUCIEN BIART, with 117 beautiful Illustrations on Wood. Edited and adapted by PARKER GILLMORE. Post 8vo, cloth extra, gilt edges, New Edition, 7s. 6d.

*Adventures in New Guinea.* The Narrative of the Captivity of a French Sailor for Nine Years among the Savages in the Interior. Small post 8vo, with Illustrations and Map, cloth, gilt, 6s.

*Afghanistan and the Afghans.* Being a Brief Review of the History of the Country, and Account of its People. By H. W. BELLEW, C.S.I. Crown 8vo, cloth extra, 6s.

*Alcott (Louisa M.) Aunt Jo's Scrap-Bag.* Square 16mo, 2s. 6d. (Rose Library, 1s.)

———— *Cupid and Chow-Chow.* Small post 8vo, 3s. 6d.

———— *Little Men: Life at Plumfield with Jo's Boys.* Small post 8vo, cloth, gilt edges, 3s. 6d. (Rose Library, Double vol. 2s.)

———— *Little Women.* 1 vol., cloth, gilt edges, 3s. 6d. (Rose Library, 2 vols., 1s. each.)

———— *Old-Fashioned Girl.* Best Edition, small post 8vo, cloth extra, gilt edges, 3s. 6d. (Rose Library, 2s.)

*Alcott (Louisa M.) Work and Beginning Again.* A Story of Experience. 1 vol., small post 8vo, cloth extra, 6s. Several Illustrations. (Rose Library, 2 vols., 1s. each.)

———— *Shawl Straps.* Small post 8vo, cloth extra, gilt, 3s. 6d.

———— *Eight Cousins; or, the Aunt Hill.* Small post 8vo, with Illustrations, 3s. 6d.

———— *The Rose in Bloom.* Small post 8vo, cloth extra, 3s. 6d.

———— *Silver Pitchers.* Small post 8vo, cloth extra, 3s. 6d.

———— *Under the Lilacs.* Small post 8vo, cloth extra, 5s.

"Miss Alcott's stories are thoroughly healthy, full of racy fun and humour . . . . exceedingly entertaining . . . We can recommend the 'Eight Cousins.'"— *Athenæum.*

*Alpine Ascents and Adventures; or, Rock and Snow Sketches.* By H. Schütz Wilson, of the Alpine Club. With Illustrations by Whymper and Marcus Stone. Crown 8vo, 10s. 6d. 2nd Edition.

*Andersen (Hans Christian) Fairy Tales.* With Illustrations in Colours by E. V. B. Royal 4to, cloth, 25s.

*Andrews (Dr.) Latin-English Lexicon.* New Edition. Royal 8vo, 1670 pp., cloth extra, price 18s.

*Animals Painted by Themselves.* Adapted from the French of Balzac, Georges Sands, &c., with 200 Illustrations by Grandville. 8vo, cloth extra, gilt, 10s. 6d.

*Art of Reading Aloud (The) in Pulpit, Lecture Room, or Private* Reunions, with a perfect system of Economy of Lung Power on just principles for acquiring ease in Delivery, and a thorough command of the Voice. By G. Vandenhoff, M.A. Crown 8vo, cloth extra, 6s.

*Asiatic Turkey: being a Narrative of a Journey from Bombay* to the Bosphorus, embracing a ride of over One Thousand Miles, from the head of the Persian Gulf to Antioch on the Mediterranean. By Grattan Geary, Editor of the *Times of India.* 2 vols., crown 8vo, cloth extra, with many Illustrations, and a Route Map.

*Atlantic Islands as Resorts of Health and Pleasure.* By S. G. W. Benjamin, Author of "Contemporary Art in Europe," &c. Royal 8vo, cloth extra, with upwards of 150 Illustrations, 16s.

*Autobiography of Sir G. Gilbert Scott, R.A., F.S.A., &c.* Edited by his Son, G. Gilbert Scott. With an Introduction by the Dean of Chichester, and a Funeral Sermon, preached in Westminster Abbey, by the Dean of Westminster. Also, Portrait on steel from the portrait of the Author by G. Richmond, R.A. 1 vol., demy 8vo, cloth extra, 18s.

*BAKER (Lieut.-Gen. Valentine, Pasha).* See "War in Bulgaria."

*Barton Experiment (The).* By the Author of "Helen's Babies." 1s.

*Verne's (Jules) Works, continued :—*

3. **A Floating City.**
4. **The Blockade Runners.**
5. **From the Earth to the Moon.**
6. **Around the Moon.**
7. **Twenty Thousand Leagues under the Sea.** Vol. I.
8. —— Vol. II. The two parts in one, cloth, gilt, 3*s.* 6*d.*
9. **Around the World in Eighty Days.**
10. **Dr. Ox's Experiment, and Master Zacharius.**
11. **Martin Paz, the Indian Patriot.**
12. **A Winter amid the Ice.**
13. **The Fur Country.** Vol. I.
14. —— Vol. II. Both parts in one, cloth gilt, 3*s.* 6*d.*
15. **Survivors of the "Chancellor."** Vol. I.
16. —— Vol. II. Both volumes in one, cloth, gilt edges, 3*s.* 6*d.*

*Viardot (Louis).* *See "Painters of all Schools."*

*Visit to the Court of Morocco.* By A. LEARED, Author of "Morocco and the Moors." Map and Illustrations, 8vo, 5*s.*

*WALLER (Rev. C. H.) The Names on the Gates of Pearl,* and other Studies. By the Rev. C. H. WALLER, M.A. Second edition. Crown 8vo, cloth extra, 6*s.*

—— *A Grammar and Analytical Vocabulary of the Words in* the Greek Testament. Compiled from Brüder's Concordance. For the use of Divinity Students and Greek Testament Classes. By the Rev. C. H. WALLER, M.A., late Scholar of University College, Oxford, Tutor of the London College of Divinity, St. John's Hall, Highbury. Part I., The Grammar. Small post 8vo, cloth, 2*s.* 6*d.* Part II. The Vocabulary, 2*s.* 6*d.*

—— *Adoption and the Covenant.* Some Thoughts on Confirmation. Super-royal 16mo, cloth limp, 2*s.* 6*d.*

*War in Bulgaria: a Narrative of Personal Experiences.* By LIEUTENANT-GENERAL VALENTINE BAKER PASHA. Maps and Plans of Battles. 2 vols., demy 8vo, cloth extra, 2*l.* 2*s.*

*Warner (C. D.) My Summer in a Garden.* Rose Library, 1*s.*

—— *Back-log Studies.* Boards, 1*s.* 6*d.*; cloth, 2*s.*

—— *In the Wilderness.* Rose Library, 1*s.*

—— *Mummies and Moslems.* 8vo, cloth, 12*s.*

*Weaving.* *See "History and Principles."*

*Whitney (Mrs. A. D. T.) The Gayworthys.* Cloth, 3*s.* 6*d.*

—— *Faith Gartney.* Small post 8vo, 3*s.* 6*d.* Cheaper Editions, 1*s.* 6*d.* and 2*s.*

—— *Real Folks.* 12mo, crown, 3*s.* 6*d.*

*Whitney (Mrs. A D. T.) Hitherto.* Small post 8vo, 3s. 6d. and 2s. 6d.

———— *Sights and Insights.* 3 vols., crown 8vo, 31s. 6d.

———— *Summer in Leslie Goldthwaite's Life.* Cloth, 3s. 6d.

———— *The Other Girls.* Small post 8vo, cloth extra, 3s. 6d.

———— *We Girls.* Small post 8vo, 3s. 6d.; Cheap Edition, 1s. 6d. and 2s.

*Wikoff (H.) The Four Civilizations of the World.* An Historical Retrospect. Crown 8vo, cloth, 12s.

*Wills, A Few Hints on Proving, without Professional Assistance.* By a PROBATE COURT OFFICIAL. 5th Edition, revised with Forms of Wills, Residuary Accounts, &c. Fcap. 8vo, cloth limp, 1s.

*With Axe and Rifle on the Western Prairies.* By W. H. G. KINGSTON. With numerous Illustrations, square crown 8vo, cloth extra, gilt, 7s. 6d.

*Woolsey (C. D., LL.D.) Introduction to the Study of International Law;* designed as an Aid in Teaching and in Historical Studies. 5th Edition, demy 8vo, 18s.

*Words of Wellington: Maxims and Opinions, Sentences and* Reflections of the Great Duke, gathered from his Despatches, Letters, and Speeches (Bayard Series). 2s. 6d.

*World of Comets.* By A. GUILLEMIN, Author of "The Heavens." Translated and edited by JAMES GLAISHER, F.R.S 1 vol., super-royal 8vo, with numerous Woodcut Illustrations, and 3 Chromo-lithographs, cloth extra, 31s 6d.

"The mass of information collected in the volume is immense, and the treatment of the subject is so purely popular, that none need be deterred from a perusal of it."—*British Quarterly Review.*

*Wreck of the Grosvenor.* By W. CLARK RUSSELL. 6s. Third and Cheaper Edition.

*XENOPHON'S Anabasis; or, Expedition of Cyrus.* A Literal Translation, chiefly from the Text of Dindorff, by GEORGE B. WHEELER. Books I to III. Crown 8vo, boards, 2s.

———— *Books I. to VII.* Boards, 3s. 6d.

**London:**

SAMPSON LOW, MARSTON, SEARLE, & RIVINGTON,

CROWN BUILDINGS, 188, FLEET STREET.

Lightning Source UK Ltd.
Milton Keynes UK
UKHW011522191118
332599UK00012B/993/P